GOING MY OWN WAY

Gary Crosby and
Ross Firestone

Going
My Own Way

DOUBLEDAY & COMPANY, INC.
Garden City, New York   1983

Library of Congress Cataloging in Publication Data

Crosby, Gary.
  Going my own way.

  1. Crosby, Bing, 1904-1977. 2. Singers—United States—Biography.
I. Firestone, Ross. II. Title. ML420.C93C75 1983   784.5'0092'4 [B]

ISBN 0-385-17055-6
Library of Congress Catalog Card Number 82-45196
Copyright © 1983 by Gary Crosby and Ross Firestone

To Andrea, the love of my life.

My wife, my friend, my lover, my tormentor, you came along when I desperately needed someone with the exact qualities in the exact amounts only you possess. You gave me the courage to share my story by telling me what I needed to hear in a way I could understand. I pray to God I can make our life together a joyful, productive adventure.

A word to my brothers Denny, Phil and Linny:

You guys walked the first part of this with me, and I love you for it. Even though you carried the weight your own way, a lot of the "I's" in here could just as easily have been "we's." I hope you like this book. If you don't, when and where's the fight?

Another word to Kathryn, my brothers Harry and Nathaniel, and my sister Mary:

This is about me and my dad and mom and my other brothers. I think you'll find the Bing Crosby here a rather different man from the one you knew, reacting to different pressures placed on him by a different time. If I've tried to do any one thing, it's to tell the truth as I experienced it. I love you all.

ACKNOWLEDGMENTS

Thanks to the following for their generous help and support: Norm Benedetti, Charlie Brill, Rosemary Clooney, Marvin Cohen, Andrea Crosby, Barbara Crosby, Steve Crosby, Muriel Davidson, Bob Dornan, Lisa Drew, Nanette Fabray, Gail Firestone, Will Friedwall, Flo Haley, Jack Haley, Jr., Phil Harris, Anne Hukill, Henry Krawitz, Gene Lesser, Mitzi McCall, Sarah Parsons, Bill Phillips, Ruthanne Ponnech, Betty Prashker, Pat Ross, Roberta Morgan Schaeffer, Moselle Seeger, Tim Seldes, Lloyd Shearer, Ilene Shifrin, Nat Sobel, Pauline Weislow and Tom Wilscam.

Contents

Prologue   1

1. Nobody Special   5

2. Getting It   23

3. "The Happy Clan Named Crosby"   43

4. Mom   68

5. The Ranch   88

6. Getting Out   110

7. Coming Back   125

8. Confrontations   148

9. Getting Out of It   179

10. The Magic Age   195

11. On the Loose   211

12. Back in the Trunk   230

13. Back on the Loose   244

14. Second Chance   265

15. Getting Straight   300

Prologue

A couple of years before my father died I found out he really did love me.

I was rehearsing a television show at NBC in Hollywood with Nanette Fabray. It was the first time we met, but like practically everyone else in show business she was an old pal of Dad's. During the break we strolled over to the restaurant on the lot to have lunch together. We gave the waitress our order and were relaxing into small talk about nothing in particular when she said she had a story about the old man I might like to hear. From the time I was a small child I never met anyone, in show business or out, who didn't have some kind of story about him, and long ago I had picked up the habit of only half listening. But this one was different.

"Back around 1957," she began, "Bing was working on a picture called *Man on Fire*. The script had been written by my husband, Randy MacDougall. He was also directing it and was one of the producers. Randy was a good fishing buddy of your father's—the first one to take him down to Las Cruces—so they had more than the usual movie-business friendship. I don't know, but maybe that influenced Bing's decision to take on the project. *Man on Fire* was a big departure from his earlier work. It was a straight dramatic film without any comedy or songs. The only singing was the title song behind the credits, and that was done by the Ames Brothers. If you remember, the story was about a divorced father's bitter struggle for the custody of his son and the strained relationship he had with the boy.

"Anyhow, one afternoon Bing came over to the house to meet with Randy about some revisions in the script. I sat in the living room with them, listening to them work. As the afternoon moved on, the conversation drifted away from the specific situation in the movie to more general talk about parents and children. The subject had a lot of personal meaning for me. Randy and I had married earlier that year, and I was now pregnant with our baby. My relationship with my own mother and father hadn't been that good when I was young, and I was full of doubts and anxieties about the kind of parent I would make now that it was my turn.

"Randy already had three children from his first marriage, and he and Bing began trading thoughts about the special problems of raising a child in Hollywood. They talked about all the poor little rich kids who grow up with parents who are wealthy and famous and adulated. What does that do to them? What are the parents' responsibilities? Should they just turn them loose and let them have everything? What do their sons and daughters feel about them if they try to put a brake on the endless privilege that surrounds the kids' lives?

"Almost thinking out loud, I said, 'God, I blamed my mother and father for so many things when I was a girl. When I look back now I realize they did the best they could, but there's still so much scar tissue. I guess we all put a lot of blame on our folks. And it kind of frightens me to think that our own kids may end up doing the same with us.'"

The waitress had come back with our lunch, but I left the food on my plate and asked her to go on.

"Now, Gary, you know your father is not much given to discussing his personal life and private feelings . . ."

I'm sure I must have smiled. I had to agree with her there.

"But there was something about the moment. Bing was sharing a camaraderie with a pal he knew on close male terms as a fishing partner. He was listening to an old friend give voice to her own uncertainties about becoming a mother. He was deep into a project that dealt with some of the same hard questions. For whatever reasons, he began to open up like I had never seen him do before.

"'Sure, I understand what you're talking about,' he said. 'I understand it very well. When you love your kids you have to do a lot of things that aren't going to make them too pleased with you. With my boys, I felt it was important to teach them that there was another way of life outside of Hollywood, and I wanted to make them strong enough to cope with it.

"'I know I was tough on them. When they were only young-sters I sent them off in the summers to work on a ranch. It was the hardest, most grueling kind of physical labor imaginable, and here they were, four soft kids suddenly thrown into a rough, completely alien world where they had to hold their own with grown-up men who had been living that way forever.

"'I forced them to do a lot of things they didn't like. And I think they must have hated me for it. I remember their anger. They tried to keep it hidden, but it wasn't hard to read. But if you love your kids, really love them, then you have to do what's right for them.

"'If I hadn't cared about my boys, I could have taken the easy way out. I could have given them everything, and they would have thought I was a great guy. But I felt this was better.'"

It was time to go back to work.

"I'm not really sure why I told you that," Nanette said as we stood up from the table, "except it had direct meaning to me and my own life and I've never forgotten it."

I didn't know what to say beyond mumbling a thank you and assuring her I was glad she did. I was too moved and confused by her story to talk about it.

"What do you know," I thought to myself on the walk back to the sound stage. "So he really had a plan. If he was trying to make it tough, he sure succeeded, but why the hell didn't he let us in on it? Couldn't he see all that stuff was making us crazy?"

It had never occurred to me that he was, in his own way, act-ing out of love. I don't believe he ever said he loved us in his life. Whatever he seemed like when he was being Bing Crosby, that just wasn't his style when he came home at night and closed the front door behind him. He was not the kind of old man who puts his arms around his sons and hugs them and kisses them and tells them how he really feels and why he is doing what he does.

I kept picking away at that last point.

"Jesus, why didn't he ever sit us down one time and say, 'Look, fellas, the world is hard and I have to be hard on you so you'll be strong enough to survive it'? Wouldn't that have saved everyone a lot of grief?"

3

The answer was so obvious that it took me the rest of the day to figure it out. He knew he was right, so he didn't feel he owed us an explanation. That was my father. He never thought he had to explain himself to anyone.

Chapter One
Nobody Special

The idea was to be ordinary. One of the troops. Nobody special.

Except for a year at Black Foxe Military Academy, an expensive boarding school where people like Charlie Chaplin shipped off their sons, my brothers and I were sent to neighborhood Catholic schools until we graduated from junior high. Our classmates included a few other show business children. I remember Jack Haley's son Jackie and William Gargan's boy Leslie. But most of the kids came from families barely middle class enough to scratch up the relatively modest tuition.

While I was growing up in the late thirties and early forties, the stars and other heavyweights in the business liked to hold elaborate birthday parties for their children, the more extravagant the better. Mom and Dad usually turned the invitations down, but every now and then they decided my brothers and I should go. That was about the only exposure I had to that world, and it didn't happen often. Which was all right with me.

I had nothing against the star kids. I simply didn't know them. And by the time I was six years old I could see we didn't share much in common. They always had money jingling in their pockets. They mouthed off at their parents and got away with it. They weren't very physical. They didn't like to play ball or do anything that might work up a sweat. From the way they talked, they seemed to spend their afternoons lounging around the house in their nice clothes or going to the movies. Regular kids didn't go to the movies in the daytime. That was only good on Saturday morning, when there were Westerns and cartoons and serials. Regular kids got a ball game going in the daytime or ran around playing cowboys and Indians.

The parties were really for the parents and press, and were orchestrated with all the efficiency of any other high-budget Hollywood production. The chauffeurs dropped the kids off in their dress-up clothes or costumes, and as soon as they stepped through the front door someone slapped party hats on their heads, stuck noisemakers in their hands and whisked them off into the prescribed routine while the photographers clicked away.

"Okay, we're going to watch the magician now. Everybody smile. Great. All right, now it's time to ride the donkey. You all line up here and this one will ride the donkey and the photographer will snap the picture. And here's the cake! No eating the cake yet, kids. We have to get the picture of the cake first. Okay, birthday boy, you stand in front of the cake. That's it. And the rest of you make a half circle around him. I said a half circle. Let's all look like we're having fun now. Good. Thank you very much."

The regulars had been through it so often that they went along with the script like the seasoned professionals they were. We never could get the hang of it. The adults led us through wimpy games, like pin-the-tail-on-the-donkey, calculated to return us back home as clean and well pressed as we left it. But if Denny and Phil and I couldn't find other kids to roughhouse with, we fought among ourselves.

I'm sure the grownups didn't know what to make of us when we went to Edward G. Robinson's house to celebrate Eddie Junior's sixth birthday. Eddie's father had become a star playing gangsters, so of course the party had to have a cops-and-robbers motif. The kids all belonged to someone famous—John Barrymore, David Selznick, Melvyn Douglas, Bob Burns—and their parents had dressed them up in snappy northwest mountie outfits, striped convict suits and the like. We got by in our regular lumber jackets and chaps over our jeans. Eddie was decked out as the chief of police and had a high time posing with the real patrol wagon and authentic Beverly Hills police captain that had been requisitioned for the occasion.

The centerpiece of the party was a wooden jail cell set up on the lawn. Eddie arrested each kid in turn and put him behind bars, then stood guard next to him while the photographer took the picture. When it got to be our turn, the twins and I entered the cell like we were told. Then Eddie snapped the lock shut, unzipped his trousers and started to pee on us through the bars.

We went crazy. Yowling in rage, we slammed ourselves against the cell door until it burst open and headed straight for the birthday boy to tear him apart. It was finished almost before it began. The adults swarmed over us at once and pulled us off the poor kid. They hadn't seen what he had done. They only knew that here were three insane desperados on a rampage, with murder in their hearts for the little police chief. We weren't invited back for birthday number seven.

Our own birthdays were different. Mom and Dad let us ask four or five school friends over on Saturday afternoon, and we played ball and ran around the backyard for a couple of hours. Because it was a special occasion, they eased up on the normal rules. As long as we were reasonably well behaved, they allowed us to enjoy ourselves. About three o'clock there was ice cream and cake and we were handed our presents. Mom always made sure we received one or two gifts we wanted, along with the usual socks and underwear. At five o'clock the company went home, and that was that for another year.

There were a few problems with being just an ordinary kid. For one thing, Dad didn't seem to be just an ordinary father.

Ordinary fathers didn't make movies and recordings and have their own radio program. Anytime I turned on the Philco, there he was, doing his show or guesting on someone else's or singing on one of his records.

Ordinary fathers didn't have their pictures in the newspapers and magazines. I'd find them scattered around the house, and one day, when I was just about old enough to make out the words, I read about what a great singer he was. It said he was the best singer who ever existed, his voice was heard by more people than any other voice in history. I thought that was really something, and the next morning I told the kids at school that the great Bing Crosby was my dad. By the time I came home that afternoon, word had already gotten back to Mom, and she sat me down for a little talk.

"Listen, Gary, you're no different from anyone else. Just because your father is sort of famous doesn't mean you're anything special. So don't get cocky. Don't get the big head. Don't start thinking you're better than the other kids. Because you're not."

Once was all she had to tell me. I never made that mistake again.

Still, it didn't quite fit. Ordinary kids didn't have to go on the radio with their father and be in his movies. Ordinary kids weren't driven to school by a man in a black coat and cap. They walked or their mothers dropped them off. Until we went out of town to high school, my brothers and I tried to con every chauffeur we had into letting us out two blocks away and meeting us back there at the end of the day. They never would do it, of course. It would have meant their jobs if Dad found out. And he would be sure to know. He knew everything.

And everyone in the world seemed to know him. That mystified me when I was small. On the way to the car at three o'clock or while we waited at the gas station for the tank to be filled—anywhere we went grownups we had never seen before came up to us and started chatting about him.

"You're the Crosby boys, right? Well, how's your father? How's your old man?"

Then they beamed as if they knew him all their lives.

"Do you know my father?" one of us would ask.

"Oh, sure!" they answered. "He's great! I heard him on the radio Thursday night. I got all his records. I saw him in *Road to Singapore* with Bob Hope. He sure did good in that, didn't he?"

Not knowing what else to do, we would smile back and say, "Yeah, he sure did."

They almost always had stories about him.

"I met him on the golf course one time . . ."

"He was walking down the street last year, and I said hi . . ."

I couldn't figure it out. They spoke about him as if he were

God. There didn't seem to be a whole lot of difference between them.

The similarity grew even stronger when Christmas rolled around. Starting about Thanksgiving, the huge living room in our house began to fill up with presents for Dad. By the week before Christmas there was hardly room for more, but the boxes continued to arrive through New Year's. There were hundreds and hundreds of them, and at least 90 percent were from people Dad didn't know, had never heard of. They ranged from golf clubs and magnums of champagne sent by companies hoping to do business with him to socks and mufflers little old ladies had knit because they loved him so much.

I knew other fathers didn't have that going for them.

I also knew it was better not to be his son. I wouldn't deny it if I were asked, but people changed as soon as they made the connection and started acting strange.

I would be at a classmate's birthday party, just another kid in a whole roomful of kids, when suddenly the grownups would come swarming in my direction and turn me into the center of attention.

"Hey, how are you, how are you? Here, want some cake? Want some candy?"

When I sneaked a look across the room, a wall of stony young faces would be glaring back in anger. There was no question that I'd hear about it later.

Sometimes a parent strolled over in the school yard while I waited for the chauffeur and struck up a friendly conversation. We would gab for a minute or two about sports or the weather, but then he would get to the point.

"Listen, Gary, I want to talk to your father about this."

An envelope would materialize and be shoved into my hand.

"Give this to your dad, will you? Just have him look at it for a second. Just have him read it."

It would be a song or a script or a piece of special material. For all the middle-class normality of the neighborhood, this still was North Hollywood, and the adults who weren't in show business kept on the lookout for the open door that would take them to the golden land of fame and fortune. And it seemed that everybody had a good joke, everybody had a song, everybody had a million-dollar idea for a movie.

The first few times it happened I brought the envelope home and turned it over to my mother to pass on to Dad. I suppose he filed it or threw it away or sent it back. He may even have read it. Eventually Mom explained what was going on.

"Look, there are some people out there, Gary, who may act real nice to you, but it's not because they like you. What they're trying to do is use you to get next to your father. Understand? So watch out when they start buttering you up."

I got the message. From then on I managed to lose the envelope or left it in the car or forgot to give it to my mother.

I didn't have to worry about my classmates buttering me up. Most of them seemed to feel that because I was Crosby's kid I had life easy and thought I was hot stuff. To even things out a bit, they took it upon themselves to make sure I paid my dues.

It started as early as the second grade. I remember being afraid to go out to recess because two of the boys in class gave me the sign they were going to whip me. I couldn't understand why they were angry. When we got outside I asked them.

"I don't like your attitude," one of them sneered and punched me on the shoulder.

"Yeah," said the other as he cocked his fist for a swing at my head. "And I don't like your face."

A confused, frightened seven-year-old had no way of knowing what they really wanted. It seemed like maybe they wanted to whip my ass because they just didn't like me or my name or my father or something, but I couldn't be sure. I only knew it wouldn't help to argue with them and that my only choices were to fight back or run.

That day I ran. I broke away from them and tried to find a safe place to hide until it was time to return to the refuge of the classroom. But I wasn't a very fast runner. They caught up with me and finished the job. So I was going to have to learn how to fight.

By the next year I had become fairly good at it. I started to win some. The school had moved me ahead a grade and I was the smallest boy in class, but I had so much anger in me by then I could whip kids twice my size.

At the first punch a red veil dropped before my eyes. Everything turned hazy and ground down to slow motion. I could see fists coming at me at half speed and bouncing off, but they didn't hurt. The next day I would be sore all over, but while the fight was on they could break my nose or bust open my eye and it didn't bother me. I just kept coming and coming and coming, and the more I was hit the harder I fought back.

When I got someone down, the other kids had to drag me off. I would have killed him if I could. If a stick or a rock was within reach, I used that along with my fists. I was a streetfighter. I was not clean. I thought fair fighting was bullshit, that there was no such thing. All I wanted was to be left alone.

Certain kids knew they could whip me, and when they realized I never backed down, it was just a lark for them. They could have me every day if they felt like it. Sometimes they did.

Most of the time, if I was able to get in some licks before I went down, the kid who started it looked for someone else to pick on who wouldn't blouse his eye or give him a bloody nose. I learned that bullies don't like to get hurt. They like to do the hurting. And they lose a lot of prestige if a little guy whacks them a few times, even if they beat him. I also saw that however it ended, my classmates' opinion of me went up. I had passed some kind of test, and they seemed to like me better. It was a good lesson. I continued to benefit from it each time I was sent off to a new school and had to prove myself all over again.

Mom was surprisingly sympathetic when I came home with my face banged up and my clothes dirtied and torn. She would put her arms around me and hold me tight so I could cry if I wanted. Then she quizzed me carefully on the details to find out how it started. That was important to her.

"Don't you ever start one," she would say. "If I ever hear of you starting one, so help me, I'll break your head. But if you can't get out of it, if you have to fight, then make sure you're still around at the finish."

She must have told the old man about the scraps. He couldn't help but notice the bruises on my face when I showed up at the dinner table, but he usually chose to ignore them. About the only time he had something to say was when I went through a period of fighting every day and the teacher sent home a note. Then he would turn his anger on me full blast.

"What the hell's the matter with you? Why can't you get along with people? Jesus Christ, you act like an animal! Why is it that you're always the one in the fight? How come other kids manage to stay out of trouble and you can't?"

When he paused for an answer, I simply shrugged my shoulders and muttered, "I don't know, Dad. I just don't know."

I never tried to explain it to him. My father could lecture and order, but he wasn't much given to listening to explanations or delving into your personal problems. I was supposed to be a regular guy. I wasn't supposed to be getting a different kind of treatment because I was somebody special. I knew he wouldn't believe me, so there really wasn't anything to say.

Every now and then one of the classmates who had warmed up to me might invite me over to his house after school or down to the park to play ball Saturday morning. I'd have liked nothing better, but it wasn't allowed.

The rule was that unless I had baseball or football practice, I had to come home promptly at three. If I got up the nerve to ask Mom why, she said, "Because you have to, that's all. I don't want to hear any more about it." And Saturday mornings were reserved for chores. The four of us were expected to rake the leaves, hose down the courtyard and trim the rose bushes and hedges. It took the entire morning—even longer once the war began and we also had to weed and water the Victory garden. We couldn't get started too early because Mom would still be asleep and the noise might wake her. So we sat around and waited for the go-ahead until eight-thirty or nine. By the time we finished it was one o'clock. The kids hit the park at eight and were done by one. They had already tucked the ball under their arms and gone home for lunch.

I never could bring myself to say, "No, I can't come because my folks won't let me." That didn't seem like the sort of answer a regular kid would give. My classmates were regular kids, and their parents let them visit each other and play in the park. The best I could come up with was, "Well, no, I don't think I want to." That wasn't a very good answer either. As the words left my mouth, I could see the change in the boy who had tried to make friends. He would pull back and throw me a funny look as if I were some kind of snobbish rich man's son who felt he was too good to play with him. I was seldom asked a second time.

Except for birthdays, inviting the kids from school to my house was out of the question. I knew they wouldn't be comfortable under our roof. None of them lived in a twenty-room mansion with a swimming pool, tennis court and half a dozen servants. And there were too many restrictions. Every move had its own list of do's and don'ts, which certainly wouldn't be suspended just because I brought some visitors home. Then, too, there was always the danger that Mom might be loaded and cause some sort of mortifying scene, and the kids might go back to school and tell everybody.

The four of us spent most Saturday afternoons at home by ourselves. We played war or cowboys and Indians or got up a two-on-two game of basketball or football, with the twins against me and Linny, our younger brother. We usually ended up fighting.

We fought in silence, without screaming and yelling. If Mom or Dad heard us, we were sure to get punished. To keep from being seen, we chased each other down to the bushes, where the view from the house was blocked, and did our scuffling there. That was about as far away as we could go. If Mom or one of the help leaned out a window and called to us, we had to be within earshot so we could answer immediately.

The big game was to get in the last hit. I was larger than the twins, but they could run faster, so most of the time they won. If I somehow managed to get in the last punch, Denny and Phil would tiptoe into the bathroom while I was taking a shower and douse me with pitchers of cold water. To this day I still lock the bathroom door behind me.

The fights were really about confinement. For all the luxury that surrounded us, we felt as penned up as cons in a prison. We had to find some way to discharge the tension and frustration. Since we were the sole inmates, we only had ourselves to work out on. We scrapped seriously and hard, but that didn't stop us from loving each other. Sometimes the twins and I carried the

13

fighting over into school, and God help anyone who jumped in between us. Instantly the three of us tightened up into a single fist and turned on him in a frenzy: "You touch one of us, you fight all three!"

When we weren't playing or fighting outside, we would sneak into the kitchen to hang out with the black help. It was about the only place in the house that had some life. Wilma, a large powerhouse of a woman, was forever working around the stove, cooking up fried chicken or biscuits or apple pie that couldn't be beat. In between his chauffering and butlering chores, Teddy would be sitting at his spot at the kitchen table reading his paper. At mealtimes they were joined by the downstairs and upstairs maids and whoever else Dad had working for him at the moment. The kitchen smelled good, and it was a pleasure just to park there for a while and watch them rapping and kidding around and being happy.

They spoke of their homes and their families and what they had planned for their day off. Wilma talked about choir practice and church. Rose, the upstairs maid, told stories about her boyfriend and ran down the spots they were planning to hit together Saturday night. We called her The Shadow because she had a way of breaking off in mid sentence and solemnly intoning to no one in particular, "Who know what evil loiks in the hearts of men—and women too? The Shadow knows!" As she detailed the pleasures of the coming weekend, Wilma might chime in, "Well, you better not let Georgie catch you," and the whole room would rock with laughter. Georgie was our grim-faced Irish nurse and Mom's strong right arm. When they heard her footsteps clumping down the hallway, they became very quiet and straight, but the rest of the time they made jokes about her.

I felt more at home in the kitchen than anywhere else. The people there weren't so solemn and uptight. They seemed to like us better. They let us act like ordinary kids. We could have fun with them and laugh and carry on, and it didn't matter. We didn't have to be on our best behavior all the time. Wilma would slip me a taste of whatever she was whipping up for dinner or slide me a couple of cookies or a wedge of pie. Teddy let the four of us gang up on him, then would chase us under the table when he had enough of our foolishness. If the coast was clear,

Rose ran us around the house playing hide-and-seek or The Shadow.

We obeyed them more than anyone else because we never wanted to get them in trouble. And when we did break the rules they didn't fink on us. They were under strict orders to report each and every transgression, but unless it couldn't be hidden they always covered for us. When we didn't finish every scrap on our plates, Wilma pretended not to notice and quickly dumped what was left. If the twins and I got into a punch-out on the drive back from school, Teddy kept it to himself. They were the only grownups I trusted.

For some reason that was never made clear, the kitchen was off limits. We knew we weren't allowed there but couldn't bring ourselves to stay away, so we cooked up an alibi in case we were caught. Our story was we had gotten thirsty playing basketball in the courtyard outside the back door and came in for a glass of water. That was okay, wasn't it? I mean, what were we supposed to do, lick the cement? If Georgie wasn't around when we peered in the door, we took our seats at the kitchen table but kept an ear tuned for the sound of her feet coming down the hall from the front of the house. The moment we heard her we jumped up, waved a quick "See you later" and raced back outside. If we were a beat slow, she might catch the door slam closed as she rounded the corner. "Those kids just in here?" she would ask Wilma and the others. "What kids?" they would answer. "Didn't see no kids."

We wanted to be ordinary. That was our goal. We thought that would please Mom and Dad and make them happy with us. It sounded like it should be simple, but why was it so complicated? They constantly preached we were nobody, yet once we set foot outside the house everyone else insisted we were somebody. They kept reminding us we were just part of the troops, yet whenever the troops took off on furlough we couldn't join up with them. And we didn't understand why. Time and again I pondered the contradiction but never could get it to yield much sense.

"If we're special, we should be special," I would reason to myself. "If we're the same as all the other kids, then we should be the same. How can we be special just at certain times and not at others? And how come we're only special when there's fun coming up and not special when we have to do the stuff we don't like?"

What lay behind the paradox, of course, was the fear about what might happen if we were let out into the world alone. And there was reason to be afraid. The Lindbergh baby had been kidnapped and murdered in 1932, the year before I was born. After that, no star in Hollywood could afford to ignore his own vulnerability.

When I was nine months old the police warned Dad they had been informed of a plot to kidnap me. According to the old clippings, a man had accidentally overheard the conspirators scheming it out together at the Pacific Electric Station in Los Angeles:

"Are you sure Crosby will pay?"

"Sure he'll pay. He's making three thousand a week."

"We'll get the money so slick the cops won't even hear about it."

Dad went straight to the newspapers and advised his fellow performers to do the same.

"A large percentage of Hollywood folk who have received kidnapping and extortion threats have adopted the attitude of silence," he told the press. "Ann Harding, Mae West, Marlene Dietrich and a number of other film stars have made known threats against their homes and lives, and I think they have been wise."

At the same time, he tried to turn away any other hungry eyes that might be lured by the glitter of the Crosby fortune.

"I believe there would be fewer threats if the unvarnished truth were told about Hollywood incomes—if the correct figures and not the phony and highly colored ones were actually stated, after deducting income taxes, commissions and living expenses necessary for the peculiar positions in which our work places us. In my own case, I feel lucky if I can save between fifteen and twenty percent of my yearly salary, over and above all normal deductions. From a financial standpoint I wouldn't be a great shakedown for kidnappers."

For the next month guards patrolled our house around the

clock. But nothing more came of the plot, and they were eventually sent away.

Mom and Dad never did let us in on their concern that the kidnappers might come back someday. All we knew was that if we weren't at school or playing around the house, someone had to be with us. When I was about five or six and we spent the summers at Dad's place at Rancho Santa Fe so he could be near his racetrack, he hired a college student named Jerry Ward to stand guard over us. Jerry became like a big brother. The day Dad decided to teach me to swim by tossing me into the pool, I wasn't all that terrified because I knew Jerry would haul my butt out if I started to drown.

A couple of years later the job was taken over by Oscar Cunningham, a former Ohio State athlete who now coached the Catholic school in Beverly Hills. Oscar was a funny, delightful guy who could outplay and outrun us and knew how to make us laugh. A few times a week he trotted us down to the park and played football or baseball with us until we were ready to drop. Sometimes he surprised us with special treats. When the Cleveland Browns hit town, he took us into the locker room and had us shake hands with Marion Motley, Bill Willis and Otto Graham.

Jerry and Oscar couldn't have been nicer. But they still were grownups. They were being paid to keep a watchful eye on us. And playing with them just wasn't the same as hanging out with the kids from school.

There were moments when Mom realized the four of us needed to taste a little more freedom from time to time. Not that she told us so directly, but years later I came across an old interview with Louella Parsons where she acknowledged her awareness of the problem. For the most part her rap was the standard fantasy about "the happy clan named Crosby" that I had been hearing all my life. But toward the end Louella dropped a surprise that got her to open up a bit more than usual. Evidently a prowler had been arrested near the house, and we had been under the protection of armed guards for over a month. I certainly hadn't known that, and when Louella asked

Mom about it she said she didn't either but thanked her for bringing it to her attention.

"I'm glad you told me. It's best that I know. Sometimes I feel so sorry for them. There are so many things that other youngsters do that they can't do. We want them brought up just like other children—but that isn't possible . . . They can't leave the house unless we know where they are every minute. Of course they don't like it—and think Bing and I are just being bossy. We don't want to frighten them or make them feel different from other boys by telling them the truth."

Every so often Mom loosened the constraints by sending us away for the weekend as a reward for not breaking the rules. Sometimes we stayed with Grandma and Grandpa Crosby. When Dad made it in Hollywood, he moved his mother and father down from Spokane and set them up in a house in L.A. They lived there until 1950, when Grandpa Crosby died and Grandma moved in with us. It was always good to be away from home, but visiting them wasn't that much of a relief from our usual regimen.

Grandpa Crosby could be fun. He was an easygoing little man who played the mandolin and taught us nonsense songs. I still remember one we would harmonize together:

She promised that she'd meet me when the clock struck seventeen
In the stockyards just nine miles out of town,
Where pig's ears and pig's feet and tough old Texas steers
Sell for sirloin steak at nineteen cents a pound.
She's my honey—my daisy.
She's ornery—she's lazy.
She's lop-eared—she's pigeon-toed and lame.
And her teeth are all phony from chewin' Swiss baloney.
She's my freckle-faced consumptive Mary Jane.

During the week Grandpa Crosby worked at Dad's office as his bookkeeper. That had been his job at the brewery back in Spokane. If Grandma wasn't looking, he would slip across the street at lunchtime and lift a few beakers at the Cock and Bull. Dad took care of him almost as if he were Grandpa's father instead of his son.

Grandma Crosby was a different story. She was a stern, strict, imposing woman without much visible emotion. Dad was a lot like her in private and treated her with great deference and respect. So did Grandpa. She was the one who ruled the roost, and whatever she said went, especially when it came to religion. Grandpa was a good Catholic, too, but Grandma made a cause out of her piety. There would be endless praying and talks about God when we came to visit. I listened to the clock tick more than anything else.

I liked it better at my other grandparents'. They lived over in the Valley in a sturdy little house that Grandpa Wyatt had built with his own hands when they moved to California to be near my mother. (Mom was born Wilma Wyatt. She became Dixie Lee when she went into the movies. She was originally from Tennessee, and some producer thought the name had a nice southern ring.) Grandpa Wyatt could do everything. He was a lawyer. He was a barber. He was an architect. He had been a soldier and fought in World War I. He was also a zealous socialist. The bookshelves in his living room were crammed with thick volumes of Marx, Engels and Lenin. When he took them down to lecture me about the injustices of the world, I noticed how he had filled the margins on almost every page with elaborate comments.

Gramps was a ruddy-faced, bald little man who wore glasses, sported a goatee and had false teeth that never quite fit. He laughed a lot and got angry a lot. Sometimes, when he got to ranting or guffawing, his upper plate dropped down onto his lower and cut him off in the middle of his sentence, but he'd just flick it back up there with his tongue. He didn't care enough about such things to take the trouble to buy himself a proper set of dentures.

My grandmother—we called her Nonie—was a semi-invalid and hardly ever out of her bathrobe. She was as quiet and gentle as Grandpa was feisty and strong, but they were both warm, loving, kindly people. When I came to visit Friday afternoon, Grandpa took me to a restaurant for dinner and then to the movie at the El Portal theater. It was late by the time we got back to the house, but Nonie would be waiting up for us and she'd sit and listen in her robe while we gabbed away into the night.

Grandpa Wyatt could be stern, too. He didn't let me get away with much. If I misbehaved, he threw me a scowl and grumbled, "Boy, if you don't stop this second, I'm gonna cloud up and rain all over you. I'm gonna hop on you like a duck on a june bug." That's all I had to hear. I believed him and straightened up on the spot. He wasn't the sort of grandparent who stores it up quietly and then goes tattling back to your mother and father. He took care of it himself. But I don't remember him ever laying a hand on me. I did what he said, and five minutes later we were back to enjoying each other again. Gramps made sure I toed the line, but he wasn't hung up on just my bad side.

The things that raised his ire usually weren't all that serious. One of the big points of contention was the way I washed my hands before dinner. Like most seven-year-olds, I simply made a perfunctory pass under the faucet and wiped off the grime on the towel. Grandpa had definite views on the subject.

"Gary, how many times do I have to show you? This is the right way to do it. Okay, first you make the water as hot as you can stand it. Got that? Now you take the soap, put it in the water and roll it around in your palms like this to get it all nice and sudsy. Now drop the soap and go over the backs of your hands. Scrub the backs of your fingers and in between 'em too. All right. When you finish with that, you wash off. Then you pick up the soap again and do your palms. And make sure to dig your fingers into the soap so it goes up under your nails. Now put your hands under the water and give 'em a good rinsing. That's it. Don't forget to get the soap out from under your fingernails. I still see some soap there. Now you can take the towel and dry off. See how nice and clean they are? Isn't that better? That's the way you're supposed to wash your hands!"

Nonie died when I was about ten. Grandpa lived by himself for a few years, then married again and moved out to Camarillo with his new wife. It was too far to travel for the weekend, so that ended my time alone with him. I only got to see him when he dropped by the house to be with Mom. He was well into his eighties when he passed away. He had suffered two major strokes but fought his way back both times and was able to get around with the help of a walker. And his mind remained alert to the end. When I visited him in the hospital as he lay dying, he recognized me the moment I stepped into the room.

"Well, hello, Gary. How you doin'? Everything all right?"

"Yeah, Grandpa, everything's good."

"Well, that's fine."

Then we just sat together for a while without speaking. When I left him I looked into his eyes and saw a kind of mirth shimmering there that I didn't understand. Eventually I may figure out what it was. To this day, whenever I'm singing to myself I find myself doing "Darling Nelly Gray," one of the old songs he used to sing. And when I'm thinking about something I always catch myself tapping the arm of my chair to the same inner rhythm that's going on inside my head, just like Gramps did all the time.

The very best weekends were spent with Alice and Hugh Ross and their son, Pat, a good athlete about two years older than I. Alice and Mom were close friends from Mom's days in the movies, when Alice helped her out as a kind of unofficial personal secretary. The Rosses lived in a small two-bedroom house in a middle-class neighborhood in the Valley. If my brothers and I weren't out of favor at home, Mom might let one of us visit them every month or so. Some weekends all four of us decended on them at the same time. Alice would put one of us in the bedroom with Pat and stash the others on the couches in the living room. We turned the place inside out, but Alice and Hugh always made us feel welcome, as though there was nothing inconvenient about having up to four more kids on their hands.

The chauffeur would drop us off Friday evening or as early as we could break out Saturday morning. Alice fixed us whatever we wanted for breakfast, then we grabbed the football and dashed outside to the wide asphalt street in front of the house. We passed the entire day playing touch with Pat, his friend Richie Chappel and a couple of other kids from the block. Sometimes Hugh put on his sneakers and joined us. When it came time for dinner, Alice cooked up a mess of hamburgers that were as good as the ones they made at the Big Boy. She dumped the food in the middle of the table, and we dug in and ate as much as we liked. There were no servants or formal dining etiquette to get in the way. Then Alice and Hugh piled us into the car and drove us off to the movies.

They were just a regular family living a regular life. Alice and Hugh loved each other and their son, and he loved them back. They were like a family was supposed to be. Pat caught plenty of hell when he stepped out of line, but there was no reign of terror. He wasn't afraid of them. When he was bad he was punished, but then it was over and they went on with life.

My brothers and I made sure to behave ourselves. We knew if we didn't they would tell Mom and Dad and that would be the end of our visits. The weekends were too important to jeopardize.

I dreaded having to leave. Sunday mornings we rode our bikes or got up another game of touch, but I wasn't able to play very well. It was impossible to concentrate. All I could think about was that in two more hours I had to go home . . . one more hour and I had to go home . . . another half hour and I had to go home. Then that big hearse of a station wagon would come crawling up the block to deliver me back to the mausoleum, and it was over again for another month.

Chapter Two
Getting It

I hated being in trouble. I was in it all the time. It's just about the earliest memory I have.

Mom and Dad had gone out for the evening, leaving us in the care of our keepers. I was six. Denny and Phil were five. Linny was still an infant and probably asleep in his crib. We should have been sleeping, too, but had kept ourselves awake whispering in the dark from our beds. It was risky—this was a whipping violation—but the danger made it exciting and the excitement was hard to resist.

I suppose that's why we plunged ahead when our thoughts turned to the canary down the hall in Mom's dressing room. We knew we weren't supposed to leave our beds but agreed we just had to pay it a visit anyhow. Taking care to muffle the giggles that might rouse our nurse, we crept down the long corridor to Mom and Dad's wing of the house, eased open the door and peered inside. The bird was chirping away in its cage.

We stood there in silence, watching it sing to itself on the other side of the doorway. But then the twins grew restless. They wanted more. They wanted to touch the canary and pet it. The caper was getting out of control. We were never to set foot in that part of the house by ourselves. It was bad enough to be up past our bedtime and out of our room.

"Don't go in there!" I hissed, hoping to scare some sense into them. "Holy smoke, don't go in there! They'll kill us!"

But my brothers weren't as terrified of them as I was—yet.

"Oh, come on, they'll never find out."

That sounded crazy to me.

"What do you mean, they'll never find out? They'll be sure to know. They'll see the footprints in the rug. They know everything."

"No they won't!"

Laughing together, they bounded across the threshold into forbidden territory. I stayed where I was, making sure to keep my feet away from the edge of Mom's white carpet, and watched them head straight for the cage. It was too high to reach, but that didn't stop them. They scampered up the back of the divan next to the stand and in a moment had the little door unfastened. One of them reached in his hand for the bird. It got to fluttering and squawking. Then suddenly it was silent.

I streaked back to my room and threw myself into bed. They were right behind me.

"Oh my God, what did you guys do? What happened?"

"I don't know," Denny sobbed. "I guess we killed it."

We tried to stay awake until Mom and Dad came home but drifted off to sleep. Sometime in the middle of the night the nurse woke us up. She got right to the point.

"Your mother and father want to see you."

I was the first to be called in.

They were in Dad's office next to their bedroom. Mom was standing with her arms folded. He was sitting behind his desk.

"What's this?" he asked, pointing to the tiny dead thing on the top of the desk. "Who was in here? You're the oldest. Why didn't you take care of your brothers?"

I had nothing to say. It wouldn't do any good to tell him we hadn't meant to harm the bird. It would be better to stay silent and just take it. I knew I was going to get it. The only question was whether it would be from the back of Mom's silver hairbrush or from Dad's hands.

I remember his hands very well. They were short and stubby, not muscular but extremely strong. That night it was their turn. When he was through, he sent me back to my room and hollered out the door for the next one.

"Philip, you get in here!"

I read the fear on Phil's face when I passed him in the hall. Denny was sitting on the edge of his bed, staring down at the floor, waiting to get it next. When it was finally over, each of us retreated into separate corners of the room to let out our tears in private. Then we pulled ourselves together and went back to sleep.

They didn't speak to us the next morning. The silence lasted the rest of the week. About all they had to say was, "Watch your step. Just watch your step now." We had to be especially careful after we got it because then their eyes never left us. They scrutinized every move we made, and it didn't take much to get it again.

Even after life returned to normal we had to keep a close watch on our actions. We could still get it at any time. All the servants were allowed to take a shot at us. The other help never did, but we had to walk softly around our nurse. If she thought we were stepping out of line, she was free to whip us or do whatever else she dreamed up. Sometimes the punishment got out of hand.

One nurse liked to use the drowning treatment. If she caught any of us talking in bed or getting up too early in the morning, she hustled the guilty party into the bathroom and ordered him into the tub. When it was filled with two feet of water, she grabbed him by the hair, plunged his head down to the bottom and held it there awhile, then brought it back up so his face went under the stream still gushing from the faucet. If you timed it right, you might catch a short breath between the faucet and the tub.

It never occurred to us to complain. We assumed the grown-ups were all in it together. There didn't seem much point in telling one adult what another was doing to you. You might even make things worse. I was more surprised than relieved when Mom happened to walk into the bathroom one morning and caught the nurse in the middle of her routine. She exploded in rage. If she could have gotten her hands on a knife or gun, I'm quite certain she would have killed the woman. As it was, she fired her on the spot and threw her out of the house.

We had so many rules to follow, it was hard not to do something wrong. Just about every waking moment was controlled by its own set of regulations.

There was a rule about not talking to each other after we went to bed at night and before we got up in the morning. Someone usually checked to make sure we obeyed. When Georgie took over as our nurse when I was eight, that became her special passion. She would set her alarm clock half an hour early, then hover outside our door so she could catch the first words of the morning tumble out of our mouths when we awoke. At the opening whisper, she came roaring in, ripped off the covers and whaled on us with a wire coat hanger. Later on she would tell Mom and, depending on her mood that morning, she might let us have it again. That's how we started our day.

There were rules about brushing our teeth, showering, making our beds, straightening our room. If the toothbrush wasn't wet or the towel felt dry, that was good for a punishment. So was not hitting the breakfast table at the right time or not dressing the right way. When one of us left a sneaker or pair of underpants lying around, he had to tie the offending object on a string and wear it around his neck until he went off to bed that night. Dad called it "the Crosby lavalier." At the time the humor of the name escaped me.

At breakfast there was a rule about finishing everything on our plates. Phil was a picky eater and had his problems with that one. But a rule was a rule. There were no exceptions. The morning he tried to get around it by hiding his bacon and eggs, Mom discovered the bulge under the rug and made him scoop the mess back onto his dish, then choke down every bite—dirt, hairs and all.

When the chauffeur drove us off to school, there was no wrestling or fooling around in the car. Nor was he to be kept waiting when he came to pick us up in the afternoon. If one of us dawdled on the way to the parking lot, Mom knew because she had the trip timed down to the minute, and he would get it as soon as he walked in the door.

In school we were expected to be model students. God help us if the teacher called home with a complaint or made one of us stay late for misbehaving. That was a certain whipping. We were also in big trouble if our grades weren't mostly *A*'s and *B*'s. A *D* got a licking. An *F* meant a licking and having to sit in the room with your books every afternoon for the next month until the new report card came home. A *C*, especially in conduct or effort, brought a loss of privileges and intimations of worse things to come if you didn't clean up your act on the spot. "Jesus," Dad would grumble, "can't you get anything better than a *C?* What the hell are you doing in there? Watch it. Just watch it, that's all."

If we played in our rooms before dinner, the door had to remain open so the grownups could listen in and see what we were up to. I didn't understand why, but it seemed to make them uneasy if we became too quiet. Of course, we couldn't be too noisy either.

Dinner was accompanied by a whole slew of rules. It was served formally in the dining room, with the table laid out in a hopelessly confusing array of plates and silverware. Mom studied us closely while we ate to make sure we used them correctly. We sat up straight on the edges of our chairs, with our elbows in at our sides and the forks held in our left hands so we could cut everything properly in the European fashion. If one of us picked up the wrong spoon or put the butter in the wrong dish, she reached over with the butt of her knife and gave him a whack on the knuckles. Dad didn't seem to take Mom's rage for good table manners all that seriously. He liked to pretend he didn't know which spoons to use either. Sometimes he deliberately irritated her sense of decorum by wolfing down his food with his mouth wide open. But that was between the two of them. We minded our own business and did what she told us. Still, there was always that devil in my brain who kept asking, "How come that's okay for him but not for us?"

The meal passed mostly in silence. They didn't have much to say to each other, and unless one of them asked us something, we weren't allowed to speak until we finished eating. There were usually one or two perfunctory questions about school, which we answered in the fewest possible words.

"So how was school today?"

"Okay."

"What did you do?"

"Went to class and played ball at recess."

Dinner seemed to take forever. It was finally over when Dad cocked back his chair, wiped his mouth, threw his napkin in the middle of his plate and said, "All right, you boys may be excused." That was the signal we were free to head upstairs to do our homework and go to bed.

I tried my best to toe the mark each day and hit all their rules and regulations. Not so much because I hoped to please them and win their approval. That seemed too far out of reach to consider as a serious possibility. It was more a matter of wanting to steer clear of the lickings and other punishments that followed fast behind their disapproval.

There was also the hope of gaining some favor at the end of the week. The lure was hard to resist, even though the chance of staying in their good graces was remote. I still remember the time the four of us asked if we could postpone our Saturday-morning chores and go to the Hitching Post theater on Hollywood Boulevard. We had heard about the place at school. The kids lined up at 8 A.M. in their cowboy outfits, checked their cap pistols on the wall, then settled in for a nonstop marathon of Westerns, serials and cartoons that lasted until four in the afternoon.

We bided our time until they both seemed in a decent mood, then worked up the nerve to make our pitch.

"Um, do you think we could go to the Hitching Post this Saturday?"

"Why, sure you can," they answered. "Just don't do anything wrong the rest of the week."

We knew what that meant. When we went back upstairs, we told each other, "Well, that's the end of that. It's a cinch there's gonna be something wrong by Friday." And, of course, there was.

It didn't help much when, on the spur of the moment Saturday morning, Mom decided that even though we had been bad she would have her friend Irma Thayer take us to *The Mikado*. Irma was a nice lady and we didn't want to hurt her feelings, so we pretended to enjoy it. But as I sat there watching the people on-stage run around and holler in a language that seemed to be English but made absolutely no sense, all I could think was, "When will I get to do what *I* like? Why is what's good for me always what I hate?"

As much as I tried to give them what they wanted, there were things about myself I couldn't seem to change or even control. One of them was my weight. From the time I was just a few years old I had a big, wide behind, and the rest of me was built like a fire hydrant. I looked like a lard bucket. Maybe because he had to struggle with his own weight problem, the old man was determined to make me slim down. He had me exercise. He put me on a diet of grapefruit and celery. When that didn't do the job, he concocted putdown nicknames that were intended, I suppose, to fuel my motivation.

The name-calling started early. It shows up in a 1937 interview he did at Paramount on a day he happened to take me with him. The clipping tells the story. I was four.

"Gary Evan is named after his daddy's pal, Gary Cooper. Bing recently brought Gary Evan down to Paramount to visit his namesake on the *Souls at Sea* set, and the tall, serious Cooper engaged the knee-high lad in conversation.

"'So we have the same first name, have we?' mused Cooper. Well, my folks call me Frank. That was my name before the studio changed it for Gary. What does your daddy call you?'

"Bashful Gary dug the toe of one scuffed sandal against the side of the other and answered,

"'Bucket Britches.'"

I guess Dad's fans thought "Bucket Britches" was cute. It didn't seem cute to me. Neither did "Satchel Ass" or "Bucket Butt" or "My Fat-assed Kid." That's how he introduced me to his cronies when he dragged me along to the studio or racetrack.

I remember tagging behind him at the track early one morning when I was about five. I was hanging in the background watching the sun rise and the steam spill out of the horses' nostrils, when some of his pals appeared and he snapped me out of my reverie.

"Hey, Bucket Butt, get over here! . . . Okay, this is Satchel Ass. Meet My Fat-assed Kid."

They laughed and enjoyed his little joke with him. All it did

29

for me was make me hurt and angry and leave me just as hungry as ever. Even then I was too afraid of him to let him see how I felt, so I tried to keep it hidden. But I wasn't a good enough actor yet. When he caught the scowl flicker across my face, he busted me on it immediately.

"Hey, what's the matter with you? Something wrong?"

"Nothin', Dad. Nothin'. Everything's fine."

"Good. Okay, then. Come on, Bucket Butt. Let's go. Move it."

The older I grew, the more of an issue my weight became. Anytime he could catch me up on it, he would. If he heard that I failed to beat out a bunt in a baseball game at school or just missed being safe at first on a grounder, he would say, "Well, if you were thinner, if you didn't have so damn much lard on you, you'd have made it." Even when I didn't mess up, he found a way to throw in a barb: "Denny says you got off a thirty-yard run yesterday. Not bad. Bet you could have gone for a touchdown if you dropped twenty pounds."

By the time I was ten or eleven he had stepped up his campaign by adding lickings to the regimen. Each Tuesday afternoon he weighed me in, and if the scale read more than it should have, he ordered me into his office and had me drop my trousers.

It didn't take a whole lot of thinking to realize this was never going to end unless I stuck religiously to the grapefruit and celery, until I finally slimmed down to his satisfaction. I couldn't do it. I could get by without the bread and potatoes. That wasn't too bad. But my craving for sweets couldn't be denied. I had to have something sweet to eat. Just had to. And since he wouldn't give it to me, I learned to take it for myself.

If I couldn't cajole Wilma into slipping me a handful of cookies or a slice of pie, I sneaked into the kitchen when she wasn't looking and stole them. I filched chocolates from the box in the living room sideboard. I became quite adept at it. I would take four or five pieces at a time, and no one could tell they were missing. To cover my traces, I made certain not to leave any empty papers in the box and moved around the remaining pieces to close up the telltale spaces. I spirited the stolen treasures upstairs and hid them behind the bedpost, then waited until later that night, when I was sure Georgie and my brothers were asleep, before I devoured them. The next morning I folded the papers and arranged them carefully in my pants pocket so they didn't form a bulge. When I got to school I slipped them into the trash can.

I wasn't trying to be defiant or flirt with danger. I hated flirting with danger. It terrified me. But I couldn't seem to stop. I thought I was insane. I would plead with myself: "You know if you don't lose weight he's gonna whip you. Are you crazy?"

But then I would think about the cherry pie in the pantry or that box of candy sitting in the living room.

Every school day I had to leave the house an hour early and walk towards school as fast and as far as I could, until the car came along and picked me up. That night Dad was told how far I made it. To prepare myself for the Tuesday weigh-in, I stopped stealing food on Sunday and began swiping milk of magnesia from the medicine cabinet in the bathroom. Monday morning I weighed myself, and if I was still a pound or two over I stepped up the dosage and didn't eat the rest of the day. Instead of going to the lunchroom, I put on a heavy sweater or sweatshirt and jogged around the track for an hour, hoping to burn off some calories that way. Monday night I took more milk of magnesia and still more Tuesday morning. I spent most of Tuesday on the school toilet. If I was lucky, when I stepped on the scale late Tuesday afternoon the needle wavered just under the magic number and, all thanks to God, I was safe again for another week. But a lot of times I didn't make it. And whether I made it or not, I'd start shoving the sugar in my face again Wednesday morning and be right back on the same terror trip the following Sunday.

I worried almost as much about school. Part of the problem was my grades. I did all right in languages and history, but once we moved into fractions I was a basket case in math. It seemed hopelessly beyond my comprehension. "You've gotta figure this out," I would lecture myself as I tried to decipher the homework assignment. "The test is coming up, dummy, and you have to pull a B or C somehow."

The sensible move would have been to ask the teacher for help. I thought about it but never did. If I admitted I was already in trouble, she would mail off a note to Mom and Dad and they might start in on me even before the grades came home. At the same time, I knew the report card better not show up with any D's or F's. There didn't seem a way out of the bind, so I resigned myself to the prospect of getting my ass whipped every month. Sometimes I managed to scrape by, but that's usually what happened.

After the lecture and whipping I would have to forget football or baseball practice for the month and sit in my room with the math book every afternoon until the next report card. It didn't matter whether or not an assignment was due.

"All right," Dad would tell me as I pulled up my pants and he returned the belt to his closet, "you go in that room with that book, and you stay there until you get a better grade. That's it."

Mom tacked on the same punishment whenever I brought home a bad mark in deportment. If I finished my homework early, she would think up extra math assignments to keep me busy without really knowing what she was asking me to do.

"Done already? Well, read the next fifty pages, then write down for me what they're about."

But my biggest problem in school was my conduct. When I was seven or eight I discovered that if I said something funny the boys in class laughed and that meant they liked me, they were on my side. That was important to me then. If I was supposed to be one of the guys, then I wanted to be one of the guys, and humor seemed to make that possible. It saved me a lot of aggravation that came with being Crosby's kid. It earned me their acceptance.

I couldn't get that by being a good student. I remember how cautious I was about raising my hand when the teacher asked a question and I had the answer. If I did it too often, the guys let me know by their looks that I was being a smartass, and later on in the school yard they steered clear of me. So I spaced my answers out to no more than one or two a week and restricted them to subjects where I was doing poorly and needed the points. And God help me if the teacher seemed to like me. Then the kids really made my life miserable.

It was better to be the class clown. I knew the risks, but if I saw an opportunity to make something funny happen I took it. I would whistle between my teeth without moving my lips, then glance around in bewilderment when the teacher tried to detect who was disrupting her lesson. I mugged and grimaced when she turned her back. I passed notes to my fellow conspirators and used my delivery to turn it into a comedy routine when I was caught red-handed.

"Crosby, are you passing a note?"

"Oh, no, Sister, not me."

"Well, what's that piece of paper doing in your hand?"

"What piece of paper? . . . Oh, my goodness, look at that. How in the world did it get there?"

I ran my mouth when I should have been listening, then played out the scene when the teacher called me on it.

"You talking, Crosby?"

"No, Sister, I wasn't talking."

"Then what were you doing?"

"Well, I was sayin' my prayers."

"Saying your prayers in the middle of class?"

"Yes, Sister. Y'see, I forgot them this morning, and when I remembered I thought I'd better say 'em now."

"Well, now is not the time."

"Yes, Sister."

When I discovered I could make the kids laugh I got to liking it and wanted to do it all the time. I realized, of course, I would have to pay the dues. They might give me a big hand for keeping them entertained in arithmetic, but they weren't going to be around later when the score was settled at home. I wasn't a glutton for punishment, so I tried to hold myself in check. Nine times out of ten I managed to choke off the wisecrack as it leapt from my throat. But then there was the tenth time. I would have myself under control for a while and start to relax, when I caught some kid's eye across the room and said or did something stupid that was bound to cause me grief.

It was like walking the razor's edge. I had to tone down my antics so they weren't offensive to the teacher but still got the desired yucks. The A-Move was to make the teachers laugh too. Then they couldn't keep me after school and start off the chain of punishments. But their tolerance level varied. One day the Sister might crack up with the rest of the class when I wised off, and later that week she might be all over me like white on rice. So it was always chancy.

33

When I was due for a licking Mom sent me outside to pull a switch off a tree in the backyard. I had to be sure to make the right choice. The branch couldn't be dead. It had to be limber, with plenty of spring still in it. She examined it carefully when I brought it upstairs to her room, then had me roll up my pants and bend over.

"Okay, don't move. And don't cry. And don't reach back with your hands. You just stay there and take it till I'm finished with you."

Then she went to work with the switch, cutting up and down the backs of my legs as fast as she could get her arm to move. It was hard to stay still. My legs felt like they had caught fire or were being jolted by a thousand volts of electricity. But if I jumped out of the way she turned into a crazy woman and whacked me even harder.

"Don't you move! Didn't I tell you not to move! Now you're really gonna get it!"

After a while I learned how to hold myself motionless until she ran out of steam and sent me off to my room.

If Dad wasn't away on location, she might offer me a choice.

"Do you want it from me or do you want it from him?"

My answer was always the same.

"I'll take it from you, Mom. I'd rather have it from you."

It wasn't that she hurt less, but she was there on the spot and he wouldn't be back until six. I hated the waiting almost as much as the whipping and wanted to get it over with as quickly as possible.

When it was the old man's turn, I waited in my room listening to the quarter hours go by on the U.C.L.A. clock over in Westwood. The clock played a tune each time it struck the hour. Every fifteen minutes it performed a different portion of the tune. The closer to six it moved, the longer it seemed to take to get from one part of the melody to the next. By five-thirty time seemed to have dragged to a standstill, and my stomach was coiled as tight as the mainspring. It was practically a relief when the front door slammed closed and he was finally home.

A few minutes later I would hear his voice calling from down the end of the hall.

"Gary! Get in here!"

34

When I came into his office he would be sitting behind his desk. He would look up with those icy-blue agates, then begin the lecture that preceded the whipping. He would be angry, but it was anger from on high, cold and dispassionate and contained, like that of a judge passing sentence on a culprit beneath his contempt.

"Your mother tells me you shot your mouth off in school again today."

"Yes, Dad."

"Well, why do you act like that? Why do you do these things?"

"I don't know, Dad."

"What do you mean you don't know? You must have a reason."

"I don't know. I just don't know, Dad."

It wasn't much of an answer, but that's all I had to say. I learned early that no reason would be good enough to get me out of the licking, so what was the point of trying to explain? Whenever I had, he cut me off before the words left my mouth: "Well, Dad, I think—" "Don't think," he would snap back. "You can't think anyway." It didn't pay to argue with him.

"You don't know, huh? Well, then you're either stupid or rebellious or just plain crazy. I don't know what it is with you. Your mother and I lay down certain rules very simply. All you have to do is follow them."

Then he would launch into three-syllable words and fancy phrases I couldn't understand, though their drift was clear enough. His point seemed to be that the particular outrage I had committed that day was only indicative of all the other things that were wrong with me. So it wasn't just my big mouth. It was also my weight and my temper and the fact that I couldn't get along with people and wasn't smart enough to handle anything but manual labor.

". . . So if you don't alter your behavior, all you're gonna do is grow up to be a fat, stupid, bad-tempered individual that no one will like or want to have around. If that's what you want to be, just continue the way you're going. Because that's what you're headed for."

I usually tuned him out by the middle of the harangue. I had heard it before and was thinking about the beating that would be coming up next. Yet as I stood there in front of him, I would nod in the right places and say yes or no precisely on cue, so that I seemed to be sucking in every word. Eventually he was ready to get to the main event.

"Okay, take 'em down."

I dropped my pants, pulled down my undershorts and bent over. Then he went at it with the belt dotted with metal studs he kept reserved for the occasion. Quite dispassionately, without the least display of emotion or loss of self-control, he whacked away until he drew the first drop of blood, and then he stopped. It normally took between twelve and fifteen strokes. As they came down I counted them off one by one and hoped I would bleed early. To keep my mind off the hurt, I would conjure up different schemes to get back at him, ways to murder him. They had to be perfect crimes so I wouldn't be caught. Maybe I could poison his coffee or "accidentally" bump him out his office window.

I was forbidden to cry or scream, so I had to hold myself together until he cut me loose and sent me back to my room. Then I went berserk. The same red veil of rage descended as when I brawled in the school yard, and I pummeled my fists against the door or the walls or anything else I could smack hard without breaking. I did have to be careful of that. If something broke, I'd be in even bigger trouble. To play it safe, I might run outdoors to the far side of the grounds and pound against a tree or the sides of the garage. If Dad heard the racket, he didn't mention it, but I suppose that's where his criticism of my temper came from. I certainly wouldn't let him see it face to face.

When my anger finally died down, I tried coming to terms with what had happened. The lectures must have sunk in more than I thought. My mind always played back the same tape.

"Jesus, I'll never get anything right. I'll never do anything worth a shit. I'll never be any good."

I didn't believe I could ever stop doing the things that were getting me whipped. I couldn't envision myself earning all A's and B's or holding down my weight or guarding my mouth twenty-four hours a day for the rest of my life. I might for a while, but then, when no one came down on my head and I started loosening up, there I would go, slipping back into my old bad habits again. I didn't see how I could control it. I didn't see how I could live up to what he wanted.

I suppose that when he kept warning me against being a certain way I felt he was saying that's how I already was. I didn't want to be like that. It was something I couldn't understand, couldn't control, couldn't change. If I knew how to fight it, I would have. Gladly. If some wise man had confided, "Okay, kid, this is what you do: Stand on your head in the corner for thirty minutes a day and you won't be that way anymore," I would have headed straight for the corner and practiced standing on my head. I would have done anything. But since I didn't know what to do, I felt I had to face up to the unpleasant fact that this is how I was and how I was going to remain.

There was no easy forgiveness after a whipping. Dad stayed cold and remote and grew very quiet when I came in his sight. His gaze followed me closely, scrutinizing every move to catch me up when I stepped out of line. And he made it clear that the punishment could happen again at any moment.

"So don't get wise," he would warn. "And don't answer back. Now that you've had the whipping, don't pull something cute or stage some kind of rebellion. Just be quiet and do what you're told."

I had to be especially careful around Mom when she wasn't feeling well.

"Gary, go clean up the yard."

"Yes, Mom."

"What's the matter? You don't like it? What's that tone of voice? What does that mean?"

If my eyes flashed in anger, I might trigger the whole thing off again.

"Don't you give me that look! Watch it now! You know what'll happen to you!"

And if I wasn't careful it would. The only way to get through safely was to keep a tight rein on my feelings and poker-face whatever either of them had to tell me.

"Yes, Mom. Okay."

"Right, Dad. Anything you say."

The twins were a year behind me in school and had a chance to profit from my mistakes. Seeing the grief I brought on myself by shooting off my mouth, they stayed a lot quieter, kept their heads down and did what they could to blend into the crowd. Phil especially didn't want to take any chances. Denny was a bit of a clown in class but never truly offensive. Most of the teachers adored him. He was a naturally likable, freckle-faced little kid who looked like Andy Hardy. Still, we all lived under the same rule of law at home, and they endured their share of terror.

Denny's heaviest burden was his grades. He was so full of ebullience and energy that he couldn't sit still long enough to stay connected to the teacher. It probably had something to do with his stuttering. That began when he was about eight and was made to keep his left hand in his pocket all the time. He had a tendency to be left-handed, and Mom and Dad thought that would cure it. Dad dealt with Denny's bad marks by laying on the lectures and lickings each month when the report card came home. Somewhere along the line he also took to calling him "Stupid." His other favorite nickname, which I don't comprehend to this day, was "Ugly."

Denny tried to avoid the old man's displeasure by staying out of his way. But he didn't know how to duck, so most of the time he took the brunt of Dad's sarcasm head on. It was easy to see how much "Ugly" and "Stupid" smarted. Denny was such an open child that anyone could read him. When he was happy, you knew it. When he was troubled or frightened, you knew it. He had the map of Ireland on his face. He hardly ever lied. If I cooked up a story to get us out of a jam, he broke down before the interrogation even began. I would rehearse him carefully, then spin out my tale while he stood by in silence. Dad might listen skeptically for a moment, but when he turned to Denny and asked, "Well, is that true?" Denny would bawl, "No-o-o-o!" and burst into tears. He was a good, straight, honest kid.

Mom was too loyal a wife to question anything Dad did, but when she saw how the put-downs were making Denny feel about himself, she went out of her way to build up his ego. She showered him with hugs and kisses. She called him into her room and sat him down on the bed for frequent pep talks.

"You're not ugly. You're handsome. You're not stupid either.

And you're the best athlete of the bunch. You're terrific. So don't pay attention to that stuff. Your father doesn't mean it. He's just kidding."

I couldn't understand why the old man didn't ease up on the name-calling when he saw how much we loathed it. Maybe, like Mom said, he was only kidding around. But that's not how it felt at the other end. It just wasn't the same as when he kidded around with Bob Hope in his dressing room at Paramount. They were equals. If he called Hope "Ski Nose," Hope could snap back with "Hippy," and they both got off on the humor and affection behind the insult. But Denny and I were his children. We couldn't do the comeback. We could only stand there and take it.

In the long run Mom's efforts with Denny worked a world of good. He lapped up her praises like a hungry puppy, and by the time he reached his teens he felt equal to anyone. Until Mom died he had more self-confidence than the rest of us put together.

Phil lucked out with the nicknames "Dude" and "Handsome." Dad began using them when Phil was seven or eight and took to standing forever in front of the mirror combing his blond, curly hair into a pompadour. Once he set it up just so, it was war if any of us messed with it. Phil was fastidious about his appearance at an age when most kids couldn't care less, so at first the names had a certain caustic edge. But after a while they lost their original sarcasm and only served to reinforce his ego. They worked out nicely for him.

When I was four and a half my youngest brother, Lindsay, was born. Linny was the only one of us with brown eyes. He differed in other ways as well. He was a quiet, dreamy, un-aggressive child who read a lot, got good marks in school and liked to draw and paint.

The quality I recall best was his vulnerability. It's the common thread running through most of the early memories I have of him. There was the time he devoured a handful of red berries from a bush in the backyard and went into convulsions. He would have died if Mom hadn't sped him off to the hospital to have his stomach pumped. As a toddler he wore a perpetual knob in the middle of his brow from falling down and striking his head on the ground. Until he grew taller, his head was much too large for his body and he was forever losing his balance. His earliest nickname was "The Head," because when he came swaying down the street that's about all you saw of him.

Linny's greatest vulnerability came from being Dad's favorite. Maybe because he was the baby of the bunch, the old man seemed to determine his preference as soon as he came along. Less than three months after Linny was born, he told an interviewer,

"Gary and the twins will probably grow up to be house-wreckers. They wreck everything they can get their hands on now. But Lindsay may amount to something. He's the quietest kid I ever saw."

My brothers and I were acutely aware of how Dad felt. We watched the two of them closely and saw that he never called Linny names and never made fun of him. He didn't seem to get as angry when Linny was bad and didn't whip him nearly as much. The reason may simply have been that Linny caused him less bother. He *was* a good kid. But, to our way of thinking, that didn't justify the favoritism and special treatment. Linny was some four years younger than us—a huge difference to a child—yet he was allowed to stay up as late, received the same allowance, got to go everywhere we went and was awarded the same privileges without having to work for them. They were just handed to him, like the special trips Dad took him on. It seems so trivial now, but the three of us were like cons in a prison who would take a knife to another inmate for scoring an extra cigarette.

Whenever Dad went off for a few weeks, Linny was left alone in enemy camp and we were free to vent our resentment. We flipped him on the back of the head as we sprinted past. We pushed him around during the games in the backyard. Most of all, we ragged him with our mouths.

"Hey, Kiss Ass, always sucking up to Daddy. Daddy's Little Boy. Daddy's Favorite. Daddy's Little Angel, who never does anything wrong. The Little King is perfect."

Linny didn't know what to do about it. None of it was his fault. He hadn't bothered or hurt anyone. When we started in on him, he just stared back in confusion with those big brown eyes of his. That's what I remember best. Those big brown eyes looking around, watching in quiet.

We had our disagreements and differences, as any four brothers will, especially when they are almost constantly in each other's faces, but we tried to take care of them ourselves without bringing in Mom and Dad and our other wardens. What kept us united was our common enemies. If a kid hassled one of the twins at school, he'd have me on his back as fast as my stumpy little legs could carry me. At home the four of us fended for each other and spied for each other and did whatever else we could to keep each other out of trouble.

That was the unspoken law: Don't let your brothers get into trouble. We didn't verbalize it. We hardly ever talked below the surface about anything important. From Dad on down, that was the style at our house. But since each of us somehow knew the others felt the same way, discussion wasn't necessary. Besides, we were too busy struggling to keep up the rules and cover our traces when we broke them.

According to our code, the very worst thing you could do was fink on your brothers. If two of us stepped over the line and one was caught, he was expected to keep his mouth shut and absorb the full weight of the punishment. And like all good outlaws, the four of us made terrible witnesses. When Mom or Dad launched an interrogation to root out the source of a felony, we suddenly went deaf and blind. Since we almost never got away with it, I suppose it was a largely empty gesture. Still, it did allow us to salvage a bit of self-respect from the inevitable moment of retribution.

It never dawned on me that I was setting some sort of example for my brothers. Years later I realized they had watched me all through high school and college and mirrored a lot of my questionable ways: the brawling, the boozing, the messing up in school. Had I known it at the time, I don't suppose I would have changed much, but it might have made some difference. While we were still young kids living together at home, though, the only example I set for them was a strictly negative one. They saw me getting my head handed to me for being the way I was and were bright enough to conclude that wasn't the way to go. I assume that's why they went in the opposite direction. All three of them turned inward, locked away their feelings so they wouldn't show, and did whatever they had to in order to survive within the structure. They adjusted.

When they were able to remember, they tried their best to steer clear of the pitfalls that landed me in the crapper. When they forgot, they remained quiet and took the punishment as it came down. We all had to take it in front of Mom and Dad, but when we got back to our rooms we could complain and bitch and moan—and I would. They would a little, but only in a token sort of way. Then they knuckled down and did as they were told. I did, too, after blowing off a certain amount of steam, which kind of made them right and me wrong. Except that for all my fear I never gave in. I couldn't disobey the old man. I couldn't mouth off at him or be disrespectful. I had to do what he said. But I made damn sure I didn't enjoy it. I didn't do it the easy way. I stayed hot and angry and sullen. I figured that was the one right I still had coming to me.

Chapter Three
"The Happy Clan Named Crosby"

We were cast as the Platonic idea of the All-American Family.

Dad played the perfect husband and father: a warm, wise, unpretentious man who was a loving companion to his wife and a pal to his sons. For all the demands of his well-earned success, he still found the hours to tell his kids bedtime stories and take them fishing and join them in singing around the old piano. Not that he couldn't be firm when that was called for. He took his responsibilities seriously, like a father should. But he was never harsh or unloving about it. The occasional spanking was for their own good and probably pained him more than it did them. Five minutes later all was forgiven, and he whisked them off to the movies or went back to roughhousing with them on the living room floor. Mostly he led them along the path of virtue through the shining beacon of his own goodness, supplemented every now and then with man-to-man chats that gently prodded them in the right direction.

Mom's role was the adoring wife who took her proper place as the woman behind the man. She may have started out as a movie actress, but soon after marrying she discovered her true vocation and put all that behind her to devote herself to providing a home for her husband and raising her four fine boys. Five boys, really. Dad's carefree, fun-loving ways made him another one of the kids, and Mom had to be there to remind him to wear a necktie, toughen up with the youngsters and take life a bit more seriously.

My brothers and I were the happy children of the family, a bit mischievous and high-spirited perhaps, but then so were Penrod, Huck Finn and the apple-cheeked youths who graced the covers of *The Saturday Evening Post*.

The family image fit in nicely with the rest of Dad's persona. The idea was that Bing Crosby was the American Everyman, just an ordinary guy who somehow managed to become a star. I suppose that's why all America loved him. Women loved him as a romantic singer and leading man, and their boyfriends and husbands didn't mind. They loved him too. His sloppy shirts, little hats and funny ears made him seem as human and familiar as their next-door neighbor. They didn't feel threatened by him as they were by the impossibly handsome matinee idols, with their custom-tailored suits, elegant manners and perfect teeth. Bing was just like they were. They liked to hunt and fish and play golf too. They also had trouble holding down their weight and keeping their hair from thinning on top. When they sang in the shower, they didn't sound all that different to themselves.

Dad knew how he was viewed by his fans. Being well liked was important to him. He talked about it regularly. Every lecture he gave me underscored the point that life would go a whole lot smoother if I made the effort to get people to take a shine to me. And he very much wanted to be seen as a family man. The image provided a good corrective to the reputation he earned early in his career as a womanizer and drinker and hell raiser. Some stars—an Errol Flynn or a Frank Sinatra—could play it that way, and if they were charming enough and cute enough the public bought it. People like Peck's Bad Boy too. But once Dad married he wanted to change all that.

I don't believe it was wholly a matter of public relations. He did take responsibility seriously. As a devout Catholic, marriage had to be an important step, and I'm sure he did straighten up after he got together with Mom. My sense of him is that he was one of those men who will carouse and carry on with the best of them when it's time to do that, but then sits himself down on his wedding day, draws up a list of how a married man ought to behave, and adheres to it as best he can from then on. He was hardly the only entertainer who felt that way about married life. Still, I can't bring to mind many others who made their families such an integral part of their act.

"WORLD'S LUCKIEST" read the caption lead on the eight-by-ten glossy mailed out by the Paramount publicity department to newspapers and wire services throughout the country. The photo shows a groggy three-week-old being cradled in his father's arms while his mother looks on approvingly. All laughter and joy, she tickles the little babe on his stomach. Is it to coax a smile out of him? As the father cuddles his son and heir, he sings to him softly. The rest of the caption elaborates on the image:

"Take a look at the most fortunate baby in the world, if you can credit the assertions of 20,000,000 Bing Crosby enthusiasts. For here is Gary Evan Crosby, three-week-old son of the crooning Paramount star, and Dixie Lee, former screen actress. Just think, every time young Gary Evan starts crying, he has Bing Crosby to sing him to sleep. What a break!"

The other shots from the session offered variations on the theme. "They'll make him a crooner," went the text on one. "Three-week-old Gary Evan Crosby, son of Bing Crosby, actor and crooner, and Dixie Lee, former actress, receives his introduction to cameras at Los Angeles. He performed well and his proud parents look forward to a successful career as a crooner and actor for him."

Three months later the photographers came back, this time to record the double christening ceremony Mom and Dad shared with Richard and Jobyna Arlen and their new son Ricky. The mothers sit on the couch balancing the infants in their laps. The fathers perch behind them on the back of the couch, completing the symmetry of the composition.

For a regular kid who was supposed to be nobody special, I was off to a peculiar start.

Phil and Denny were heralded with the same attention when

they came along the following July. "Bing Crosby, Dixie Lee Parents of Twin Boys," the headlines announced. "It's a Record in Hollywood; Singer Plans Golf 4-Somes." When Dad returned to his radio show that September, the twins provided his writers with a natural subject for banter with announcer Ken Carpenter on the opening show.

BING: Did your summer go well, Kensy?

KEN: Oh, it was one of the best. What about yours, Bing?

BING: The greatest summer of my life. First, there were the twins.

KEN: Ah, yes, the twins. Say, have you learned much about them?

BING: No, it's a new racket for me. But what would you like to know?

KEN: Well, tell me something about them. Anything.

BING: Well, twins usually look alike, having been born more or less under the same conditions, having no particular preference in the matter.

KEN: You don't say.

BING: Sure, and if they resemble the mother they have what might be called a flying start in life.

KEN: What if they resemble the father?

BING: Well, in that case they should be held right end up and patted lightly on their respective . . . um, backs.

KEN: You don't say.

BING: I do say.

KEN: Well, how about the upkeep on twins? Must be staggering, Bing.

BING: No, no. The overhead on a small pair is much less than on a singleton. Now your greater buying power enables you, naturally, to do your shopping wholesale. The tidy sum you save this way may be set aside for a marching fund to send them to military school.

KEN: After they grow up, what sort of careers do you have in mind for them?

BING: Well, I don't quite know. I haven't thought of it. But if they were girls instead of boys and triplets instead of twins, they could sing like . . . three girls with but a single thought: harmony.

SEGUE INTO BOSWELL SISTERS' SONG

Even before Lindsay arrived and turned the three of us into a proper quartet, Dad was honored by the National Father's Day Committee as "Hollywood's Most Typical Father for 1937." If the title held a certain ambiguity, I'm sure it was unintentional.

The image worked well for him, and the people who handled his publicity found all sorts of clever ways to implement it. The next year they had him do a special fifteen-minute Christmas-morning radio show from the house so he could hand us our presents over the air. *Variety* complimented its effectiveness:

"The mikes, apparently hidden in the Crosby Xmas tree, picked up the audible reactions of three of the four children, with papa Bing and mammy Dixie doing a little ad libbing. The mother contented herself with seasonal greetings, but Crosby's admonitions to the kids—'Come on you guys,' 'Get into it, men,' etc.—as they went for their Xmas presents was sound seasonal sentiment on the air . . . It's a cinch no actor at any time anywhere got such favorable national publicity . . . It was great sentimental pushover stuff, well attuned to the season, and as the kids tried out their accordions, horns, drums, etc., the world came into the Crosby home, apparently to share Xmas cheer with them."

Then, of course, there were the interviews. Dad could sound as though he liked nothing better than to talk about his family, and it didn't take long for his fatherhood to become as much a part of the Crosby image as his passion for golf and the race-track. He was forever regaling the press with amusingly bewildered tales about the demands of raising four high-kicking hooligans who seemed to be the only people in the world who didn't regard him with total reverence. "Bing Crosby Without a Fan in Own House" ran one story. "Gary, His 4-Year-Old Son, Prefers Air Story Teller to the Crooner; Angered by Dad's Screen Kisses." It was a nice, humanizing touch, not unlike the running gag about his inability to field a winner out of his stable of race-horses. Both details revealed that for all his great good fortune he was still as subject to the minor frustrations of life as the average Joe on the street.

The little joke that Bing Crosby was a prophet without honor in his own country was always good for a chuckle and made its way into most of the interviews he gave about the family during the years we were growing up. In 1944, when I was eleven, he told Louella Parsons about how he found himself with a minor insurrection on his hands when he sent the four of us over to Paramount for two days to do a scene in the movie of *Duffy's Tavern.*

"The night after they finished the first day's shooting," Louella wrote, "the twins said, 'We're not going back unless we get more lines to say.' 'Remember you have a contract, and you're going back!' their father told them. It was then Dixie said, 'We'll have no more of this nonsense.' 'I guess,' Bing grinned, 'she thought one ham in the family is enough.' "

Needless to say, the anecdote was pure fantasy. We were much too afraid of him even to consider getting up the nerve to proclaim what we would or would not do. If he told us we were going to shoot a scene in a movie, we shot the scene in the movie, whether we wanted to or not. And we never did want to. Acting in front of a camera was no place for a regular kid. We found it embarrassing, frightening and, given the long hours of waiting around on the set, more than a little dull. But I suppose the story had its charm.

Six years later Dad was still at it when he talked with Louis Berg of *This Week Magazine* for a Sunday-supplement feature on "Bing and His Boys."

"Out near the Bing Crosby ranch in Elko County 12-year-old Lindsay, youngest of the 'Groaner's' four sons, was singing in the local church choir for the first time with the other members of the singing Crosby family. Bing was soloing. 'When do we join in?' Lindsay whispered to his nearest brother.

" 'After a while,' was the answer.

" 'Okay,' said Lindsay, settling back in his seat. 'He's off key anyhow.'

"This apparent lack of respect for his celebrated father, who is the idol of millions and a multimillionaire besides, characterizes the relationship between Crosby and all his kids. It is casual to the point of seeming indifferent, but it's all part of the Crosby plan for bringing up his boys. The four youngsters have been allowed, without undue interference or encouragement, to develop their own separate personalities and have never stood in awe of their fabulously successful father. . . .

48

"He's not overly sentimental about the boys—'the Irishers,' he calls them—once swore he couldn't stand being with them for more than 30 minutes at a time. He was kidding, of course. The affection is there—and their easy relationship and constant ribbing only proves it. . . .

"Their lack of reverence for their father has a healthy quality. In the process of kidding Bing, and being ribbed by him, they have been taught not to be snooty. . . .

"[They] live in an atmosphere of easy friendship. There's plenty of give and take on both sides and no standing in awe of Dad—even if he is the idol of millions!"

Louis Berg may have thought that "strict disciplinarians might object to the Crosby method of bringing up children," but Dad usually made it clear to his interviewers that however much he tolerated our occasional cheekiness, he very definitely maintained the upper hand. When Louella asked how he kept us in line, he told her, "Good old spanking routine. There isn't a week goes by that one of 'em doesn't get a good spanking, but I leave their upbringing mostly to their mother."

"Spanking" was an interesting choice of words. He almost always used it when answering that question in the press, but that's not what we heard at home. With us it was a licking, a whipping or a beating—harsher terms that generated a lot more fear.

Louella concluded, "He's a far stricter father than the average and the kids hop when he says something. But in his seemingly careless way he's crazy about them."

Which is what she was supposed to conclude. The idea was that he did put out punishment to keep us from running wild, but then he was a good guy too. It allowed him to have it both ways. Fans who were tough with their kids could read that Bing shared the same no-nonsense views of child raising they held. More relaxed types could see that it pained him to be hard and he really wasn't. All in all, it made a good story.

As my brothers and I moved past the arm-cradling stage, we were conscripted to make our own small contributions to the Crosby family mystique.

We were told the night before that the photographer would be coming to the house in the morning. That meant instead of our usual jeans and sneakers we had to dress up in our good clothes and best smiles. We usually put on matching outfits, I suppose to emphasize the harmony of Crosby family life. When I was six, the twins and I wore white Buster Brown shirts, navy shorts and socks, and spotless white shoes. A few years later, when Linny was old enough to join in, all four of us were decked out in identical checkered sport coats or, less formally, leather jackets and cowboy shirts. The most important item of apparel, though, was the smile. We were expected to look ecstatically happy. Life had to seem wonderful.

"Look at your dad," the photographer would cajole as he arranged us on the couch or next to the huge oil painting of an English hunting scene that hung in the den. "Now look at your mother. Now smile. Okay, that's good. No, you're not smiling enough. Come on. Get happy. Make it a big smile now."

If we failed to give him what he needed, Mom might squint down at us and, without altering her own happy face, whisper under her breath, "Smile, dammit. Do what he tells you."

When we finally got it right, he broke into a big grin himself and began snapping away, taking hundreds of shots to make sure he had the four or five good ones that captured us in all our joyful radiance. Then he moved us off to another part of the house and snapped another hundred. A month or so later, there we would be in the movie magazines and newspapers—four terrific, happy kids, the wonderful offspring of their wonderful father and his wonderful wife.

Sometimes the photographer brought along a reporter to do a little interview with us. When that was to happen, Mom prepared us in advance.

"They're coming to interview you in the morning. They'll be asking you questions. You just answer them the way you're supposed to. And don't forget, nothing that takes place in this house is ever to go outside this house. Remember that."

We knew that meant nothing bad. By the time I was nine or ten I had myself fully primed to field the very worst a reporter might throw at me. Not that it ever happened, but even if he had asked, "Does your mother drink?" my answer would have been ready. "Drink? I don't know what you're talkin' about. I can't imagine where you heard that. Mom's fine."

It wasn't hard to figure out what the reporters wanted. We had seen their articles in the papers and magazines and knew what we were supposed to be like, so that's what we became as soon as they cracked open their notebooks and took out their pencils.

"Did you enjoy your dad's latest picture, fellas?"

"Sure did. Boy, it was really neat."

"Was it funny?"

"Oh, yeah, it was really funny!"

"What was really funny?"

"Well, when the ape chased Bob Hope around the ring and caught him and sat on him, that was really funny, that was really neat. And Dad was good, too, in the part where he went by the skeletons in the graveyard and said, 'Don't get up.' That was real funny. Wasn't that funny, guys?"

"Yeah, that was really funny."

We gave them just what they wanted to hear. If they smiled at the end of an answer, the rest of us chimed in, "Yeah, that's right. Sure." If they frowned a little, we quickly made the adjustment and got back on the right track without missing a beat.

There really wasn't much to worry about. We were in completely safe hands. The story wouldn't be printed until Dad looked at it first and gave his approval. A few days after the interview a copy of the manuscript arrived at the house. Dad checked it over that night and made whatever changes he wanted in the margins. When it had been carefully manicured and dressed up so that everything was presented in the best possible light, it was sent back to the paper and that's how it appeared in print. All the big stars did the same thing. They were all given the opportunity to make sure the stories about them came out exactly the way they wanted. The gossip columnists often didn't even bother talking to us. They simply dreamed up little anecdotes and then called Dad on the phone to ask if he had any objections.

Anytime I ventured out in the world and crossed paths with strangers, they began feeding me back the fairy tales just as soon as they made the connection.

"You're Bing Crosby's son, right? Well, it's certainly a pleasure to meet you. I know you're a good boy. You couldn't be anything but. Not with your old man. Gosh, he's such a terrific guy, so warm and understanding. Your whole family is wonderful. I read about you and your mom and your brothers in the magazine. Yessir, you all sure got a great relationship going."

I would stand there like an idiot, nodding my head in agreement.

"Yeah, yeah, yeah. Right, right. Yes, he sure is great. I know it, I certainly am lucky."

It was the same way at school. The nuns were mystified that I could flunk a test or get into a fistfight or misbehave in the classroom. They would look at me with the sorrow of Mary on their faces and shake their heads slowly in disbelief.

"How can you be such a problem? I don't understand it. You're Bing Crosby's son. Why, Bing Crosby's son wouldn't act that way. You'll disappoint your father. Your father will be hurt. You don't want to do that, do you? Why would you want to hurt your father?"

The subtext of the sermons was clear enough. I had all the advantages. I came from a wonderful home brimming over with piety, money and love. So why didn't I appreciate what a marvelous man my father was and straighten up? It could only be because I was a bad kid, a rotten apple, the spiny crown of thorns the saintly Bing Crosby was forced to suffer.

The possibility had to be considered. Could everyone in the world be wrong? There were moments when that didn't seem possible. Then I would have to conclude, "Well, it must be me then. I'm the one who's wrong. I must just be a bad-ass, a bad, fucking guy. That has to be why I bring out the bad side of him."

And, in truth, no one except me and my brothers did seem to bring out his bad side.

Along with the pictures and interviews, the image of Bing-as-family-man was enhanced by having us perform with him. In my case it started shortly before my eighth birthday, when he had me tested for a part in *Birth of the Blues*. I was to play him as a kid in the prologue of the movie. I suppose he thought it would make a cute gimmick.

He brought home a few lines for me to memorize, then drove me over to Paramount the next morning, where the director handed me a clarinet and stuck me in front of a camera. I didn't know anything about acting or even how to hold a clarinet, but I was too frightened to ask. The closest to acting I had come was playing out fantasies of cowboys and home-run heroes in the backyard. It was all I could do to get the words out of my mouth in the right order. The screen test was miserable, and the part went to someone else, which didn't disappoint me in the least. It would only have given the kids at school one more reason to knock me in the head.

Two years later, when Dad was shooting *Star Spangled Rhythm,* he tried it again. This time I did a little better and made it to the screen. The picture was a glorified variety show, with cameos of every star on the Paramount lot: Bob Hope, Dorothy Lamour, Alan Ladd, Veronica Lake—the list went on and on. Dad topped the whole thing off at the finale with a patriotic salute to Old Glory. I had two tiny scenes and managed to stumble through them without embarrassing myself too badly. In the first I walked through the Paramount gate with him, and when the guard asked me, "I suppose you've come to watch your daddy making pictures," I answered, "Naw. Dorothy Lamour's working today," and then made a wolfish click with my tongue. My irreverence toward the old man was of a piece with the breezy quality of Crosby family life depicted in the interviews. So was his bemused response. "This is to hope too much." In the second scene Betty Hutton planted a big wet kiss on my cheek when she found me bouncing a ball against the wall outside Dad's dressing room.

There was no feeling of accomplishment when the day ended, only relief that I hadn't messed up. Dad seemed reasonably pleased, so I figured I wouldn't be punished later on at home. Most of all I wanted to get back to school and my regular routine. I hoped the kids wouldn't find out I had been pulled out of class to be in a movie. The next morning I told them I was sick and had to stay in bed.

Two years after that Dad put me in another one, *Duffy's Tav-*

ern, this time along with my brothers. The four of us showed up in our good clothes and tried to stay clean while we waited out the long hours it took them to get around to our scene. We did a skit with Robert Benchley. He read us a bedtime story about the life of Bing Crosby. I was twelve now, but the fear was still the same. So was my apprehension about what would happen when I was sent back to school.

During the early years of the war Dad took me out on the road for two weeks on a tour of bond shows and military camps in Arizona and Texas. About the middle of his turn he would call me out onstage, exchange a bit of patter, then have me sing a little nonsense song with tricky words like "Rose O'Day" or "Mairzy Doats."

My brothers and I all liked to sing. We picked up harmony, phrasing and rhythm fairly easily, I suppose from listening to the music that was played around the house when we were small. Our home wasn't exactly the happy abode of perpetual harmony written about in the papers, but while we were growing up Mom and Dad did keep the phonograph in the den spinning much of the day and night. Their taste ran to big bands—Tommy and Jimmy Dorsey, Harry James, Duke Ellington, Count Basie—and technically good pop singers like Buddy Clark, Perry Como, Jo Stafford and Kitty Kallen. Mom was also big on Dinah Washington, Billie Holiday and Lena Horne. Johnny Mercer and Hoagy Carmichael were special favorites. I loved them too. And, of course, they always played a lot of Dad's records—his current releases and some of the old classics. So there was no shortage of examples to emulate. Mom liked to tell her friends how when I was still being toilet trained she would come into the bathroom and find me singing "Miss Otis Regrets" while I was taking care of business on the potty.

I sang to myself all the time just for the fun of it. Performing before an audience, though, was something else. I still remember how choked up I became when I was about seven and Dad made me stand up at a party and do a number in front of his pals. I looked across the room, and there sat Bing Crosby and Judy Garland and one or two other great singers. I felt like an idiot.

I felt the same way the first time I sang in public a couple of years later. It was at a talent show in school. Naturally, Crosby's kid had to do a song, so I rehearsed "An Apple for the Teacher" with a classmate who played the piano. Dad had recently put out a record of the tune. The night of the show I told him over dinner what I had picked to sing, and he made a suggestion.

"Why don't you do it like this. Sing it through once straight, like you rehearsed it, then come back to the bridge. Now, when you go into the last chorus, instead of just singing 'an apple for the teacher,' double up the phrasing and sing, 'I want an apple a-big-red-apple for the teacher,' and move on through the rest of the chorus the same way."

I tried it for him once, and it seemed to work fine. I was a pretty good rhythm singer for a kid and could cram a lot of words into a brief space without losing the beat or tripping over the phrasing. So I went along with what he told me and sang it that way at the show. But I made one little mistake. I forgot to tell the piano player about the change. The moment I began doubling up, he went to pieces. He hadn't the foggiest idea what I was up to. He stopped playing and I stopped singing and we had to turn back to the bridge and start all over again. The audience fell out of their seats. They were probably laughing with me, but I felt so demoralized I was certain they were laughing at me. My humiliation was even worse when I came home and told the old man. He seemed to get a big kick out of it. He laughed. He thought it was funny too. I guess it was, but at the moment I only knew that even though it was a big thing to me, to him it was nothing.

The memory of that disaster was still fresh when Dad announced one summer evening that he was taking me along to sing for the troops and the people who bought war bonds. I certainly didn't want to go, but I kept my apprehensions to myself and did what he told me.

We toured with a band and a comic. As I recall, the comedian was Bob Burns, the funny Arkansas hillbilly who was a regular on Dad's weekly radio show. The rest of the troupe traveled by plane, but Dad preferred not to fly, so we drove or took the train and caught up with them later. When we arrived at a stop, after making sure the show was ready to go, he occasionally took me horseback riding at a nearby dude ranch or played a round of golf while I caddied for him, but we mostly spent the day alone in the hotel room. We put in a lot of time together. That was another thing to worry about. An entire morning could pass without a single word of conversation. He was perfectly comfortable with long silences, but they made me edgy. I was afraid that for lack of anything better to do he might dredge up some past misdeed and start in on me again. Actually, that never happened. He kept himself busy reading, writing letters and dictating memos into his dictaphone. But to my way of thinking the possibility always lurked behind the next moment of quiet.

About noon he would turn to me—perhaps for the first time that day—and say, "Mmm, come on. Let's get something to eat." At the restaurant, when strangers walked over for his autograph he would suddenly light up and kibitz with them for a few minutes with all the warmth and humor they expected from Bing Crosby. I sat there with my head down, munching the salad he ordered for me instead of the burger and fries I was dying for. Then we would return to the hotel room, and more silence, until the driver picked us up for the show.

When I wasn't onstage I was expected to stay quiet and do what I was told, to be seen but not heard. If out of exuberance or sheer boredom I forgot myself and let the wrong words slip out of my mouth at the wrong time, he would throw me a cautionary look and mutter, "Uh-uh, back in the trunk." It took me quite a while to figure out that what goes back in the trunk is the ventriloquist's dummy, but the gist of his meaning was clear enough.

About the same time as the tour, Dad began bringing my brothers and me onto his radio show. The twins were still small enough at the start to have to stand on baffle boxes to reach the microphones. Again, there was no discussion about whether or not we wanted a taste of the limelight. Mom simply announced, "Okay, you're going to be on your father's show this week," and that was that. The night before a broadcast, when the script had been timed out and edited, Dad brought home the relevant pages and ran us through our lines. At first we only did a short segment of dialogue, usually on his Christmas show. A few years later he added a song or two. When that was to happen, his pianist, Buddy Cole, or John Scott Trotter, his musical director, dropped by the house the day before and rehearsed us around the piano until we sounded more or less passable.

The evening of a show, Mom sent us off with a little lecture. "Don't do anything bad down there. Behave yourselves. Just listen to the man and do what he tells you. Make your father proud of you."

On the ride to the studio my heart would be pounding. I was terrified that I might miss a word or fluff a line. The programs were still broadcast live, so there was no taking back a mistake once it left your mouth. And since the entire country listened to Bing's show, my incompetence would be exposed to an infinitely larger jury than the hundred or so students and parents who had watched me make a fool of myself in the school auditorium. There was no question in my mind that Dad expected me to perform my lines perfectly and would let me hear about it later if I didn't. Even before we reached the studio, I anticipated the scene that was sure to take place when we returned home.

"Did you hear the dummy?" I imagined him telling my mother. "Couldn't say the line right. Did you hear this genius?"

Like my fear about his laying into me in the hotel room, that never once happened. Yet I was always certain it would. Looking back now, I realize I put the pressure on myself. I was so conditioned to his disappointment over my inability to live up to his expectations that I didn't need him whispering in my ear, "Now, don't you miss it. You better get every word exactly right." I supplied my own dialogue. Just the fact that he was there and it was his show and he was Mister Perfect in the world's eyes and I was his son was enough to make the thought of messing up absolutely cataclysmic in my own mind, the very worst thing that could possibly occur.

Predictably, I was so frightened of the world caving in on me if I blew it that there were programs when I did blow it. Sometimes the rhythm of the words turned out to be awkward and I couldn't get my mouth around them once we went on the air. Everyone who works in radio has run into that one and knows how to head it off at rehearsal. Just tell the director. He'll talk to the writer, and two minutes later they'll have the wording changed around to fit more comfortably. Dad did it all the time. But I didn't realize that as a kid. I felt I had to struggle with the phrasing until I had it licked. But the harder I fought, the more panicky I became and the worse it got. Mostly, though, I messed up not because the words were hard but because I lost my concentration. I would see the old man sitting there right in front of me, my attention would shift over to him, and before I knew what happened I had blown something easy.

I wasn't expecting him to be kind and understanding when I messed up on the air, but he invariably was. He made it easy for me. He covered up so well that at least one critic assumed the mistakes were deliberately written into the script. If his line came up next, he might pretend to fluff it too, saying, "Well, you're not the only one with lip trouble today." Or he would improvise a wisecrack to the audience to get them laughing and buy me some time, then throw another ad lib in my direction to loosen me up. "Want to take another run at it?" I would try again, and when I got it right everyone laughed even harder because they were happy for me. But by then I had worked myself into such a frenzy that I was sure they were hooting at the dummy.

Dad's tolerance for my mistakes constantly surprised me, even though I saw he was just as loose with the other performers when they messed up. What I didn't put together was that he was a lot more easygoing about the normal, natural blunders that will happen in the business than he was about breaking the rules at home. In the studio he was Bing Crosby, not my father. When he was Bing Crosby, anyone could make a mistake, even his son. I figured that no matter which person he was, it wasn't all right for me to make one.

On the drive back home I took care of my own punishment. Nothing showed. I sat there stone-faced. But underneath I let myself have it good.

"Idiot. Dummy. You moron. You goddam klutz. You can't do *anything* right. What's the matter with you? You really are terrible. You don't belong on this earth."

My brothers and I were supposed to be playing ourselves on the show, but the dialogue and situations bore only the flimsiest relation to the reality of our lives. For the most part they were straight sitcom fantasy. The scripts had me smartmouthing and one-upping the old man like the bratty nephew on *The Great*

Gildersleeve. My lines were so cheeky that at first I was even afraid to read them out loud when Dad ran me through a rehearsal. But he egged me on, so I had to assume that's what he wanted. Then when we went on the air I understood why. The audience laughed. That was the justification. "Oh, I get it. This is a joke. People think it's funny. It's not supposed to be the truth. It's just a story."

Dad was perfectly content to be the butt of the gags. As long as the people stayed entertained and kept on laughing, he didn't much care who had the punch lines.

Our personalities on the air were cut from the same cloth as the feature stories about us in the press. We were the Crooner's very own Katzenjammer Kids, lovable little roughnecks who had the old man climbing the walls from our mischief.

KEN: You know, you're looking great. Your vacation did you a lot of good.

BING: My vacation is just starting.

KEN: What do you mean, just starting? . . . You were away with your kids all summer.

BING: See what I mean? . . .

KEN: Oh! Y'know, Bing, with your kids away at school now, I'll bet the house must seem empty.

BING: It *is* empty when they leave . . . That's quite an evacuation. It's like the Eighth Army leaving. But even though they're gone, I keep finding many reminders of the little—darlings . . .

KEN: For instance?

BING: Well, there's the cute little hole that Dennis hacked in the roof to let his pigeons in . . . And then there's the other hole that Philip chopped in the roof to let the pigeons out.

KEN: Oh, clever.

BING: Thorough these boys, real thorough. Their brains are thinking every minute . . . Little wheels are wheeling and turning . . . Then every time I step in the bathtub, there's Gary's pet snapping turtle to give me a pedicure. Isn't that nice? . . .

KEN: A rather rugged reminder of the lad.

BING: Ah, yes . . . And then at the end of the day when I sit down

to relax, there in my easy chair I find little Lin's submarine
—the one with the periscope. Ah, I love them all . . . But
the pain of it.

KEN: Well, they may be a bit of a problem now, Bing, but they'll
be a great comfort to you in your old age.

BING: Yes, but why should they bring it on so soon?

KEN: Oh look now, Dad, they can't be that much trouble.

BING: Oh, no? Ken, when the four kids are home, our mailman
mails our mail to us so another mailman will have to deliver
it.

Our ventures into show business were actually rather few and
far between. They happened when they happened, and then they
were over and we were put back in the trunk and made to forget
them. A month later it was hard to remember that we had ever
been out there.

But the gags about us continued as a staple of Dad's show.
After a while Bob Hope picked them up and began using them
as ammunition in his friendly feud with the old man. His mono-
logues in those days were loaded with lines like, "Did you hear
that Crosby's next movie is *Birth of a Nation?* We have to keep
him away from home more." Then the other radio comedians got
in on the act. When I heard the wisecracks coming out of the
radio in my room, I tried to shrug them off. I told myself it didn't
matter. It was only stuff someone made up to get a laugh. Jokes
didn't have to be true, so it wasn't as if they were talking about
me or putting me down. Still, I knew I would be in for a ragging
at school the next day. Some kid was bound to stop me in the
hall and say, "Hey, Crosby, I heard all about you on the radio
last night. Listened to your old man's show, and he said something real funny about you." To keep him from making a big
deal of it, I would cut him off. "Yeah, yeah. So what?" If that
didn't shut him up, I walked away.

In 1948, when I was fifteen, the critic John Crosby devoted a
column to the Crosby kids' gags. He wrote, "Crosby's four sons
have been more widely publicized even than the former Crosby
racing stable or Crosby's present affiliation with the Pittsburgh
Pirates. As joke material the kids flourished only a little way
behind Eddie Cantor's five daughters and Jimmy Durante's nose.

They were always good for a laugh simply because they existed. It must be rather odd to grow up in the knowledge that every mention of you will provoke a bellow of laughter, but this is the American way of life and the boys had better get accustomed to it."

I never did.

In a way, I did understand why Dad's fans loved him so. When I saw *Going My Way* I was as moved as they were by the character he played. Father O'Malley handled that gang of young hooligans in his parish with such kindness and wisdom that I thought he was wonderful too. Instead of coming down hard on the kids and withdrawing his affection, he forgave them their misdeeds, took them to the ball game and picture show, and taught them how to sing. By the last reel the sheer persistence of his goodness had transformed even the worst of them into solid citizens. Then the lights came on and the movie was over. All the way back to the house I thought about the difference between the person up there on the screen and the one I knew at home.

When he came back from the studio that night, I made a point of telling him I had seen the picture.

"Caught your flick today, Dad. It was great. It was really great."

"Oh, good. Glad you liked it."

That was the extent of the discussion.

A few months later Louella Parsons quoted him as saying that he hadn't watched *Going My Way* yet because he wanted to see it with his kids. He hoped we would be as proud of him as he'd like us to be. I remember tossing away the magazine in disgust.

But the persona wasn't simply an act. That side of him was real too. Once he left the house and stepped into the world, he became another man—that same nice guy everyone loved in the movies.

There was nothing unlikable about him. He was always pleasant to people. He never turned snippy or angry or hard. When something went wrong on the set, he kept his patience and waited calmly until it was put right. If he had to play a scene that made him uncomfortable, he didn't become difficult or stormy like most stars will under that kind of tension. They will yell and scream, then stomp off to their cars and drive home, putting an end to the day's shooting and costing the company a fortune. Dad got what he wanted in a fraction of the time by being nice.

Very softly he would say, "Well, gee, I don't think I can do that. It just isn't me. How about trying it this way?"

Then he would suggest an alternative. He had thought about it beforehand and had something positive to offer beyond the usual bitching and moaning.

At first the producer and director might try to cajole him into shooting the scene as planned.

"Oh, come on, Bing, you can handle it."

But then he would answer, "Mmm, I don't think so. I'm pretty sure the other way would go a whole lot better. Listen, fellas, I'll tell you what. I'm gonna go to my dressing room. You guys think it over and let me know what you decide. We'll work something out."

That's about as heavy as he got. Instead of taking off in a huff, he stayed close by so he could return to work just as soon as they decided to change their minds.

Back in his dressing room he practiced his putting, hung out with his pals or took care of some of his other business. No more than half an hour later the men in charge would come knocking at his door.

"All right, Bing, I guess we'll do it your way."

Dad was all graciousness and tact at those moments. He charmed the pants right off them.

"Well, okay. That's nice. Thanks a lot. That really helps me out. I was having a heck of a time with that other thing. You really made it easy for me. I appreciate it."

And when they tried it his way, it worked at least as well— usually a lot better. Half the time the producer or director probably ended up believing he had thought up the improvement himself.

Every now and then he took me along to Paramount, and I would see him change into Bing Crosby the moment he stepped from the car. On the drive over he would still be Dad and I would still be afraid of him. He'd sit quietly behind the wheel, occasionally breaking the silence by whistling to himself or singing a few bars of a song. Then, as we approached the studio, he would turn to me for the first time and deliver the customary lecture about how he expected me to behave.

"Okay, now don't speak until you're spoken to. Call the people sir and mister unless they ask you to call them by their first names. And I want you to pay attention to me and do exactly what I tell you when I tell you. I don't want to have to yell at you. I don't want to have to say something twice. Just watch what we're doing. You'll have fun. You'll like it."

"Yes, Dad."

It was a relief when we finally passed through the Paramount gate and pulled into his space in the parking lot. The first person who saw him would yell, "Hey, Bing!" and that's who he became.

"Hey-y-y, whaddaya say? How are ya? Good to see ya. What's goin' on?"

As soon as he made the transition, I felt I was safe. He wouldn't turn on me now. Though he did have a way of letting me know when I stepped out of line. If I did anything that interrupted the flow of activity in his dressing room and called attention to myself—if I talked when I wasn't supposed to or accidentally dropped a cup of water—he would throw me a steely look with those blue agates that told me in no uncertain terms that I was in deep trouble. He wouldn't make a scene about it in front of the others. He would still be Bing Crosby to them. Nothing more would happen until we got home. But I would hear about it then.

As long as I was a nice, quiet, polite kid who sat in the background, Dad was relatively happy, so that's what I tried to be. I found myself a spot in the corner and disappeared into the woodwork. Occasionally he might tell me to fetch something or give a visitor my chair—"Satchel Ass, get up from there. Move. Move"—but most of the time he ignored me. Which was fine with me. I didn't want his attention. I wanted him to keep doing what he was doing and forget I was there. If I was invisible I was safe. And as a spectator I could enjoy him.

And when Dad became Bing Crosby he *was* enjoyable. He

laughed and sang and swung his golf club and traded wisecracks with his cronies. Barney Dean and Leo Lynn, two funny show business characters who worked for him, were usually around. Another regular visitor was Jimmy Cottrell, a propman who was a close personal friend. The door of his dressing room stayed open so he could toss a quick hello to whoever passed by on the street. He knew everybody—the grips and the other working men on the crew—and they all loved to stop and hang out with him for a minute. The most fun was when he spotted Bob Hope ambling along outside.

"Hey, Ski Nose!" he would yell. "Come over here. I want to talk to you."

When Hope came in, they went after each other like they were shooting another "Road" picture.

"Hiya, Hippy. Say, I gotta tell ya, your last performance left a lot to be desired."

"Well, that's only because I was working with you. You don't give me much. You know I have to invent when I'm out there."

When they worked their way through the acting put-downs, they moved on to the gags about their physical appearance and their money and their golf scores.

"Saw you on the course last week, Dad," Hope would say. "You were hitting the ball like an old lady. You have no distance, but you sure are crooked."

"Uh-huh. Well, you know how it is, the old thing of drive for show and putt for dough."

They kept the *tummel* flying, breaking up everyone within earshot. Whoever got in the first line put the other on the defensive, and they continued working it that way until the one who was down moved on top. Then they reversed positions and went at it like that for a while. Hope usually got off more gags because Dad was a strong counterpuncher. He would wait until he saw an opening, letting seven or eight of Hope's zingers pass by, then he'd hit him with a big one, back off and wait some more. Hope would go and go and go, and then Dad would hit him again.

I laughed as hard as everyone else. I only wished he could be like that all the time. *That* person was great.

In the midst of the socializing and kidding around, Dad was

getting himself ready for the day's shooting. First Wally Westmore would come in with his toupee. Dad detested the thing. He hated even looking at it and would try to contrive a scheme to get out of wearing it.

"Goddamit, Wally, can't I put on a hat in this scene?"

"C'mon, Bing, you're in the living room."

"Well, let's play it out on the porch. Someplace. Just let me wear my hat and forget all this shit. Whaddaya say?"

"No, Bing."

They would both be smiling. It was a standard routine they went through every morning they worked together. After a few more attempts Dad invariably gave in and resigned himself to the indignity.

"All right, put it on. Lay the mucket on my dome. Here we go. Okay."

Wally would take out the gum and go to work, while Dad sat at his dressing table and watched in the mirror. If the toupee was crooked, he would say, "That's great. Perfect. Don't worry." He couldn't care less how it looked.

For all his nonchalance, the old man managed to take care of an extraordinary amount of business over the course of the day. And he never appeared to. His manner was so loose and cool that it was easy to miss how much he accomplished unless, like me, you sat in the corner and watched him. He could talk with a dozen different people about a dozen different things without becoming the least bit ruffled or strained.

During the morning breaks, John Scott Trotter or Buddy Cole might stop by the dressing room to go over the songs for the next radio show. They would choose the tunes together, then Buddy or John Scott would sit down at the piano that was always there and work out the format for the arrangements.

"How do you want to do this one, Bing?"

"Well, let's do the verse and then the chorus, then back to the bridge and out."

"Okay, what about the key?"

"Oh, I don't know. Just throw it out there, whatever it is. Don't make it too high, and don't make it too low."

That was nearly all Dad knew about keys, and it worked out fine. A few minutes later, and the music for the show was set.

During lunch someone might see him about playing a benefit. Then, as soon as he left with Dad's decision, a group of men in suits might turn up to pitch him about a business proposition, to be followed by one of Dad's lawyers, who had to go over some fine points in his taxes. If he wasn't in the first shot after lunch, he might meet with his record producer about the session that was coming up later in the week, or work with the demos of the songs he planned to record. On and on the action would go. Even when he went on the set it didn't stop. Between takes people were forever running up to him with little, quick questions that needed answering.

"Bing, do you want your car back tonight washed and gassed up?"

"Yeah, sure. Thanks a lot."

"Bing, Dixie needs some stuff at the store. Should I get it for her?"

"Okay. Fine. Get it. Whatever."

Then, when it was time to go before the camera, he hit the mark and said the lines as if he had been working on nothing else the entire day.

Shooting stopped about five. Back in his dressing room, he took off his costume, makeup and toupee, changed into his street clothes, and with a toss of his head motioned me to follow him out to the parking lot. The exhilaration of the day kept him in good humor during the drive home. He would be quiet but content. He didn't stop being Bing Crosby until he arrived at the house.

The transformation was most extreme when Mom had been drinking. She was easy to read when she was stoned. It was obvious to both of us the moment we stepped through the door. A shadow of disappointment flickered across Dad's face, then he closed off and withdrew. Mom wouldn't or couldn't acknowledge that he knew and would try to engage him in conversation.

"Well, did you have a good time at the studio today?"

"Yeah, it was okay."

"What'd you do?"

"Nothing. We just did the scenes. And Gary was okay. He didn't knock anything over or bother anyone. Look, I'm kinda beat. I'll see you at dinner."

66

Then he retreated into his corner and left her alone in hers until we were summoned to the dining room.

Mom still wasn't aware Dad saw she was whacked. All through dinner she played out the charade that everything was fine. My brothers and I kept our eyes riveted to our plates so we didn't have to look at either of them. Dad ate without saying a word. When he wolfed down the last bite, he left the table.

"I'm going to bed now. I'm tired."

Once he disappeared up the stairs, she let go of the smile she had fixed on her face. The tension and gloom welling up out of her suffused the entire room. Because then she knew for sure. She hadn't been able to bring it off. She hadn't fooled him.

Chapter Four
Mom

It wasn't until I was eleven or twelve that I realized Mom drank. When I was very young and she still left the house, sometimes she took me along when she spent the afternoon boozing at a girl friend's, but I was stashed out of sight in the backyard. During the drive home I would notice how her speech had become so slurred she could hardly talk, but I didn't know why. I figured she just wasn't feeling well again. That's what our nurse told us whenever Mom closed the door behind her and disappeared into her room for the day. "Your mother doesn't feel well right now. She's taking a nap. Don't play too loud or you'll wake her." We didn't have to be told twice. When Mom got like that, we made sure to keep our distance.

When she wasn't sick she could be a pleasure. My brothers and I would tiptoe into her room in the morning, and she would throw her arms around us and motion us to sit on the bed beside her while she sipped her coffee. She would laugh and joke with us and ask us about our plans for the day. If we didn't have to dash off to school, she might think up a special treat, something she knew we'd enjoy.

"Well, how'd you fellas like to go out this afternoon? How about a movie? There's a Roy Rogers over at Westwood. Would you like to do that?"

"Great, Mom. That'd be terrific."

"Fine. Finish up your chores and come see me after lunch. I'll have someone take you."

But a few hours later her mood was likely to have changed completely. By the time we were ready to leave for the theater, she might not even remember what she had told us.

"Okay, Mom, we're all set to go."

"Go? Go where?"

"To the movie show."

"What movie show?"

"But, Mom, didn't you say . . . ?"

"No. Don't know what you're talking about. Bullshit. You can't do that. You're staying right here in the house where you belong."

There was no arguing with her, so that was the end of it. I only hoped she wouldn't think to summon me back to her room later on, because then she was certain to be worse. Even when she was three quarters in the bag, she could still feel the reserve in me pulling away. That would hurt her, then make her angry, and that would set her off yelling and screaming and cursing. I would have to stand there and listen until she was done. If I made a move to edge out the door, she spotted it at once.

"Just a minute! Where the hell do you think you're goin'? I'm not through with you yet! Sit down!"

"Yes, Mom."

When she got to ranting like that, she slurred and mumbled so badly I could barely make sense of her rage. I was able to decipher that somebody was a "no good sonofabitch," but wasn't sure if it was me or someone else. Whoever it was, when she paused in her tirade, stared me straight in the eye and asked, "Right?" I knew I had better agree with her. "Right, Mom. Right. Right."

Sometimes she ended one of those mumblings with just a question mark and waited for my answer. Then I couldn't fake it. A simple "Right, Mom" wasn't enough, and I didn't know what else to say. That would make her even more furious.

"Jesus Christ, what's a matter with you? You stupid? What? You must be stupid!"

"Yes, Mom, I'm stupid."

I couldn't explain I hadn't understood her. Then she would growl, "What's a matter? You deaf? You're not paying attention to me when I talk to you?" Any answer I gave was wrong, so stupid was fine. Okay, I'm stupid. At least that didn't get me a whipping.

It didn't take much to bring one on at those moments. The slightest wrong expression or inflection was enough to trigger her wrath. "I told you not to let me hear that tone of voice!" she would yell, ordering me outside to pick a switch off one of the trees.

Yet I could never be sure when that was coming. She might seem to be heading that way, when she would shift gears abruptly and veer in the opposite direction.

"Get 'em all dressed!" she might suddenly shout out the door to Georgie, our nurse. "Kids are all goin' to the Ice Follies. That's it. Get 'em all dressed in their good clothes and take 'em."

One time she stopped cold in the middle of a harangue and decreed that we had to learn tennis. "I know what you need. *A sport you can play with decent people later in life.* Georgie, call up the tennis pro. Kids are gonna take lessons!" And for the next few months that's what we did, two afternoons a week.

Often, when I saw her the next morning it was as if nothing had happened. I would sidle into her room expecting the worst and be greeted with outstretched arms and a radiant smile.

"Aw, honey, how are you? It's so good to see you. Come over here and let me give you a hug."

She was all gentleness and warmth then and didn't seem to remember anything at all about how she had raged and cursed and maybe even worked me over less than twenty-four hours before. I think that frightened me even more than the yelling and whipping.

Making my way to her bed, I would go through the motions of returning her affection and hold up my end of the conversation with as much naturalness as I could simulate. But I wasn't that trusting. I still remembered even if she didn't. It would take me two or three days to stop flinching. And just about the time I began to open up to her again, she would fall sick again and turn back into that other person.

I could never be sure where I stood with her, so I had to learn to read her quickly. At the first sign of a slur I tried to get out of her way, go someplace, hide out. I constantly tested the wind. When I came back in the house I listened for voices and watched the help, pumping them with questions to find out what sort of mood she was in. "How's Mom?" I would ask. "How's it going? Is she feeling okay?" It was a relief to hear, "Oh, she's fine today, just fine." But I still kept my guard up. There were moments when she was loving and funny and marvelous to be with, but those moments were sure to end.

I had no idea what was wrong with her, but whatever it was seemed to grow progressively worse. By the time I was nine or ten, the good moments early in the day had all but vanished. She was sick a lot more, and the sickness was making her act stranger and stranger.

One night, as my brothers and I were getting ready for bed, she burst into our room and began flailing away at us while she ranted about something or other we had done wrong. Dad heard the commotion and rushed in a minute later. Without speaking a word, he pried her loose, scooped her up in his arms and carried her off. That was the last we saw of either of them that night, and there was no mention of it the next morning.

Another morning I came into her room and discovered her sprawled out, unconscious, on the floor of her dressing area. Everything there—the counter, the drawers, the walls—was mirrored glass, and her motionless body reflected into infinity. She must have passed out while sitting at her dressing table and tumbled off the stool. But I still didn't know about drinking and passing out. I only knew she was far sicker than she had ever been before. Maybe she was dead.

I went screaming off to Georgie in terror.

"Georgie! Help! Come quick! Mom's sick or something! She's lyin' on the floor in there!"

Georgie hurried to her and immediately took charge.

"It's all right, Gary. Don't worry about a thing. Go downstairs. I'll see you in a few minutes."

Miraculously, an hour later Mom was up and about again. But I had to wonder, "What kind of sickness is this? And why doesn't the doctor make her better?"

It was an enormous relief to discover that the trouble with

Mom was booze. At least that made some sense out of her illness.

I figured it out from watching the parties at the house. Every so often, when Dad was between pictures and didn't take off out of town, he would have a few dozen people over for the evening. By the standards of Hollywood entertaining, they were just casual little get-togethers. The men wore neckties and the women put on their jewelry and furs, but there were no tuxedos or evening gowns or heavyweight producers who might do Dad some good. The guests were mostly friends in the business who were fun. Some were stars, like Bob Hope and Judy Garland, but there were also propmen, stunt men, songwriters, second leads and a good assortment of the show business characters Dad enjoyed.

About the time they got into their first drinks and hors d'oeuvres, my brothers and I were shipped off to bed. But if Georgie wasn't standing guard, we would sneak down the long hall from our room, hang over the banister at the top of the stairway and spy down on them as they laughed, sang around the piano and swapped stories about the old days. By the peak of the evening, the serious drinkers would have gotten themselves thoroughly loaded. That's how I made the connection. One night I finally figured out that when Mom became sick she was just like them. There was the same slurred speech, the same peculiar expression on her face, the same strange behavior, so that's what it had to be. That ended my confusion and dispelled most of my fear. As long as I knew what it was, I could more or less handle it.

My brothers assimilated the knowledge about the same time. We didn't talk about it, but we didn't have to. I don't recall ever discussing it with Dad either. The closest he came to directly acknowledging Mom had a problem was that night he stopped her from whacking on us and carried her back to her room. Yet we knew that he knew, and somewhere along the line he figured out that we did too. When he returned home from a trip, he would ask us, "How's your mother been?" I would answer, "Okay" or "Well, she was good for some of the time and not too good for the rest." That ended the discussion, but each of us was perfectly aware of what the other was saying.

Dad was away a lot those years. If he wasn't making movies and records and doing his radio show, he was touring military bases, playing war-bond rallies or off with his cronies on hunting and fishing trips and golf excursions. We didn't see that much of him, which was all right with me. I thought of him as God Almighty, the Great Circuit Court Judge. It seemed to me that he came into town just to pass judgment on all the bad things we had done; then he would punish us and go off again.

I always breathed more easily when he packed up his bags and golf clubs and left for a while. It meant there was one less person to mete out punishment, another pair of eyes that wouldn't be scrutinizing me to find something wrong. And when he was away, Mom might start hitting the bottle early and be in bed for the night by the time I got back from school. Then I wouldn't have to face either of them. There was still Georgie, their surrogate when they weren't around, but she couldn't keep up with all four of us all of the time. It's a terrible thing to say, but I liked it better around the house when Mom was drinking and passing out early and Dad was gone.

Two or three days before he was due home, Mom would try to straighten up and pull herself together. But that's no time at all to dry out, and it would leave her in a state of whoops and jingles. Her nerves were so raw that the slightest wayward look or comment was enough to throw her into a black depression, and she would jump right back into the jug again.

Mom's drinking must have mystified the old man. To his way of thinking, everyone had the strength to do anything, so it was simply a matter of wanting to stop. From the stories I heard years later, that's what he did early in his career when he was well on the way to the same problem. Evidently he was quite the carouser when he sang with Paul Whiteman's band in the late twenties, and the heavy partying took its toll on his work. That's supposed to be why Whiteman fired him. Yet shortly after he married Mom he decided to turn it off, and that was the end of it. When she wasn't able to do that, I'm certain he didn't know what to think.

Part of Mom did want to stop. She had a Freudian psychia-

73

trist, Dr. Tony Sturdevant, come to the house to work with her, and he did manage to help her somewhat. There were weeks and even months when she didn't touch a single scotch. But sooner or later she invariably went back to it. Dad had to be beside himself when he realized the doctor wasn't able to fix her up for good. I can imagine his frustration. "Jesus Christ," he must have said to himself, "what the hell am I paying him all this money for if he just keeps coming here and nothing gets any better?" I don't know if the doctor ever could make him understand why she was having such a hard time. Dad knew a lot about a lot of things, but he didn't have much feeling for psychological complexities and for how dark and fearsome life can sometimes seem.

I remember his response, a few years before he died, when one of my brothers flew off into the manic phase of the manic-depression that bedeviled him. I was trying to explain why his son was under sedation in the hospital, when he stopped me in mid sentence, stared me straight in the eye and asked in all sincerity, "Tell me something, Gary. How the hell does anybody have a mental problem? What's that about?" Mental problems were all around him. I had them. My brothers had them. His own wife had them. But he was so strong and self-assured and so blessed in his professional life that they remained beyond his comprehension. I didn't know what to answer. I simply said, "Well, I guess everybody ain't as strong as you are, Dad. That must be it." He threw me a funny look, shook his head and changed the subject.

At times Dad ran out of patience with Mom's boozing, and I would hear their voices rising and falling in anger down the hall. They did their scrapping in private and attempted to keep it cool in front of the kids. When Mom was in an especially bad way she might slip a little and let out eight bars at the old man while we stood within earshot. But her mutterings were largely unintelligible, and the moment she started we automatically excused ourselves and beat it out of the room. I tried not to listen in on their arguments, partly because I didn't want to hear them and partly because I was afraid of being caught. There were too many people working around the house. God help me if one of them found me eavesdropping and decided to turn me in.

If I accidentally surprised them in the middle of a quarrel, they threw up an instant cover. One evening I rounded the corner into the den and found them going at it full blast. I slammed on the brakes but was already too far into the room to back out. Yet they straightened up on the spot and, almost in unison, began firing questions in my direction about how I had done at school that day. Put on the defensive, I forgot about everything except what I could safely tell them and what I had better keep hidden. It wasn't until they were through with me and sent me off to my room that I realized what I had witnessed.

Most of the time I knew they were angry with each other only because they seemed more distant than usual and particularly formal and polite.

In public they made a special point of presenting a united front. When friends came to the house, or on the rare occasions when they went out together, it would be impossible to tell they weren't getting along. There was never a cross word. They did a hell of an act.

Dad and Dr. Sturdevant weren't the only ones who tried to get Mom to stop. From time to time some of her women friends also took a shot at it. Mom had two sets of girl friends. They could be divided neatly into those who drank and those who didn't. The drinkers were mostly the wives of stars and other men in the business. They would hit our house late in the morning and spend the day in her room or the den gossiping and laughing while they slugged it down. Many of them were bright, beautiful, funny women who seemed to have everything, yet all they liked to do was go to someone's home and get loaded. I couldn't understand why. By five o'clock they would be gone. Even when they were completely bombed they still had enough wits to take off before Dad came home.

The other, smaller group consisted of friends from the old days before Mom was married, women like Pauline Weislow, who had gone to high school with her, and Alice Ross, her pal from the years when she was still making movies. Mom usually didn't drink as much when they came to visit. When she did, they might risk her ire by saying something about it. They wouldn't come right out and flatly tell her, "Dixie, don't drink." No one except maybe my father talked to her like that. But as the afternoon wore on and they watched her become more and more wasted, she would read the unhappiness on their faces and call them on it.

"What's a matter with you?"

"Well, gee, Dixie, you know. Why don't you lighten up on that stuff?"

Not that the suggestion did much good. It just put her on the defensive.

"You don't tell me what to do. I'll live my life, you live yours. You want to drink, you can drink. You don't want to drink, you don't have to drink. If I feel like drinking, I'm gonna drink."

There was nothing more to be said, so they backed off until the next time. But they loved her in spite of it. They never let their disapproval build to the point where they stopped coming around. And she loved them too—better, I think, than her drinking buddies. At least they showed they cared about her. And Mom appreciated that, even though she knew they weren't ever going to make her change.

Grandpa Wyatt didn't know what to do about her either. Her boozing must have broken his heart. Mom was the only one of his children still alive. His other two daughters had both died of rheumatic fever. His wife, Nonie, was on the way out, too, so Mom was about all he had left.

She hated for him to see her when she was in her cups. It made her too guilty. But when she was on a long binge it couldn't be avoided. She didn't try to hide what she was up to. She drank in front of him. It had to make him crazy. I'm certain they fought about it. Knowing Gramps, he wouldn't let that slide by for a second.

Georgie loved Mom too. I remember her as a short, stocky, fanatically devout Irish Catholic with a Boston accent, wiry hair and a grim face. She was hired on as our nurse when I was about eight and quickly became the lord high executioner of all my mother's rules. The instant one was broken she went running off to Mom or, more and more frequently, took care of the punishment herself by going after us with wire coat hangers. Georgie was bound and determined that Mom's commandments be carried out to the letter. She ran us out of the kitchen so we wouldn't hang out with the help, whacked us when she caught us whispering in bed in the morning, forced us into Mom's bedroom to say hello when we came back from school, even though we tried every ruse in the book to keep away because of our fear about what we might find. Georgie never would admit Mom drank. According to her, some days she just didn't feel well. Through all this Georgie kept saying how much she loved us, which made me really wonder what love was all about.

After a while Georgie took over the running of the entire house, acting as my mother's voice when Mom withdrew into her room and wouldn't see anyone else. If the hallway had to be cleared, the floors scrubbed and waxed or the car taken to the garage, Georgie was the one who delivered the orders, then stayed on top of the staff to make sure it happened. She did the work of two or three people—all out of love. Her devotion to Mom was so complete that she had no life of her own and didn't seem to want one. When the time came for her vacation, she wouldn't know what to do with it. I don't believe she ever took a day off. She was a middle-aged woman, years older than my mother, but it was almost as if she were her daughter.

When Mom was on a heavy bender, Georgie vanished into her room and played backgammon with her for days on end. They played through the night without stopping. In the morning she reappeared long enough to pack us off to school and get the house running, then went back inside and continued the game. Sometimes Mom yelled and hollered at her, but Georgie took almost any abuse she heaped on her without a complaint. One afternoon when Mom was in an especially bad way, she became so frenzied about how Georgie had played a double six that she picked up a shoe and hurled it at her, smashing her hard on the face. But Georgie kept on playing.

Every great once in a while she stomached as much as she could bear and threatened to leave.

"That's it! I'm quitting! I'm getting out of here! I can't take it anymore!"

But all Mom had to do to turn her around was apologize.

"Aw, come on, Georgie. I'm sorry."

"Well, okay."

Then they went right back to the backgammon board.

God never created a more perfect partner for an alcoholic.

I'm not really sure when my mother started drinking. One of the earliest memories I have about anything is the nurse's admonition to play quietly because Mom was feeling sick, so she must have been into it by the time I was four or five. But I'm fairly certain she didn't start until she got together with Dad.

They met in 1930, when he was singing at a nightclub in Los Angeles, and married before the year ended. Dad was about twenty-nine. Mom was ten years younger but was already becoming established as a featured actress and singer in the movies. The head of Fox had brought her out to California just the year before from New York, where she was playing the lead in *Good News,* singing the hit song of the show, "The Varsity Drag." He signed her to a three-year contract, put her in the Fox *Movietone Follies* of 1929, one of the first talkies, then followed that up with a slew of other musicals and comedies. Some of the pictures starred top performers like Janet Gaynor, Will Rogers and Clara Bow; others were amiable quickies with titles like *Cheer Up and Smile, The Big Party* and *Let's Go Places.* In something like a year and a half she made eight of them. Her personal notices were good, and her career was building nicely.

All this happened so fast that her head must have been spinning. When Mom was whisked off to Hollywood she had been on Broadway all of seven weeks. In typical show business fairy-tale fashion, she had been called in from the road company when the star fell ill and couldn't go on. The road company job was her first show, and she had been doing it for only five weeks when she moved on to New York. Before that, her professional experience was pretty much limited to singing at the College Inn in Chicago for a month. Her folks had moved there from Tennessee three years earlier, and she was still in high school. The engagement was her prize for winning an amateur contest judged by Ruth Etting. From the stories I've heard, a high school classmate entered her name in the contest without telling her, and either Grandpa Wyatt or Nonie had to talk her into showing up. She was so young and had so little ambition and self-confidence that her agent had to force her on the train to Pittsburgh when he got her her first real job with the road company of *Good News*.

When Mom met my father he had recently been fired by Paul Whiteman for spending too much time partying and not enough taking care of business. Dad had worked with the Whiteman orchestra for about three years, singing with Harry Barris and his childhood pal Al Rinker as the Rhythm Boys trio. That was his big break, but he seemed to care more for wine and women than he did for song, and Whiteman finally ran out of patience. For a while the trio worked on their own at the Montmartre Café in Los Angeles, then moved over to the Cocoanut Grove, where Dad began to attract a good bit of attention for his solo spots in the act. He was becoming the hot new singer in town to the show business insiders who patronized the club, but he hadn't yet broken through to a larger audience.

According to a frequently told story, when Mom informed Sol Wurtzel, her boss at Fox, that Dad had proposed to her, the producer shook his head in disapproval and said, "If you marry that Crosby character, you'll have to support him the rest of your life. He'll never amount to anything." The state of their respective careers is summed up nicely by another tale that's been passed along through the years. The headline of the Associated Press release announcing their wedding read "Dixie Lee, film actress, today married Murray Crosey, orchestra leader, at a simple church ceremony."

Supposedly, before Mom consented to marry Dad she made him promise to quit boozing and knuckle down to work. A feature story published in 1952, the year of her death, stated that during their courtship she had launched a one-woman campaign to straighten him out. "She'd break his gin bottles and cart him off to a Turkish bath every time she thought it wise. She laid down pretty strict rules of deportment and was a stern disciplinarian whenever Bing broke them."

The campaign did not succeed until after the wedding day had come and gone. Dad had Sundays and Mondays off from the Cocoanut Grove, and he took to spending his weekends partying at Agua Caliente, a resort just over the Mexican border. Sometimes he got back too wasted to put on much of a show. Sometimes he didn't get back at all. Eventually his boss tried to fine him for missing work, but Dad wouldn't put up with it and quit.

I can only wonder if that was the reason, but right about this time Mom took off by herself and headed down to Ensenada, Mexico. The Associated Press reported the story on March 5, 1931: "Dixie Lee, featured film player, and Bing Crosby, orchestra and radio singer, have separated and she soon will sue for divorce." Mom told the reporter, "We have been married only about six months, but already we have found we are not suited for each other. Our separation is an amicable one."

According to one account, Dad followed her down to Mexico, promised to straighten up and prevailed upon her to come back to him. Ten days later, on March 15, another Associated Press dispatch reported the reconciliation:

"Dixie Lee's five months' marriage to Bing Crosby seemed short enough when she announced a week ago that they had parted, but they hung up a new record today when it was learned they were reunited. The reconciliation between the crooning member of Gus Arnheim's band and the Fox film commedienne was brought about in the most approved motion picture scenario manner. They just kissed and made up."

From what I've been able to piece together, Dad kept his promise. He didn't exactly join the temperance union, but he did cut back on the heavy partying and began to attack his work more seriously. Putting the Rhythm Boys behind him, he decided to go out on his own and brought in his older brother Everett to guide his new career as a soloist. Everett had been selling trucks in Los Angeles and handling bits and pieces of Dad's business on the side, but now he took over managing him full time.

Dad's career took off almost at once. About six months before the separation, he had gone into the studio with Gus Arnheim's orchestra, which had backed him at the Cocoanut Grove, to record a song written by Harry Barris, his partner in the Rhythm Boys. The tune was "I Surrender, Dear," and when it turned into Dad's first big solo hit, Everett rushed a copy to William Paley, the head of CBS, and sold him on Dad as a radio singer. In the fall of 1931, just half a year after he and Mom reconciled, he began his own national radio show from New York. That November Everett parlayed the program's success into a ten-week appearance at New York's Paramount Theater. The run was extended to an unprecedented twenty-nine weeks at a hefty four grand a week, and Paramount Pictures signed him to star in *The Big Broadcast* of 1932. While he was shooting the movie back in Los Angeles, the studio was so delighted with his work that it grabbed him for five more pictures at sixty thousand dollars a copy. By 1933, the year of my birth, he had already become the Bing Crosby everyone in the world knew and loved.

I don't know if he asked Mom to give up her career when her contract with Fox expired. I doubt whether he had to. For all her feistiness, there was an introverted, painfully shy and uncertain side to my mother that made performing an agony. She was good at it, but she told me more than once how much she hated it. I saw that for myself some years ago while watching a clip from one of her old movies. At first I just listened to her voice. Her singing was free and effortless and, within the confines of the arrangement, unusually creative. She bent notes and added little embellishments and sounded like she was having a marvelous time. But then I looked up at her image on the screen. Her arms were fixed rigidly at her sides. Her fists were clenched so tight I could almost make out the whites of her knuckles. Her whole body seemed to be screaming, "I am frightened to death."

She had absolutely no confidence in her talent, a trait she passed on to me. When she looked back at her career with reporters, she almost always found a way to put herself down. Reminiscing with Hedda Hopper about the amateur contest that started the whole thing off, she told her, "I was so bad and nervous that Ruth Etting must have known that I was a real amateur. She voted for me." Her recollection of her performance in *Good News* was equally self-deprecating. "The band was hysterical over my dancing. The boys just hoped that I'd do one number right." She talked the same way with Louella Parsons about her movies. "When I was with the old Fox company I made the world's worst picture, *Follies* of 1929. If they didn't know how bad I was—I *did*. I hadn't been so bad on the stage. But I knew a movie career was not for me. When I was right at the height of my flop—Bing and marriage came along."

I'm certain the bullshit of the business also had her climbing the walls. My mother was an outspoken, irreverent woman with a mind of her own. She couldn't endure anyone who wasn't straight and honest. When gossiping with her girl friends, she saved her most acid barbs for the stars and other high rollers who were overly impressed with themselves. She simply didn't have it in her to go through the ass-kissing and false friendships necessary for a young actress trying to build a career. When she found a reason to give it up, she could only have been relieved. Not that she married Dad for that reason. She had to be in love with him. She had to want a home and children and all the rest of it. But marriage also gave her a way out of the jungle.

To this day I don't know what to make of the fact that she went back to it, however briefly, shortly after Phil and Denny were born. If life at home isn't working out for a married actress, the first thing she's likely to do to salvage her ego is pick up her career and throw herself into work. But even in her most down moments Mom never once mentioned the possibility. On the other hand, maybe she came back when she did just because the first years of marriage were so happy that they made her feel strong enough to handle it. Maybe she thought, "Now that I have love and a husband and a home, it won't be so hard to get out there."

Whatever the reason, in January 1934, when I wasn't quite seven months old, the papers printed the news that she was returning to the movies to co-star with Lanny Ross in *Melody in Spring*. The return was postponed, I suppose because she discovered she was pregnant with the twins. But she did make it back a year later in a picture with George Burns and Gracie Allen titled *Love in Bloom*. "Mrs. Bing Crosby has taken Hollywood's biggest risk and decided to combine marriage with a career," the interview proclaimed, and then went on to list all the two-performer marriages that had failed. Mom seemed fully aware of the risk. "Just because a wife has a career," she told the reporter, "is no reason she should lose sympathy for her husband's. This is an experiment in every sense. I'm keeping an open mind about what happens to my home. I think I'll be able to feel which way the matrimonial wind is blowing. And you can bet that if it looks like a squall, Dixie Lee will trim her sails for Mrs. Bing Crosby."

Love in Bloom was trashed as a "complete waste of time,"

though Mom's personal notices were good. One reviewer thought she gave a "winning performance." Another wrote, "Miss Lee's performance and beauty make up for a lot of things." The results were pretty much the same with the other movie she shot that year, *Redheads on Parade*. The critics treated her kindly, but their response to the picture must have made her think twice about going on. It certainly didn't do her ego much good. And then, after trying it a few times, maybe she found that performing was still murder for her. Maybe Dad also pressured her to quit. Louella seemed to think so. When she announced that Ethel Merman had been brought in to replace Mom in the film of *Anything Goes*, she wrote, "I thought Bing Crosby gave his consent for Dixie Lee to appear opposite him in *Anything Goes* a little bit too easily. He probably realized he could talk her out of it later, and that is just what he has done." In any case, that ended it. In 1935 Mom retired for good and disappeared into the house.

For all intents and purposes, she was left there. I suppose that's when the heavy drinking began. Not that Dad was entirely to blame for leaving her by herself. Some of it was her fault. He would invite her along on location or to the studio or over to a friend's for the evening, but she always turned him down. By my early teens they had long since settled into a predictable routine where they both just went through the motions of playing out the script. When he came home he would say, "Hey, there's a thing at seven over at Van Heusen's. Would you like to make it?" She would answer, "Oh, gee, I don't know. I don't think so." And then his line would be, "Well, okay. I'll see you later, 'cause I'm going." That would be the end of it. It was no big thing as far as he was concerned. He had asked, and if she preferred to stay home, well, that was fine. But as soon as he took off, she collapsed into the dumper. And when she was drinking, she vanished into the bottle.

Sometimes the booze made her let down her guard, and I would overhear her grumbling to herself that he never wanted to take her along or do anything together. When I was about seventeen I started looking at him from that standpoint, asking myself,

"Well, does he or doesn't he?" I saw that he always asked and she always refused, so I thought at first, "Well, what the hell is she complaining about?" Then it finally dawned on me that although he made the advances, she wasn't reading them. He would only take one step, and that wasn't enough for her.

Mom was shy. She had to be coaxed. Otherwise she felt she was in the way and was just being asked along out of politeness. Once she was forced into a corner and had to talk with people, she held her own beautifully. She was funny and warm, and everyone loved her. But when it was left up to her, she agonized over leaving the house. What she needed was for Dad to grab her by the arm and tell her in no uncertain terms, "That's it. I'm not listening to any more of this nonsense. You want to go and you know damn well you want to go, so come on, get dressed." But he didn't know how to reach out that far. He didn't recognize her need for constant reaffirmation or recognized it but couldn't give it. He was not a demonstrative man. And Mom couldn't tell him. It would have been impossible for her to sit him down and say, "Look, I'm shy. You have to coax me." So he went out alone, and she stayed home, got depressed and drank.

Dad wasn't able to express it directly, not face-to-face, but I know he loved her deeply. Mom told me how, when he went out of town, he wrote her long, marvelous love letters that were full of feeling. Yet once he came back, the best he could do was speak to her in a kidding, wisecracking manner from which she was supposed to deduce, "Oh, yeah, Bing loves me. That's just him." But for her that wasn't enough. And that was her problem. I can't attribute it all to him. She needed more affection than most people require. And she did her own job of hiding it. Most of the time she was equally off the cuff with him. When things were bad between them they hardly spoke at all, but when they were good they masked their real feelings behind a facade of banter and comic takes.

"Ah, the Romantic Singer of Songs You Love to Hear is home," is how she would greet him when he returned from the studio.

He would break into a tune and sing, "Yes, I'm home, and it's lovely to be here."

"That's marvelous, dear. Just marvelous."

"And what did you do with your day today?" he might ask. "Anything earthshaking happen?"

"Oh, Alice and Pauline dropped by."

"Oh my God, that's wonderful. That's terrific."

"And how was your day?"

"Oh, well, I did the usual thing. I was my usual charming self at all times."

Often, when he came down for breakfast in the morning, they did a few minutes of stand-up comedy on the way he was dressed.

"Mmm, magnificent. Marvelous outfit today."

"Wha-a-at? What's wrong with this?"

"I don't think the yellow socks really show off your blue suit to best advantage, do you?"

"Well, I just thought they were light. I didn't know they were yellow."

"Uh-huh. Well, don't you have a dark pair somewhere up there in your dresser?"

"Why, yes, I think so. I suppose I could rustle one up."

He would go upstairs to change, and when he came back down wearing brown ones, she would shake her head in mock exasperation.

"It's such a good thing that that's part of your image. It's so smart of you to incorporate that in."

On the humorous level they got along fine. Everywhere else the gap between them continued to widen as the years passed. She became increasingly reclusive and drank more. He was gone for longer and longer stretches of time. When he was home they merely coexisted behind the walls.

More than anything, the picture I have of my mother is that of a rich man's wife sitting around her huge barn of a house by herself. The closest she came to breaking out of her seclusion was during World War II. What with the bond shows and the tours of military bases added on to his other activities, Dad was hardly home at all. Mom's heart went out to the servicemen, too, and she managed to rouse herself from her depression to do something about it. She wasn't a joiner, but on her own she sent a constant flow of checks to hospitals and charities, planted Victory gardens in the backyard and threw open her doors to anyone in a uniform who was passing through town.

She virtually ran her own Hollywood Canteen at the house. She gave the GIs parties, fed them, fixed them up with dates with single women she knew in the business, handed over whatever money she had in her purse if they were broke, lent them her Packard convertible for the evening and listened to their troubles when they wanted to talk. One badly wounded kid, a paraplegic who got around in a specially built car, visited regularly. He would lift out his wheelchair, then drag himself out with his arms and roll himself up the driveway. He and Mom talked together for hours. I imagine she helped him more than a little.

It's a peculiar thing to say, but the war was a good time for her, in the sense that it made her busy and productive and fired with purpose. She was needed. She could do something for someone. There wasn't much she could do for Dad. He was too self-sufficient. He never seemed down or troubled or frightened. And it's hard to keep taking from someone like that without giving anything back.

Whatever the problems that kept them apart, Mom adored my father. If she was drinking, her voice might take on a sarcastic edge when his name came up. Every great once in a while, when she forgot I was sitting there in her room, she might get a strange look on her face and mutter the names of some of the actresses in his pictures. But that was about as close as she came to talking him down. And God help anyone else who found fault with him. It would be instant war. If my brothers or I had the poor sense to try to criticize him, she laced into us before the reproach cleared our lips.

"Geeze, it was bad that Dad did—"

"Don't you dare say anything bad about your father! You just keep your mouth shut."

When she was angry she had a mouth like a truck driver. She could level anyone with it—and she would. I saw her come close to throwing girl friends out on the street when they were kidding around and took a more or less playful swipe at the old man.

"Well, let's face it, Dixie, he's not the greatest singer in the world."

That was all she had to hear.

"Bullshit he's not! Long as you're in this house, you don't say one word against that man. You do and you're out on your ass."

They shut up on the spot. They knew she meant it.

Mom's loyalty carried over into the way she played out her assigned role as Mrs. Bing Crosby. The part was difficult for her. She was only at ease on her own turf with people she felt close to. I doubt if she ever knew for sure what was expected of her. The role wasn't spelled out in so many words. It simply evolved. Dad wouldn't have said, "Look, I'm a celebrity and this is how you have to act." He didn't play it like a celebrity and never quite believed that he was. He had a certain ironic detachment that kept him from taking it all that seriously. I remember him joking that he expected to hear a knock at the door one day and there would stand the man in the suit, who would tell him, "Okay, Bing, the game is up. We found you out, and you have to give it back." Not that he felt guilty or insecure about his success. He was grateful for it and enjoyed it. It fit him as comfortably as one of his Hawaiian sport shirts.

But from the way Mom handled herself with the press, she seemed to feel that what she had to offer wasn't enough or was not what people wanted. So she had to transform herself into someone else. I watched her try to appear educated and well rounded and outgoing and unfailingly optimistic—all the things she wasn't—and I know that had to hurt. She couldn't abide sham and deceit, especially in the business, and here she was as full of it as every other Tinseltown phony. But she did it. She gave them what they were waiting to hear, and she carried it off without muffing a line.

"Oh, yes, it's wonderful being married to Bing. He's such a wonderful actor and singer and a wonderful guy, a great father and a warm, wonderful human being. I want for nothing, and life is rosy and terrific and wonderful. It couldn't be better."

Chapter Five
The Ranch

The ranch was supposed to make a man of me. That's what Dad had to say when he summoned me into his office one February afternoon and announced he had bought a spread up near Elko in the northeast corner of Nevada and would be taking me up there for the summer when school let out in June.

"You're ten years old, Gary," he intoned from behind his desk in that same stern voice he used when I did something wrong. "It's time you realized there's a lot more to life than Beverly Hills. You're going to have to work hard for a living when you grow up. There won't be any ne'er-do-wells in this family if I have anything to say about it. You're big enough to start now. I'm putting you to work this summer on the ranch. You'll be just another hand, treated the same as everyone else. You'll learn how to take care of horses and cattle and find out what it's like to work up a sweat in the hay fields. It'll be good for you. It will teach you a sense of responsibility. It will build your character. It will turn you into a man. When your brothers get a little older they'll join up with you, but this summer it'll be just the two of us."

The prospect of a summer alone with him in the great outdoors was more than a little frightening. It sounded too close to what it was like when he dragged me along to play golf or go fishing with his pals. That was also supposed to build my charac-

Dixie, 1930. (courtesy Maurice Seymour)

Gary and Bing, 1933.

Richard, Joby, and Ricky Arlen with Bing, Dixie and Gary on Gary and Ricky's christening day.

Dennis, Gary, Dixie and Philip, 1936.

Patty Taurog and Gary, 1939.

ter and teach me how to work, but all it did was make me more afraid of him than ever.

When he played golf I caddied for him, and God help me if I had trouble lugging his bag up and down the links, handed him the wrong club or got in his way. He would throw some acidy line at me like, "Hey, Bucket Butt, wake up, will ya!" and his cronies would double over laughing in appreciation of his wit while I attempted to disappear into the soles of my sneakers. It was even worse when he walloped off a long drive and I lost sight of where the ball landed. Trying hard to control my panic, I would scurry down the fairway praying that the Lord would take mercy on me and grant me sight of that little white bastard before the old man caught on and roasted my ass for spoiling his game.

"Please, God, I've got to find that sonofabitch and I don't know where it went, I just don't know where it went!"

Sometimes my prayers were answered. A guardian angel would materialize in the form of another caddy and clue me in on where it was hiding.

"Hey, kid, see that bush over there? It's just about three steps to the right of that bush. Take a look and you'll find it."

But most of the time I was left to search it out on my own while Dad grumbled and cursed away at my incompetence.

"Jesus Christ, what the hell's the matter with you? Can't you do *anything* right?"

The fishing trips would start with the customary litany of do's and don'ts he laid on me whenever he took me somewhere.

"Don't be wise. Don't be fresh. Don't speak unless you're spoken to. Don't fool around with the fish. Don't fool around with anything. Just stay out of the way and do your chores and you'll enjoy yourself."

When the old man was in an especially good mood he might put out a pole for me, but that brought its own possibilities of danger. I never forgot the first time he took me deep-sea fishing. I had gotten seasick and was sprawled out on the top deck trying to puke when I heard his voice shouting up to me.

"Hey, Gary, come quick. You got a fish on your line. Looks like a big one."

I wobbled over to the side of the boat and, sure enough, my

pole was bent double from the weight of the thing. I reeled it in about as far as I could and then he said, "Okay, jerk him in now. Just give it a big yank and jerk him in." I snapped the pole back with all my strength, and a large plastic fish that had been tied to the end of the line came flying up and whacked me hard in the head. The boat rocked with laughter, but I was too sick and my head hurt too much to share the little joke.

"What's the matter?" Dad demanded when he finally simmered down. "Can't you take it, spoilsport? Don't you have any sportsmanship?"

Exactly how these outings with the old man were supposed to improve my character was a mystery beyond my comprehension. I hated every minute of them, and he seemed just as unhappy to have me tagging along behind him.

A whole summer together at the ranch sounded like a guaranteed misery for both of us. But, giving myself over to the fantasies of the cowboy life that floated around in my head from my favorite Roy Rogers and Gene Autry movies, I cheered myself up with the possibility that, well, maybe it wouldn't be so bad after all. I would climb out of my bedroll about nine in the morning, put on my woolly chaps and ten-gallon hat, and then, after a hearty breakfast of flapjacks and biscuits, strap on my six-shooters, hop on my trusty horse and spend the day riding the range looking for damsels in distress and bandits. When the sun went down I'd mosey back to the ranch house for more grub and pass the evening harmonizing around the campfire. The fantasy carried me through the rest of the winter and didn't crash up against reality until the morning after I actually set foot on the Cross-B.

A few days after school ended, I tossed some clothes into a suitcase, said good-bye to Mom and my brothers and climbed into the front seat of Dad's car. He threw it into gear and headed north toward Elko, some seven hundred miles away.

We drove for two days without speaking. The silence was filled by the whirring of the tires against the asphalt and whatever music I could dredge up from the car radio. The farther we traveled, the hotter and dustier it became. As one station after another faded into the distance and I searched out the next one, the music changed from records by Dad, Como and Sinatra to a different kind of singing I had never heard before by people with strange-sounding names like Hank Williams and Ernest Tubb. Eventually the radio conked out altogether, and I passed the hours watching the mileage signs speed by, ticking off the distance to the next stop for gas or food.

We pulled into Elko late in the afternoon. Dad telephoned the ranch to alert the foreman we had arrived, then took me to the general store for the extra jeans and shirts I would need to see me through the next eleven weeks. He also bought me two cowboy hats: a plain straw job I'd use for work and a fancier felt number to be saved for church on Sunday.

Dad's place that first year was a relatively small spread only seven miles from town, and within the hour I was seated at the dinner table in the main ranch house with Johnny Eacret, the foreman, his wife Doris, ramrod Jim McDermott and the rest of the hands. That was one part of the cowboy existence that lived up to my fantasies. The table was loaded down with huge bowls of vittles: biscuits and gravy, mashed potatoes, big chunks of steak and chicken, corn on the cob, carrots, homemade breads and pies. Unlike mealtime at home, everyone dug in with abandon, and the only utensils they seemed to need to work their way through the mounds heaped on their plates were a spoon, a knife and a tin cup for the coffee to wash it all down. But when the old man saw my eyes bulging from the display of abundance passing under my nose, he threw me a look that made it clear I'd better hold myself in check. I grabbed a piece of meat and a portion of carrots and let the rest slide by.

After supper Dad strolled out to the porch with Johnny and the other hands and sat around swapping small talk about the cattle and the weather and the neighboring ranches. As usual, he fit right in. Dressed in his plaid shirt and faded Levi's, with his cowboy boots propped up against the porch railing, he seemed like just another good old boy who had been living that way all his life. About the only thing missing to complete the image of "Bing Out West" was the harmonizing around the campfire.

I kept myself occupied by breaking in my new hats the way one of the hands showed me. I wet down the straw job at the water pump, curled the brim just right, then closed my bureau drawer on it so the curl would be pressed in permanently by the time it dried in the morning. For the rest of the evening I sat off to one side of the porch, kneading the brim of my felt hat with my fingers to work out the stiffness and mold it into shape. By eight-thirty Dad was ready to call it a night, and everyone sauntered off to their rooms. The moment my head hit the pillow I collapsed into a deep sleep.

I began to get some real idea of what the summer held in store when someone's hand shook me awake at five o'clock the next morning. As I stumbled into my new Levi's, I could smell the bacon and flapjacks already frying away on the kitchen griddle. An hour later I was on the back of a horse heading toward the government range in the nearby mountains where the cattle had been put out to graze for the summer. The amount of dust I swallowed on the ride out easily made up for the flapjacks, biscuits and mounds of potatoes I kept myself from devouring at the breakfast table.

Once we reached the range I bounced along behind the hands as they cut out Dad's cattle from those that belonged to the other ranchers. I had ridden a little at the old man's breeding farm near San Diego, but I never spent a full day on a horse before. When we finally trotted back to the ranch house late that afternoon, it felt like my new jeans had rubbed just about all the hide off the insides of my thighs. I peeled them off an inch at a time, then sat on my bunk for an hour dabbing my legs with ointment. The rest of the night I walked around straddle-legged to keep my thighs from touching.

"How'd it go?" Dad asked on the way to dinner.

"It went okay," I answered.

"Well, good. Glad to hear it."

The next day was more of the same, and so was the day after that. By the end of the week my legs were finally in shape, and I was ready to get down to serious work.

I spent the summer learning how to drive cattle, clean out barns and stables, take care of the horses and chickens, and bale hay. Dad made it clear to Johnny that I was up there to work and learn and wasn't to receive any special favors because I was his son. He wanted me treated just like any other green kid from the city who had never set foot on a ranch before. Johnny passed the word along to the hands, and that's exactly how they treated me.

I had a lot of learning to do, and I learned mostly by making mistakes and getting yelled at so I wouldn't make them again. I'd be toting my bucket and broom into the barn to swab out the stalls when a sudden shout would jolt me out of my daydreams.

"Stop! Goddamit, don't you move another step!"

I'd freeze dead in my tracks without having the slightest idea what was wrong.

"What? What's the matter?"

"Look what you're doin'! Stand still and look where you are!"

When I glanced around I couldn't see anything but the ass end of a horse a few feet away.

"What is it?"

"Jesus Christ, boy, you're about to take off and walk behind that fuckin' horse there! That horse don't know you. That horse is standin' there tied up, and it's about half hinky anyway. You want to get your brains kicked out?"

"No."

"Well, then get the fuck out of there! Don't you ever walk around behind a horse like that again."

"Oh, okay. Sorry."

Or I'd be ambling along in the hayfield watching the shadow of a cloud play over the mountains in the distance when someone's fist would snatch me by the collar and toss me off to one side.

"Look what the hell you're walking under, idiot!"

A boom was swinging a huge bale of hay over the exact spot where I had been standing.

"Look around you, boy. You can get yourself killed out here. Pay attention to what the hell's goin' on. Don't be stargazin' or thinkin' about somethin' else. This is important."

The reprimands were different from what I got at home. They weren't weighed down with the same cold disapproval and contempt. They didn't carry the same threat of punishment. They were always for a good reason. No one was chewing me out just to chew me out. Being yelled at made me feel silly and stupid, but when I looked around I realized I *could* have been kicked by that horse or flattened by that bale of hay. A ranch *was* a dangerous place. I'd heard the hands swapping tales about pals who had been killed in stampedes or mangled in machinery. I saw for myself how some of the guys I worked with were missing fingers and toes. So instead of turning off and retreating into my secret anger and fear, I found myself actually grateful that they yelled at me for messing up. It made the mistakes stick in my head, and I didn't mess up the same way twice.

During the early summer we spent six days a week out on the government range working with the cattle. The first big job was to round them up. We had to drive them down from the hills where they had spent the winter grazing, herd them into the rodeo grounds, a corner where two fences met at a right angle, then—and this was the trickiest part—separate ours out from those that belonged to the other outfits.

There was still plenty of work to do once the roundup was finished. The calves had to be castrated, branded, earmarked and wattled. The beef had to be cut out and moved to market. The calves, cows and bulls had to be kicked back out on the range again, then checked every day to make sure they stayed healthy and hadn't used up the salt licks and were getting enough to eat. When we found a large bunch congregating in one space, we'd cut it in two and drive half over to a grassier spot, then move on to the next bunch and repeat the process. It may have been on horseback, but it was hard, hard manual labor that didn't end until five in the afternoon, just time enough to ride the twenty miles back to the ranch before the sun went down. The rides home were the murderous part. The day's work was exhausting, but there were still two hours to go of steady trotting along, broken only by occasional pauses to open and close the range gates we passed through.

Every so often the work took us too far away from the ranch to make it back the same afternoon. Then we carried our bedrolls with us and either flopped on the bunkhouse floor of a nearby spread or slept outdoors. The nights outside were the ones I liked best, maybe because they came closest to whatever fantasies of the cowboy life I still had in me.

When we finished up for the day, we pulled the saddles off the horses and threw them on the ground, where they became our pillows for the night. After the horses were hobbled to keep them from wandering off, someone would build a campfire and we'd break out the biscuits and heat up the cans of pork and beans we brought with us, washing it all down with tin cups of steaming black coffee boiled in an ordinary kitchen pot so that you had to strain the grounds between your teeth. The very best part was after supper, when the hands sat around the fire for an hour or two swapping yarns about their homes and their lives and the people they had known.

There were stories about pals being shot, mauled in machinery or run over by stampedes, and tales about barroom brawls, bad checks and gambling debts—all of them human stories that spoke of real life and hard times and making it through no matter how rough it got. That's what impressed me most. Those men were survivors. I could see it for myself. They sweated their butts off sixteen hours a day for their hundred dollars a month, and they had so little to show for it that when one job ended they put everything they owned under one arm and had to jump a freight train to move on to the next one. But they never complained and never dogged it. If one of them did cop out and made someone carry his load, the others just walked away from him. They took pride in their work and knocked themselves out to do it well.

That was their life, and it wasn't easy. There wasn't a whole lot of room for pleasure. Yet they could get joy out of a sunset or their coffee after dinner or a clean pair of Levi's. Maybe once every six months they scraped enough money together to go into town, where they'd blow it all in a week. They would gamble it away, drink it away, party it away at one of the local whorehouses. Then they'd come back to work and wouldn't see a drink or a woman again for another six months. But that was all right with them. As long as they had a little left over for tobacco, a new pair of pants when the old ones fell apart, and a couple of shirts they could wash out at night, they were content. They accepted their existence on whatever level they found it and had themselves as good a time as they could with whatever they had.

I would sit around the campfire listening to the tales unfold and say to myself, "Gee, you may think you got problems, but look at these guys. And they're makin' it, they're goin' through it. Because they're tough. They just ain't ever gonna quit. They ain't ever gonna say die." I learned to respect survivors real early.

The feeling around the campfire was so close that sometimes I found myself chiming in with stories about my own home and family. Even then, though, I made sure to edit my words carefully to keep up the front that had been cultivated in the press. Mom had warned me so often, "Nothing that takes place in this house goes outside this house" that it had become second nature by now. It seemed strange that these grizzled cowboys living out their lives a million miles from Hollywood were so interested in gossip about people in show business. Not that they pressed me, but one thing would lead to another, and before long they'd be throwing questions at me about the old man just like the fans back in Los Angeles who went to the movies three times a week and devoured Louella Parsons along with their cornflakes at breakfast.

"Is that feud between your pa and Bob Hope for real? Is it true that they don't get along too good?"

"Did they have fun workin' together in that *Road to Zanzibar* picture?"

I'd answer as best I could, then try to move on to some other subject without making myself seem curt or uppity.

"Nah, Dad and Bob Hope are good buddies. They get along just fine. They only do that feud thing for laughs . . . Well, I wasn't there, y'know, but I hear they had a whole lot of fun workin' together."

Then I'd shift the conversation to the movie stars I cared about, the cowboy actors in the Westerns. They didn't think a whole lot of most of them.

"Bunch of damn drugstore cowboys prancin' around in those flashy getups and ridiculous pearl-handled six-guns. Why, they couldn't keep their ass on a horse or rope a steer if their lives depended on it."

The only cowboy actors they respected were the few who actually were what they seemed to be, and they had no trouble picking them out. One look was enough to tell them if a man knew anything at all about horses.

"Well, Roy Rogers is okay. Roy can ride. He used to cowboy a little before he went off to the pictures. But just about all the rest of them guys are bullshit."

One afternoon, toward the end of July, I came in from the range and found the rooms and storage areas in the ranch house being filled up with extra bunks. The haying season was about to begin, and a dozen or so temporary hands had just been hired on to help out with the work. Johnny Eacret, the foreman, called me over and told me that for the rest of the summer I'd be out in the hayfields with them.

The worst part of haying was the boredom. There were no horses to ride; no nights out under the stars, sitting around the campfire listening to stories; no new things to learn once you got a handle on your particular job. It was just endless repetition of the same monotonous chore seven days a week. Except for the fact that we were outdoors, we could just as well have been working on an assembly line. It seemed to take a week to get through a day, an eternity to make it through to Labor Day.

As the summer turned out, I saw less of the old man than I had feared. He spent most of his mornings hunting and fishing or dictating letters back to his office on his Dictaphone. In the afternoons he hung out with the other ranchers or rode around with Johnny, playing lord high overseer of his domain. Every now and then he descended on me without warning while I was hard at it. His great agate eyes swept across the terrain, noting each and every thing I was doing wrong. Then he galloped off into the distance and I could start breathing again.

"Hey, whaddaya say?" he would greet the foreman of my crew as he rode up. "How are ya?"

"Great, just great," was the inevitable reply.

"Good. Well, how's he acting? Is he giving you any trouble?"

"Nah, he ain't no trouble."

"Uh-huh. Well, if he gives you any trouble, just let me know."

About all he had to say to me directly was, "How's it going?" And about all I had to offer by way of an answer was, "Fine." I didn't want the special attention and kept the conversation to a minimum. Whenever he came around I suddenly turned into the boss's son. The rest of the time I was just a dumb kid from the city trying to learn something, and I liked that a lot better.

I was only alone with him when he took me off to church Sunday morning. I'd scrape the cowflop off my boots, put on clean jeans and my special Triple-X beaver felt hat, and we'd drive the seven miles to Elko in our customary silence. As usual, he came to life the moment he stepped from the car. Dad fit right in with the townspeople. He became just another good old boy, and they all loved him. I saw it on their faces from the way they said hello. Unlike how it was back in California, though, they left him his privacy and didn't pester him for his autograph or try to engage him in conversation unless he indicated he wouldn't mind shooting the breeze for a couple of minutes. I suppose that was one of the things he liked best about the place. Westerners know how to respect a man's space. Occasionally Dad did play a benefit for the local hospital or the town fair, but only because he wanted to help out, not because some local promoter sold him a bill of goods.

Several times during the summer Dad's business took him back to Los Angeles for a few weeks. Then he would write out a long list of do's and don'ts—covering everything from brushing my teeth to finishing my chores and going to church—and hand it over to Johnny and his wife Doris.

"Just don't step out of line while I'm gone," he would warn me before taking off, "because if you do they'll tell me. You do anything wrong and I'll know every detail. Don't worry about that."

There was no doubt in my mind that he would. If I even considered the possibility of not toeing the mark for a second, I felt the long arm of the law seven hundred miles away tugging me back.

Actually, Johnny and Doris didn't much care for being made my wardens. Johnny didn't talk to me about it. He hardly ever said more than "yep" and "nope" about anything and his face didn't show much. Yet a lot of warmth shone through his eyes, and the prospect of playing the heavy to a small kid must have been distasteful. To save himself the bother, he turned me over to his wife. Doris stayed on my case a little, but she was no Georgie. I expected the old man to blow his top when he heard how I had overslept fifteen minutes one morning, but she kept it to herself and I actually got away with something.

The summer finally ground to an end after the Elko fair on the Labor Day weekend. Like all the other kids in the area, I had been given a calf to take care of and, surprisingly enough, when I entered it in the 4-H competition I won third or fourth prize. One of the cattle brokers, a nice man who was a friend of Dad's, bought him for so much a pound, and I got to put the money in the bank. I suppose I should have felt a sense of accomplishment. I didn't. I knew the guy only bought it to please my father.

About five years ago I started to think back on all those summers I spent on the ranch and realized they could have been a lovely experience. There was so much that was good about them. The country itself was so beautiful. I loved taking care of the horses and the other animals. I loved getting out early in the morning, wrangling horses and punching cattle. Most of all, I loved the people I came to know—Johnny and Doris, Jim McDermott and all the other hands. But because I *had* to be there, because the old man just jammed it down my throat and forced me to do it, I hated every minute of it, hated everything about it and couldn't wait to get away.

The next summer I was back, as I was every summer but one after that until I reached my twentieth birthday. I never did come to like it any better, but that didn't seem to matter. The old man's attitude continued to be, "You *will* enjoy it. You *will* learn." Once he made up his mind, that was it.

Dad, though, was so taken with the ranching life that after the first year he traded in the Cross-B for a much larger spread about sixty miles northeast of Elko, up around the Owyhee Indian reservation. The new place was put together from a number of ranches bordering each other that happened to go up for sale at the same time. I remember the Spring Creek, the Evans Ranch and the Quarter Circle S, and there may have been one or two others. Altogether, they added up to about twenty thousand acres and somewhere between three and four thousand head of cattle. The place became a refuge for him, and he spent as much time there as he could. When he finished a picture or came off a heavy tour, he liked nothing better than to toss his fishing gear and hunting rifle into the backseat, step on the gas and head north.

Mom braved it a year or two, but it wasn't her style.

"Where'd everybody go?" she would laugh, looking around at nothing but sagebrush and mountains. "There's nobody here. What is this? No Chasen's? No Lucy's? No shows? Please, please, I'm not country. Leave me alone. I don't want to know from this. I don't need to be out here in the wilderness watching crickets."

After giving it a couple of tries, she opted out for good and stayed home by herself in Los Angeles.

"Sorry, fellas, you have to do this one on your own," she would tell us as we loaded up the car. "So long, guys, have a nice summer. See you in the fall. Aloha."

When my brothers received their sentence, they took it a lot better than I did. They bitched and moaned almost as much beforehand, but once we were there they accepted the inevitable and served out their time without complaining. I suppose it was the sensible way. They didn't like it either, but there were moments when they actually seemed to be having fun.

On the rides up, the four of us whiled away the long hours seeing who could spot the most out-of-state license plates or singing along with the radio. Sometimes Dad started up an old campfire song—"I've Got Sixpence" or "There's a Long, Long Trail"—then one of us picked up a harmony part and the rest joined in. The harmonizing helped. It kept our minds off where we were heading, and whenever Dad started singing he turned into Bing Crosby and we could get along with him as easily as everyone else in the world.

Once we hit the ranch, Linny took off to the main house with the old man, and the twins and I went to our room in the bunkhouse. We threw our sleeping bags down on the iron beds, hung our clothes up on the pegs in the wall, then settled in for the long summer before us. Dad liked to tell the press how the ranch helped bring his kids closer together. In a sense it did. Except for haying season, when we all had different jobs, we were with each other a lot and didn't fight nearly as much. I suppose that was because we had more time to ourselves and fewer rules to follow than back home. As long as we did our work, the old man was reasonably satisfied and left us to ourselves.

For the most part, I saw even less of him in the new place than I had at the Cross-B. We no longer lived under the same roof, and I spent many of the nights in one of the outlying line camps. Every now and then, though, when he was in an especially good mood, he took it into his head to instruct us in the manly pleasures of the outdoor life. After dinner, when there was maybe an hour of twilight left, he would call us together and say, "Come on, fellas, let's go hunting. Let's shoot some sage hen." We were exhausted from working all day but dutifully followed him outside and into the pickup truck. Hunting consisted of watching him gun down these large, floppy chickens, then scampering out to retrieve them. When he had had his fill, we dragged the carcasses back to the ranch and pulled out the feathers. It reminded me of the good old days when he took me fishing.

When I was about thirteen he decided I was ready for bigger game. He stuck a 217-B in my hand and took me out to hunt deer. We crept up on our victim in the quiet of the evening, and he gave me the privilege of firing off the first shot. He seemed delighted when I made a direct hit, but I was almost sick to my stomach. As I watched it take its final breaths, I said to myself, "I can't do this no more. This ain't for me. Hell, I can kill anything that's fighting me or threatening to mess me up, but I just can't take a gun and shoot some poor fuckin' animal that ain't doing nothin'."

After that I tagged along when the old man told me but refused to shoot anything. "Why not?" he would ask, and I'd arch my back and answer, "Oh, I don't know, I'm just not that crazy about it." After a while, when I had bogged down my heels and bulled my neck enough for him to get the message, he stopped dragging me with him and found some other companion to share in the kill. From then on he told everyone I didn't like hunting because I was lazy.

As one summer led to the next, I graduated from riding drag behind the cattle to riding the sides to riding point at the front of the herd. The one thing that didn't change was my attitude. I stayed hot and angry the entire ten years I was up there. It seemed to me that was about the only right I had left. I couldn't disobey the old man. I had to be there. I had to do the work. But I damn well didn't have to pretend to enjoy it.

Predictably enough, the only person to suffer from my rage

was myself. You don't think well when you're angry, and you make stupid mistakes. That's what happened one Sunday afternoon when I was about sixteen and damn near sent a whole stack of fence posts up in flames.

Dad had decided, on the spur of the moment, to hold a picnic on top of one of the mountains on his property. He rounded up my brothers, Johnny and Doris and some of the hands, but I begged off, telling him I'd just as soon stay back at the bunkhouse and rest. It rubbed him the wrong way. His voice turned cold, and he said, "Well, all right, if you don't want to come on the picnic with us, you'll just go down behind the barn and creosote posts for the rest of the day. That'll be it." I was furious, but it was too late to change my mind.

Not paying much attention to what I was doing, I flopped down the four railroad ties that support the creosote barrel, built up the fire to get the stuff boiling, then rolled the barrel onto the ties and went to work as soon as it started to bubble. Each time I waited out the five minutes it took for an armload of posts to soak in the creosote, I looked up at the mountain and watched the trail of dust from the old man's horse as it made its way up the side.

My anger kept me from realizing that I had built the fire on an incline instead of level ground, and that two of the ties were partly burned out from having been used before. Just about when the picnic party was finishing the fried chicken and moving on to the berry pie, the ties suddenly collapsed, the barrel crashed over on its side and the boiling creosote spilled up the incline, then came pouring back down into the fire, sending a huge cloud of black smoke up into the sky. I tossed a sack of dirt on the flames and shoveled the creosote away from the stack of posts so it wouldn't start something serious, then the hands came running from the bunkhouse and pitched in to help.

The first thing I did, once we brought it under control, was check out the mountain to see if the old man had spotted my smoke signal. And, sure enough, there was the dust trail racing back down the side. "Oh, shit!" I said to myself. "I'm in for it now." I felt like an idiot and had already tried, convicted and sentenced myself by the time he came roaring over. It was one of the few times I saw him lose his composure. He gave me a good dressing down on the spot—"Jesus Christ, you leave him alone for five minutes and he burns the whole fucking place down!"—and for the rest of the summer kept hammering away about what a dummy I was and how I did things that were so stupid they defied credibility.

If there was a lesson to be learned from the incident, I missed it. All it did was stoke up my rage and make me even more furious than ever.

I counted off the days until I could get out of there, and when I worked on the tractors I ticked off the hours until the day ended. To keep from going crazy from the monotony, I played little mind games with myself. If I was running a mowing machine, I looked ahead to when I would have to change sickle blades. If I was driving a rake, I looked forward to running a tooth into the ground so I could interrupt the routine for as long as it took to put on a new one. When it got to be ten-thirty I began counting off the minutes to lunch.

To move the hours along I tried finding ways to keep my mind off the clock. I fantasized ball games I was going to play when I returned to school in September. I'd conjure up scenes of executing the perfect tackle that saved the game or making the hit that kept the other side from getting a touchdown or intercepting a pass or beating the blocker to the ball carrier. I fantasized about the girls in the movies—Betty Grable and Rita Hayworth and Lana Turner—and how I was their boyfriend and was taking them out on dates. That started even before I knew what sex was. I listened to how the guys in the bunkhouse talked about them and figured that was something worth latching onto even though I wasn't clear exactly why.

Mostly I sang. Over the roar of the tractor I belted out the words to every song I had ever heard—the records Mom and Dad played around the house, the tunes I remembered from *Your Hit Parade,* the country songs that came over the bunkhouse radio at night from the station in Del Rio, Texas. The longer I spent at the ranch, the more that country music got to me, especially the lonesome, down, wailing numbers that mirrored exactly how I felt. I would pick out a couple of my favorites—T. Texas Tyler's "Remember Me," Lefty Frizzell's "Always Late," Little Jimmy Dickens' "Please, Mama, Please Stay

Home with Me"—and see how long it took to sing them back to back. Or I'd focus on one tune and keep singing it over and over again, doing it different ways to find things in the music I hadn't heard before. When I discovered something new I'd go for it and keep working on it until the original melody fell away and I had my own version. By then I'd be sure half a day had passed, but when I checked my watch it was only thirty or forty minutes, so I had to come up with a lot more songs, a lot more ball games, a lot more girl friends to make it through the rest of the afternoon.

The summer I was fifteen I paid my first visit to Maude's. I knew it was a mortal sin and the old man would kill me if he found out, but horniness conquered all. Sex had most definitely raised its furry head by now, and my fantasies on the tractor had turned considerably less innocent. But that was about as far as it went. There was no chance to even take a walk with a girl at home. I went to all-boys Catholic schools where the only females were the nuns. And in the unlikely event I did get to meet one somewhere else, I certainly couldn't ask her for a date. You can't invite a girl out if you have to be back in the house by ten o'clock. She'll only laugh at you. Dad never did get around to the standard lecture about the birds and the bees. I suppose he thought I'd pick up the essential information in the school yard and from watching the animals go at it on the ranch. That's about how it worked, though I was still somewhat sketchy on the details. When I listened to the cowboys weigh the virtues of the various whorehouses in Elko—Maude's and The Classy Inn and The Sheik—I decided to fill in the blanks the first chance I got and see what it was all about for myself.

My only opportunity was after church on Sunday. Until haying started and we had to put in seven days a week, Dad would drive my brothers and me into Elko every Sunday morning to attend mass. By the time I was fifteen the routine had been going on long enough for him to cut us loose for a few hours in the afternoon. After lunch at the Commercial Hotel he would give the twins and me money to go to the movies or the local baseball game, then take off with Linny to pay some business calls, hang out with his cronies or try his luck at the hotel casino. I figured that if I got Denny and Phil to cover for me I could sneak enough time to beat it over to Maude's before we had to meet him back at the hotel and return to the ranch.

In front of the theater I handed the twins their share of the movie money and stuck the rest back in my pocket. Added to what I had saved from my allowance, it gave me the five dollars I needed for the tab.

"Okay, guys, there's something I want to do. See you later."

"What do you mean? Where you goin'?"

"Oh, I just gotta see someone. I'll meet you here after the show."

I was so nervous and guilt ridden that I didn't want anyone to find out what I was up to, not even my brothers. It was Sunday, and I knew I was being disrespectful to God and the Church. The next week, when I showed up at confession, I would have to tell the priest and, Jesus, what would he think? Even worse, what would the old man do if he found out? But there wasn't any other way. This was the one day I had, and I just had to do it, I just had to see what it was all about.

To minimize the risk of being busted, I had carefully mapped out my route in advance so I'd spend the least amount of time out in the open. Following my plan, I headed down the main drag to the Stockmen's Hotel, scooted inside and cut out the back door, then sneaked my way down alleys and over fences until I reached the street next to the railroad tracks. Sticking to the shady side of the walk, I moved from elm tree to elm tree until I reached the intersection just across from Maude's.

I don't know if I could have held up under Dad's cross-examination, but I had an alibi ready for every step of the way. I had told myself, "Look, you're gonna get caught. There's no question about that. So this is what you were doing if you get caught here, and this is what you were doing if you get caught there." I was looking for one of the ranch hands. I was heading for the soda shop. I took a wrong turn and got lost.

I paused at the intersection until the coast was clear, then took a tentative step off the pavement. Just as I reached the middle of the road, a squad car rounded the corner. When the cop beeped his horn at me and called out, "Hey-y-y, how are ya?" in a voice that seemed all too knowing, I figured the jig was up. "Oh, shit! He'll tell the old man for sure." But he kept on moving and nothing more came of it.

With the neon sign in front still turned off, Maude's looked like an ordinary house. I climbed the four steps to the entrance and rapped on the screen door. It took an eternity for someone to let me in. I was the first customer of the day. After a big Saturday night that didn't end until seven in the morning, most of the girls were still asleep. While I waited for the few early risers to get themselves together, I sipped on a 7-Up—Maude wouldn't serve me a beer—and checked out the jukebox next to the dance floor. Thank God all it had were country records. If I had found any by the old man, that would have been enough to send me flying. As it was, I figured he was coiled right outside on the front porch, just waiting to spring. Eventually some of the ladies were ready for business and yawned their way downstairs. One was dressed in a tutu. Another had on a black leotard. The third had decked herself out in a circus rider's outfit. I guess the costumes were supposed to be sexy, but who knew? At the moment a burlap sack would have been sexy to me.

Time was awasting. I made my selection and followed her upstairs. Maybe ten minutes later I was back down again. "My, that was fast," she teased, but when she saw the hurt on my face she tried to make it better. "Nah, come on, I was only kiddin'. You were great." It was nice being fondled and touched and held by a woman even that briefly, but I was too worried about the consequences to really enjoy myself. I looked over my shoulder the entire time, and as much as I wanted to stay I also wanted to get the hell out of there before someone caught me.

Moving fast now, I retraced my steps down the street, across the intersection, through the alleys and fences and out the front door of the Stockmen's Hotel. Ah, yes indeed, a wonderful afternoon at the Stockmen's. When I caught up with Denny and Phil in front of the theater, I grilled them about the movie to get my story together for the old man. If he had wanted a scene-by-scene rundown of the plot, I could have given it to him.

Once we pulled into the ranch and I knew I was safe, I offered up a silent prayer. "Dear God, thank you for letting me get away with it this time. I pray from the bottom of my soul I never get horny again." Two weeks later, when I had scrounged up enough loot, I was back.

As it turned out, the old man never did quiz me very closely about how I spent my afternoons. That should have been the tip-off, but as long as I seemed to be getting away with it I wasn't asking any questions. The town was really too small to hide a secret, and there wasn't much he didn't know. Years later—well after I was married—he finally let out that he had been perfectly aware of what I was up to. We were sitting around reminiscing about those summers when he turned to my wife and said, "Oh, yeah, Gary saw a *lot* of movies and a *lot* of ball games—*a whole lot* of ball games on Sunday." Then he threw me a take and almost smiled. In spite of myself I had to laugh.

The fact that the four Crosby boys spent their summer vacations busting their butts on Bing's ranch was too good an item for Dad's PR people to ignore. It fit right in with the rest of his image as a tough but concerned and loving father. Every so often a photographer would fly up from Los Angeles and we'd be excused from our usual chores for the morning to pose for pictures. That meant taking a bath, digging out clean cowboy shirts and Levi's, and dusting off our best smiles. The photographer would hunt up some picturesque backgrounds, then put us up on horses next to the old man or group us together, straddling the corral fence. The imagery was straight out of Max Brand's novels and Gene Autry's *Melody Ranch*. It had nothing to do with the reality of our lives. I don't think anyone believed for an instant that we worked as ordinary laborers, even though that's what the stories accompanying the pictures always claimed.

Dad liked to tell the press how much good the ranch was doing us. "Ranch life is part of Bing's idea of toughening his sons for the future," read one feature article about "how a famous star is training his children in the fundamentals of Americanism." "'They've got to get along with the cowboys,' he says, 'or they'll get a fast brush. They wouldn't learn how to face the world by staying in Beverly Hills. They've got to grow up with a correct set of values and I think ranch life will help them.'" To make sure the fans didn't get the wrong idea, the writer went on to point out the warm, affectionate side of life-with-Bing-on-the-ranch: "All this is not to say that Crosby rules with an iron hand. Bing is a pal to his sons, and the weeks at the ranch provide both time and place for close association." The balancing act was typical. After telling the reader how hard we worked, the stories invariably added some details about how we still had time to go fishing with Bing or catch a movie together or join him in the evening for a community sing around the campfire.

I have to admit I contributed my part to the myth of "Crosby family togetherness in the great outdoors." A reporter wanted to do a story on the subject and made up some quotes for me. I gave him my okay, and a couple of months later there they were in one of the Sunday-supplement magazines. "At the ranch in Elko, Nevada, Dad is a firm believer that all play and no work makes Phil, Dennis, Linny and Gary dull boys," he had me saying. "We are all up at five for breakfast and then into the hayfields lifting our own weight on the end of a pitchfork. But Dad's no Simon Legree—he always lets us have Sundays off. However, he doesn't lay around the ranch in a hammock. He gets out at the crack of dawn, too, and helps mend fences, brand stock and do other chores. He's quite proficient with a whitewash brush, and he likes to paint fences—probably the Tom Sawyer in him."

Somewhere along the line Dad got it into his head that the twins and I would take over the ranch when we finished college. I guess he loved the place so much he thought it was just a matter of time until we came to love it too. That's what he wanted, and it never dawned on him that he might not have it his way. "They're going to own the ranch someday," he'd tell reporters, "and I want them to know what the men who will work for them have to do."

Denny and Phil made it easy for him to sustain the fantasy. One morning, when they were about seventeen, he walked in on them as they were finishing breakfast in the ranch house and suddenly demanded, "Well, what do you want to be?"

That was the first time the question had been raised, and it caught them with their pants down.

"Huh?"

"What do you want to be in life? What are your goals? What career? 'Cause I've got to figure out what to do with you."

Denny exchanged glances with his brother, looked around, saw where he was and said the first thing that popped into his head.

"Uh, we want to be ranchers. Yeah, Dad, we want to be ranchers."

Dad was pleased to hear it.

"Okay. Good. Well, then, I'll send you to agricultural school. You'll go to Washington State."

Then he turned on his heels and left. That was that. Their fate was sealed.

When we were outside, I grabbed hold of them and said, "You zombies, you've got to wake up when he asks you questions like that. You could wind up knee deep in cowshit for the rest of your lives."

"Well, what the hell. We didn't know what to tell him, and we had to tell him something."

"Yeah, well, I agree with you there. You can't stall Dad when he asks a question. You've got to come up with some kind of answer."

I handled the situation differently when he asked me what I had in mind for my future. "Oh, show business," I answered, and that stopped him cold.

Chapter Six
Getting Out

That wasn't what I had in mind at all.

I loved to sing, but only for the fun of it. From the time I was a small kid I enjoyed singing to myself around the house or filling in a harmony part with my brothers, but the last thing I wanted to do was follow the old man's footsteps into the business. I was looking to find my own place in the world, a place that had nothing to do with him.

Besides, I didn't feel I had anywhere near the talent, confidence and ego drive you need to be an entertainer. My imagination was never stirred by the fantasy of standing out there in the spotlight all alone, sucking up every drop of attention and praise that washed over the stage. When I finished a song on Dad's show and the audience applauded, I usually didn't even hear them. I was too busy asking myself, "Okay, did I do it all? Did I get it right? Did I miss a word here or blow a note there?" Even when I didn't mess up there was very little satisfaction or sense of accomplishment. If the audience seemed especially enthusiastic, my eyes went straight to the applause sign, and when I saw it was lit I figured they were just following orders and doing as they were told. Applause was a kind of flattery, and by now I knew I was nothing special and wasn't to get the big head when people started sweet-talking me and saying how much they liked me.

Then, when I went out of town to a high school full of ordinary kids who weren't anything special either, they looked at me a little funny when they found out I was from Hollywood. That wasn't the real world for them. The father of one of my friends steam cleaned trucks for a living. Another was a farmer. My roommate's mother supported the family by running a small grocery store. Except for big stars like Bing Crosby, show business was strictly for sissies.

The only reason I told Dad that's what I wanted to be was to end the discussion. I had no intention of letting him in on what I really had in mind. I was afraid he'd screw it up the way he did most everything else I looked forward to as soon as he found out about it. Show business seemed like a reasonable stand-in for my real plans. I figured that if the prospect didn't make him especially happy, it would at least buy some time, which is just about what happened. "Show business, huh?" he answered, throwing me a take that seemed to say he was fairly certain I couldn't do anything anyhow. "Well, finish school first and then we'll see." He didn't sound like he was entirely against it, but he didn't sound like he was going to be leading the cheers on the sidelines either.

Like every other Catholic boy sent off to the nuns and priests for his education, I had moments when I seriously considered entering the priesthood. Religion was important to my father. He made sure we attended church on Sunday and had us sign up as altar boys by the time we were nine or ten. Some of the indoctrination took hold, and some of it didn't. High mass at the Church of the Good Shepherd left me cold. It was too filled with pomp and ceremony, too much of a Beverly Hills social event. Dad would march my brothers and me down the main aisle in our Sunday best, and although the pews were crowded with movie stars like Ray Bolger, Jack Haley and William Gargan and behind-the-scenes moneymen who controlled the business through their banks, every head would turn at the sight of Bing Crosby putting in a personal appearance with his brood. And, of course, we were expected to hold up our end of the performance. With Dad sitting next to us, there was no nodding off or spacing out, even when the priest ticked off the same old sermon he had been repeating for the past twenty years.

Yet when I served the early mass at 6 A.M., the superficialities fell away and an authentic religious feeling broke through. With no large crowd of rich people, no special vestments and grand gestures, the ritual narrowed down to what was truly important, the actual taking of the Body and Blood of Christ, and I was glad to be there. I knew I was part of something good, and that made me feel peaceful and confident everything was going to turn out all right. When I went away to high school, I always tried to serve the mass that was said at the priest's house at five-thirty in the morning because then it was just the two of us and God, and I felt close to my Maker.

I had enormous respect for the nobility of some of the priests. They possessed the same feelings I did, yet they sacrificed that part of their nature to serve God, to devote themselves to performing Jesus' work for the rest of humanity. They had to go through life without female companionship. They would never have any of the material possessions and creature comforts the rest of us hope and strive for, and if they did get something they promptly gave it away to people who needed it. "Can I do that?" I would ask myself. "Can I be like them? Is it possible?"

I mentioned the thought to my mother once or twice and could see that she wasn't too taken with it. Not that she came right out and said so. Mom never bad-mouthed the Church. On the contrary, even though she wasn't a Catholic, she was the one who stayed on our case about showing up for mass on Sunday and meeting all our other religious obligations. "If you're going to be in a religion," she would lecture us, "if you're doing something you believe in, then you do it all the way." Whenever Grandpa Wyatt started one of his tirades against the pope and big-time religion, she shushed him up on the spot.

But she was still her father's daughter. I only remember a single time she actually set foot inside a church herself. It was a Friday morning during Lent. I was a ten-year-old altar boy assigned to carry the candle next to the priest as he moved through the stations of the cross, and Mom decided to come along to see what her son was up to. I tried to block her out so I could concentrate on holding the taper in front of me just right, but about halfway through the ceremony a fly landed in the hot wax and burned itself up. I stood there while it struggled, doing my best to keep a straight face, but then I caught a glimpse of Mom in the front pew. For all the solemnity of the occasion, she was giggling away at the absurdity of the sight. "How did he do?" Dad asked her later. "Great!" she answered, still grinning. "Cremated a fly. He had a wonderful time."

When I was still living at home, I asked one of the priests what it took to join his order, hinting broadly enough for him to catch on that I was thinking about it for myself. He paused for a moment, then went right to the heart of the matter.

"Look, Gary," he told me, "don't be jumping in here to hide. Don't be jumping in here to run away from life. Because that isn't what it's about."

I carried his words with me into high school, doubting and probing and questioning whether or not I had a true vocation. Eventually I realized I didn't. After a while, when I found myself still full of doubts, I had to conclude, "Well, if I was really meant to do this, God would have cemented it into my head by now. And I'm still shaky. So I guess it's not for me." When I took a good hard look at myself, I had to face the fact that I wasn't ready to give up life's pleasures. I hadn't had enough of them yet. I still wanted more.

I began playing sports in the fourth grade, when Mom and Dad sent me off to Black Foxe Military Academy, a posh boarding school for the sons of the Hollywood gentry. In keeping with the overall tone of the place, the kids were decked out in fancy baseball and football uniforms and were organized into regular teams. In that respect only, it was a bit of a letdown when we moved to Beverly Hills the following year after a fire destroyed our house on Camarillo Drive, and I was brought back home to attend the local Catholic school in our parish. There were no uniforms, organized teams or neatly lined playing fields at Good Shepherd, just a small dirt playground and Roxbury Park across the street, where the boys tossed the football around after school or chose up sides for an impromptu game of softball. When I wasn't in trouble with my folks, sometimes they let me join them.

I saw right away that if I was playing sports I didn't have to come home at three o'clock, and that was a big selling point. I enjoyed the games, too, but the best thing about them was they kept me out of the house a little while longer.

By the time I graduated from Good Shepherd and moved on to the seventh grade at St. John's, I knew for certain that sports were my escape route to freedom. I had to do what they told me at home and was just as locked up in school. St. John's was a Catholic military academy, and between the nuns and priests and the saluting and close order drills, the discipline was enough to drive you batty. But for two hours a day I could break loose from all that. I could put on a uniform and kick ass and hit and run and learn things that were important and enjoyable. And the ball field was the one place where my name didn't count one way or the other. It didn't matter who my old man was. I either produced or I didn't, and I found out that I could. I wasn't much of a basketball player—my behind was too big and I wasn't fast enough—but I made the baseball team as a catcher and played blocking back and single-wing quarterback in football.

For the first time in my life I seemed to have a natural bent for something. In baseball I was a pretty good hitter and didn't have much trouble learning the headwork you need to catch. In football I seemed to have a feel for what plays to call when, and I also blocked well on defense. Most of the time no one could get a good full piece of me and stop me from coming on. I usually managed to put an arm on the ballcarrier or get in on the tackle or pile on top of the fumble. I had absolutely no respect for my body. I would throw it in front of anyone any way I could. I didn't care how bruised and busted up I would be the next morning.

I wasn't looking to be a star. All I wanted was to hold up my end and do my job the way I was supposed to. I was happier playing defense than any of the glamour positions on the offensive team, and even there I was just as satisfied plugging the hole so someone else could make the tackle instead of making it myself. If the spectators in the stands gave him the cheers, he was welcome to them. When I messed up I felt every bit as crummy as blowing a line on the old man's radio show. But when I did my job absolutely right, it was the greatest feeling in the world. No one had to praise me or make a big deal over me. Just the pure joy of it was enough.

What began as a standard childhood fantasy—not much different from wanting to be a cowboy or fireman—gradually evolved into a real plan. I saw I was fairly good for my age and figured that with more experience and the right coaching I was bound to improve. I wasn't at all confident about how far I might actually go, but when I looked at it hard it seemed to me that, well, maybe I did have a shot, maybe I could make it all the way and play football as a professional. That would be my way out.

In the eighth grade I started plotting the moves that would take me there. After finishing up at St. John's the June after next, I would need a full four years in high school. That would let me pick up the year I skipped a grade when I was eight, put me back with guys my own age and physical development, and give me time to grow. The school should have good teams and coaches and play a good brand of ball. That would give me the experience I needed and a chance to be noticed by the colleges. I realized there was no way to win a college scholarship, not with my old man's money, so I would have to gain their attention through the press or by making All High School Something. That seemed possible. Then, after four years of college ball, if everything worked out I should be ready for the pros.

I began putting my plan into effect the following Thanksgiving vacation when I ran into Emmett Dougherty, a former student at St. John's who now went to high school at a place called Bellarmine Academy. As he described Bellarmine to me and carried on about all the fun he had there and how much he liked it, it seemed to be just what I was looking for. The school had a strong sports program. It was run by Jesuits, which meant you received a good education and wouldn't have that much trouble being accepted into college. And, best of all, it was located up north in San Jose, a full three hundred and fifty miles from Los Angeles—and my father. That was a big selling point, ranking right up there with the winning record of the football team.

I waited until Dad was in a decent mood, then pitched him about Bellarmine, stressing the point that the place was run by

Jesuits. I had heard the affection in his voice when he reminisced with his cronies about the Jesuit schools he attended back in Spokane, so that seemed my best shot. The part about football I kept to myself. I knew he was reasonably pleased that I played sports. When he was feeling chatty he might ask me what string I was on or how the team was making out, and once in a while he would pop by St. John's unannounced to watch the game. But he was hardly your standard Little League father, full of pride in his kid's accomplishments and egging him on to excel. On the contrary, his zingers about my weight always seemed to underscore my limitations as an athlete. "How you gonna play football with your fat ass? . . . Jesus Christ, you're the only guy I know could hit a triple and not get to first." I could imagine what he'd have to say if I let him in on my plan to become a professional. Nor did I want him associated with that part of my life. Sports were the one place I could stand or fall on my own, and I wanted to keep it that way.

Dad checked out the school, found it up to his standards and agreed to let me go. From the morning the letter of acceptance arrived in the mail, I counted off the days until it was time for me to leave. Finally the day arrived. The chauffeur drove me down to the station, saw me on the train, and I was gone.

I dropped my suitcase at the dorm, then hunted up Emmett Dougherty, who took me around to meet some of the guys. Fifteen minutes later I was playing touch football on the lawn. That was my first test. A couple of the kids doubled up on me and made an extra effort to knock me on my ass to see if I would cry or quit or complain. When I picked myself up, came back and gave it to them just as hard, they found out what they wanted to know and the test was over. By the end of the game we had started to become friendly.

The next few weeks followed the same pattern. My three roommates had never met me before, so naturally they all hated me at first until I was able to show them that I wasn't some snotty Hollywood rich kid, or whatever it was they assumed Bing Crosby's kid had to be. In the same way I had to prove myself to the rest of the school. Whatever went down, I handled it as best I could without trying to be something I wasn't. If I had to fight, I fought. If it was humor time, I did jokes. It took a while, but eventually the guys who were going to like me liked me and those who weren't didn't.

Bellarmine was made up mostly of tough working-class Italian, Portuguese, Mexican and Irish kids from San Jose. There was also a sprinkling of first-time offenders from San Francisco who had been dumped there by the courts instead of being sent to jail and, at the other end of the spectrum, a few boys like myself and William Gargan's son, Les, who came from wealthy families in Los Angeles. But all of us lived under the same rules of discipline laid down by the Jesuits. That was the great equalizer. Everyone went to study hall from 7 to 9 P.M., Sunday through Thursday. No one got to stay out past ten-thirty on Friday nights and eleven on Saturday. For the first time in my life my rules weren't tougher than anyone else's. Come nine o'clock I didn't have to act like a snob and go home early, pretending I wasn't interested in hanging out because I was too ashamed to let on that the old man would lay in a whipping if I failed to make it back to the house by ten. My classmates bitched and moaned about being locked away in prison, but as far as I was concerned the place was Freedom City.

The first part of my plan bore fruit when I went out for football and managed to make the B team as a tackle. Just as I had hoped, the only thing that mattered was what I did on the ball field. As long as I produced, the coach and the other guys couldn't have cared less what my last name was or where I came from or how much money my old man had in the bank. The one time that seemed to count was when we went up against another team. Then I was always my father's son. "Get Bing Crosby's kid!" I would hear them snarl as I squatted down and took my position on the line. "Kill that Hollywood cherry! Murder that fuckin' faggot!" But all that did was whip my teammates into a rage, and I suddenly had ten guys fighting *for* me for a change. It was a strange but beautiful feeling to know there were ten kids out there I could count on, who would be behind me, who were as busy kicking ass for me as I was for them.

When baseball season came around in the spring, I tried out for the team and made catcher. That was the backup part of my plan. The way I had it figured, if I wasn't good enough to go all the way to the pros in football, maybe I could do it in baseball. Our head coach was an old scout for the Yankees named Bob Faggio. The first day of practice he walked me over to home plate, pointed down and said, "Now this is yours. Anybody coming in here is trying to take it away from you. The question is, are you gonna let 'em or not?" Once was all he had to ask me.

In the middle of June I returned to the clutches of the Great Bald Eagle and spent my usual summer working as a manual laborer at the ranch. While I sweated away I kept fantasizing about how at this very minute the other kids were taking off for the beach and hanging out with girls and getting themselves ready for football in September. I hoped to make the regular team as fullback and play linebacker, so I invented my own training program to whip myself into shape. When I finished my chores for the day I lifted weights, improvised out of anything heavy I could find, and forced myself to run a couple of miles. Then, when haying season began I asked to work on the stacker. For the rest of the summer I spent seven days a week building up stacks of hay fifteen or twenty feet high, taking the loose hay the stacking machine kept dumping down on top of me and dragging it around with my pitchfork to make the butt of the stack level and the sides neatly squared. My legs sank down in the stuff to my knees, so that every step was a major effort, and I had to work fast and without letup so as not to drown in the stinging shower of vegetation constantly pouring down on my head. I hated the drudgery of the work but figured it would be great for building up my legs, shoulders and chest. And it paid off. When I came back to school that fall I alternated starting fullback and became the outside left linebacker.

By playing ball with the other guys and living under the same rules and pressures at school, I was able to develop my first real friendships. My closest buddies were all jocks like myself. Norm Benedetti, my roommate, played tackle. Tom Wilscam was a guard. Jim Donovan and Tom Seeger were halfbacks. The five of us would hang out together after a game, rehashing it endlessly, and the night before we had an especially tough team to face we would share our apprehensions about what the next day might bring. That was a new experience for me. For the first time I wasn't alone. I had someone to talk to, someone to go through it with. I could tell they were just as nervous as I was, and I knew I could trust them enough to drop my defenses and let them in on my own hidden uncertainties. And just as we confided in each other about football, we also talked together about girls and exams and all the other things that loom large in the life of a high school kid.

Wilscam's old man steam cleaned trucks. Jim's father was a successful insurance broker. Norm's mother was a widow and ran the grocery store in Pescadero, a small fishing village up the coast. But we all thought and acted and looked the same. Like the other hard kids in San Jose, we decked ourselves out in school jackets or letterman sweaters, greasy D.A. haircuts helped along by gobs of El-Dee Hair-In-Place, khaki or denim pants pegged down to the ankles and worn low around our asses, shiny shitkicker shoes with two-inch-thick soles and lots of metal around the heels, and Mr. B. shirts with the top buttons unfastened and the collar rolled up in back. We were bad-looking sonsofbitches. Next to us Fonzie was strictly a choirboy. When I went home on vacations, my getup had Mom climbing the walls. "Pull your pants up for Chrisake," she'd complain. "Button your shirt. You look like a bum. Haven't you got another jacket but that goddam dirty thing?"

Back in my room at school, the normal clothes Mom had bought me in Hollywood gathered dust in the closet I shared with Benedetti. About the only time they came out was when Norm spotted something he liked and decided to wear it for a while. I wore his clothes, too, even though his pants were so long I had to hitch them up to my armpits to keep them from dragging on the ground. That's how we all were with each other. We shared whatever we had. Now and then we even borrowed each other's identities.

That started in a piano bar the night of the junior prom, when one of our gang overheard some grownups buzzing, "Hey, Bing Crosby's kid is supposed to be with that bunch over there." By now, whenever a stranger asked me, "Are you Bing's son?" I never knew what was going to come out of my mouth, but it was definitely not "Yes." Sometimes I denied it. Other times I turned hostile. "Are you a detective? You the fucking FBI or what?" When I flashed on Tom Seeger sitting across the table, I saw a way to avoid the aggravation. We both had light hair and blond complexions and were built about the same, so I figured, "Hell, if someone walks over I'll tell him it's Tom. Let's see how he lies, how much bullshit he's got going." The way the evening worked out, Seeger had the time of his life basking in the spotlight and I was able to enjoy my anonymity. We tried it again once or twice, and Tom got to liking it so much he wanted to make it permanent. "Hold it, Tom," I had to tell him, "let's don't get crazy. If you have to go to my home, you won't think it's so great." But from then on, whenever anyone stopped me and asked, "Are you Gary Crosby?" I pointed to whatever friend I was with, whether he looked like me or not, and answered, "No, he is," and then he carried the ball for me.

Beginning with the sophomore year, boarders were allowed to check out from Friday night to early Sunday evening. The last thing I wanted was to return to the mausoleum in Beverly Hills, so I talked Mom into giving me permission to spend the weekends visiting my friends. It was like staying at the Rosses' when I was small. The parents welcomed me like a member of the family and treated me the same as their own kids. The visits were the high point of my four years in San Jose. I haven't found anything like them since.

Every couple of weeks I traveled up to Pescadero with Norm and stayed in his mother's apartment above the grocery store. At first he was a bit embarrassed to show me where he lived, but I thought the place was neat and was happy to be there. Norm's hometown buddies were all cowboys and farmers. When he took me around to meet them, he made a special point of introducing me simply as "Gary," and it took them a while to figure out my last name. I certainly didn't act like some kind of Hollywood big shot and try to buy their acceptance by spreading around my old man's money. I couldn't have done that if I had wanted to. I received the same five-dollar-a-week allowance Norm did. Dad made sure of that. When we started rooming together he telephoned Norm's mother and questioned her carefully about the amount of spending money she put in her son's pocket. By the time Norm's pals finally caught on that I was Bing Crosby's son, it was too late; they already liked me.

The weekends Norm went home alone I stayed with one of my other buddies in San Jose and hung out with Tom Wilscam, Jim Donovan and our two pals from Lincoln High, Wally Perry and Sam Bruno. After supper one of the guys would borrow his father's wheels and pick up the rest of the crew. Then we'd take off for a liquor store in Chinatown that would sell us quarts of Lucky Lager even though we were underage. We spent the early part of the evening chugalugging the stuff down and cruising San Jose for girls—with our usual lack of success. Invariably we made a pit stop at the Hawaiian Gardens, the one bar in town that would let us in, so we could come on to the sensational-looking blond waitress. We tried every ruse in the book of teenage lust to talk her into going out with us, but somehow she never would. Of course we didn't stand a chance. She had to be over twenty-one just to work there, and when she got off she was being picked up by grown-up men in suits and jewelry and shiny cars. She'd have had to be crazy to climb into a beat-up Chevy with five horny kids with greasy hair, but that never occurred to us.

Around twelve o'clock, after we had gotten a good buzz on and the kids with dates had left their movies and dances and taken their girls home, we headed for Tiny's Drive-In, the local late-night hangout. The burgers and shakes interested us less than the tough guys from the other schools who were looking for action. They weren't hard to find. San Jose was loaded with big, strong country boys who loved to fight. That was their main recreation, and they were good at it. They were tough. They could lift trucks. One night I saw a kid literally tear the back door of a car off its hinges when four guys gave him and his friends some lip and tried to lock themselves inside when he came after them.

A few minutes after we parked, a carful of kids would glide up next to us.

"Okay, men, here they come."

At first we'd pretend not to notice, but then the tension would start to build and someone would look over as casually as possible to check them out.

"Who are they?"

"Rizzo and Connelly and a couple of other wiseguys from Lincoln."

"All right. Be cool. Let's see what happens."

Now we'd begin staring out the window to face them down, and they'd do the same with us. When the moment had reached the proper pitch, maybe one of them would give us the finger or start running his mouth at Tom or me.

"Hey, Crosby! Yeah, you, the singer's little boy. You from Hollywood? Where all the fuckin' fags live? You a fag?"

Those were the magic words. Anytime someone wanted a piece of me because of my name, he was welcome to it. If he thought he was picking on some little Hollywood cherry who didn't know how to defend himself so he could show off in front of his friends, he had another think coming.

"Well, why don't you take a fuckin' swing at me and find out? What do you do to fags, asshole? Why don't you try it and see if I'm a fag or not? Let's see if your guts are as big as your big fuckin' wideass mouth!"

By now we were all out of our cars, lined up in front of each other, ready to uncoil. While the insults escalated to the inevitable conclusion, I kept my eye fixed on the kid's right hand. Finally it cut loose and we were into it.

We would go at it then and there, and the moment it was over we'd jump back in our cars and speed off. The idea was to do it now, do it fast and get the hell away before the fuzz came. I wasn't looking to get busted, not with my old man. I wouldn't have known where to get bail money. He sure wouldn't have sent it.

I always waited for the other guy to throw the first punch. I had to make myself feel justified, and that seemed to do the trick. I suppose it was something I carried with me from grammar school days, when Mom lectured me, "If you ever start one I'll break your ass, but if somebody else starts it, make sure you're around at the finish." When I went to confession Sunday morning, I had a lot of sins to get rid of, but fighting wasn't one of them. If the priest had cornered me on it, my answer would have been ready. "I didn't start it, Father. I was minding my own business and this kid took a swing at me, so I hit him back." That wasn't bad thinking for someone in my position. However much they loved the old man, I'm sure any number of parents would have been all too happy to haul him off to court for the damage his out-of-control child inflicted on their innocent sons. Given the opportunity, the prospect of shaking loose some of the Crosby bucks would have proven too great a lure to resist.

I know it's a disgrace to say so, but I loved every minute of it. I was a living, breathing volcano from having to hold everything in for so long, and I welcomed the chance to explode. It didn't much matter if I won or lost, as long as I got it out. Afterwards I felt as though a tremendous pressure had been lifted, and I was happy and relaxed. I hurt, but not much worse than after a hard scrimmage or game. Only this time I got to use my fists, and nobody was dictating rules to me. And I found out that even when I lost, it helped my reputation.

"Hey, don't mess with that cat," I heard a kid tell his friend, who was looking to start in with me. "He's crazy. That mother-fucker may kill you. You're gonna have to knock him out or someone's gotta break it up before he'll quit. And if he hasn't beaten you by then, he may just come lookin' for you tomorrow."

That was exactly the reputation I wanted. If you don't like me, if you don't want to be nice, then leave me alone. Because I will hurt you. If you don't want to get hurt, then don't fuck with me. I don't want any more aggravation from anyone.

The twins didn't seem to relish the fighting quite like I did. They were both a lot more easygoing and wouldn't force a confrontation to its conclusion if they could avoid it. When a tough guy from another school started in on Denny, he'd usually say, "Oh, fuck you, man," give him the finger and walk off. If the kid came after him, Denny would run and duck and dodge around him until he was insane with frustration but too wasted to take another step. He'd stand there with his tongue hanging out, swearing and wheezing, while Denny just laughed at him. It wasn't that Denny was afraid to fight. When pushed to the wall, he was a maniac. He fought back with everything he had.

Whenever I got into a scrap, I took it for granted Dad knew about it three hours later. And, sure enough, within a day or two the call would come over the telephone.

"Okay, Gary, I'm gonna have to talk to you when you get home. I have a few things to say to you about your temper."

"Temper" was his code word for fighting. He hardly ever mentioned it directly. But I was perfectly aware of what he was saying. Then, when I came back to Los Angeles the next vacation, he would march me into his office and run me through the customary lecture.

"People don't like a guy with a bad temper. First thing you know, you're not gonna be invited anywhere. Nobody's gonna want you. You've got to get control of this thing. You can't be so damn hostile and angry all the time."

Strangely enough, that's about as heavy as he got. There was no licking or any of the other usual punishments. Which makes me think now that maybe he understood what the brawling was all about. I'm sure he would have busted my behind if I had gotten into trouble with the law, or if the priests had complained that the scrapping was more than they could handle. I know he wouldn't have tolerated it for a second if I had instigated the fights or surrounded myself with a couple of bodyguards and sicked them on people like the sons of certain other Hollywood heavyweights were in the habit of doing. He probably read into the reports that got back to him exactly what was there: His kid was walking around with a chip on his shoulder from being who he was, and when someone tried to knock it off he spilled him on his ass. To his way of thinking, that was better than running away or crying. But since he never sat me down and talked it over, I assumed he didn't have the least understanding of what I was going through and automatically tuned him out. While the lecture droned on, I would nod my head in agreement, then wait until his voice dropped so I could get the hell away from him and his irrelevant moralizing.

Chapter Seven
Coming Back

I hated coming home on vacations. Up in San Jose I was a tough guy in stompin' shoes who nobody messed with, who got half-juiced every weekend and rode around in cars and raised hell. But the moment I stepped inside the house I was back to being ten years old again. It was all "Satchel Ass" this and "Bucket Butt" that and "you can't" and "you have to" and "if you don't, you know what's going to happen."

The only kids in town I felt comfortable running with were Jackie Haley, Les Gargan and Bob Dornan. Since they all came from show business families, they knew my story from their parents and nothing had to be explained. When I broke off the evening early to get back to the house by ten, they accepted it without putting me through any phony excuses. They had whatever hours they wanted and kept right on going, and when I caught up with them the next day they'd fill me in on whatever I had missed.

My reputation for scrapping seemed to follow me down from San Jose. Haley and Dornan were forever trying to set me up with some musical comedy hood from Beverly Hills High. They would get into a hassle with a kid at Simon's Drive-In, then tell him, "Okay, you just wait till Christmas when our friend Gary hits town. He'll take care of you. You'll see. Don't worry. Gary will fix you good." They built me up like I was this great avenger from the North descending on Hollywood to kick ass. Then, when I came home they filled my ear full of stories about all the rotten things this guy did and how he was out looking for me, and tried to hustle me over to the drive-in, where they could feed me to him like cannon fodder. I never would go for it. Nobody was hitting on me, and it was a matter of principle never to start anything. Fighting was serious business. I wasn't interested in Beverly Hills dramatics.

The strangest part of the vacations was doing the radio shows with the old man. When he brought a script home and I read it over, I'd say to myself, "Let's see, can I get my mouth around this idiot line without puking? 'Gosh, guys. Golly, gee whiz.' Okay, I'll pretend I'm cherry again." Those shows contained some of the best acting I ever did.

It seemed to take forever until Easter or Christmas finally dragged to a close and I could hightail it back to San Jose and leave this life behind. When kids at school asked me about being on the radio, I pretended I didn't know what they were talking about. I flat out denied it ever happened.

"Hey, Crosby, I heard you on your old man's Christmas program."

"Nah, you didn't hear me on no fuckin' Christmas program."

I did everything I could to keep those two parts of my life separate. San Jose was my turf, my territory. I was known only one way up there, and that's how I wanted to be known. I didn't want anyone from show business or my family stepping in and confusing things. It made me feel threatened.

When my Uncle Bob came into town to play a one-night stand, I made a fast trip to his dressing room to say hello but turned down his invitation to hang out afterwards. It had nothing to do with Bob personally. I loved my uncle. I felt closer to him than any of Dad's other brothers. Bob was the only one who didn't work for him and was far and away the most easygoing and approachable. He was funny and told good stories and was a pleasure to be around. I knew he had his own problems living in the old man's shadow, and that gave us a common bond. Not that there were heavy discussions about it. We were both still Crosbys, and that just wasn't the family style. But he would toss off one-liners about Dad that made it clear how he felt, and he always gave me the sense that he had a pretty good understanding of my position. When I brushed him off that night, I could tell he was a little angry and hurt, but it couldn't be helped. If I was seen hopping around town with him and going into fancy restaurants, it would only trigger off more of the celebrity wisecracks when I returned to school.

I was the same way with my San Jose friends when I had to go back to Los Angeles. I visited Norm, Tom or Jim almost every weekend but practically never returned the invitation. I didn't want them to see Dad eating my ass out—"Hey, Bucket Butt, get your behind over here. Move it. Look at this fuckin' bum"—while I just stood there meekly taking it. The few times I did risk bringing someone home, I knew for certain Dad would be away and I wouldn't have to eat as much crap. I figured that without him around, Mom might ease up on the rules and let us stay out past my ten o'clock curfew. And if she didn't, well, there was a good chance she might be drunk and asleep by the time we came in. That's how it worked out when I asked Tom to visit over one Christmas weekend. The evening he checked in we found ourselves some beer and a fight at a local hangout and staggered back home at 2 A.M. By then Mom had long since passed out, and she never called me on it.

Tom played the tough guy like I did, and it wouldn't have been cool to show too much reaction, but his eyes bugged out of his head for the entire visit. Living as he did in a little two-bedroom house, with a living room full of bric-a-brac his mom had collected, he couldn't get over the size of our place. Years later he told me how strange it seemed to him that he saw my mother for the first time when he bumped into her in her peignoir and sunglasses while he was wandering the halls the next morning, but because there was so much space he didn't meet her again for another three days, when she gave a dinner party. Her guests that night included Lana Turner and her husband of the moment, Bob Topping. I don't know which impressed Tom more, the fact that Lana Turner was there or that she had half a bag on. As usual, I excused myself from the table as soon as I could get away, but Tom hung in a while longer to savor the experience of her company. Twenty minutes later he came bounding out of the dining room, his eyeballs as big and round as half dollars.

"Jesus Christ!" he giggled. "Lana Turner just called her old man a dumb shit and told him to keep his fuckin' mouth shut!"

"So what?" I answered. "Those people are just people. They aren't any better than anyone else."

I never could understand why my friends were so blown out by so-called celebrities. That kind of gush was strictly for bobby-soxers. On the other hand, they thought I was a little strange for refusing to be impressed. When Dad showed up at the house for New Year's Eve and invited over Dean Martin, Jerry Lewis, Marilyn Monroe and Joe DiMaggio, Tom couldn't believe it didn't mean anything to me, that I'd rather take off and catch a flick with him.

"Man, you don't have to go to the movies," he told me. "You can stay home and see all those people right here."

Once or twice a year Dad called me at school to say he had some business in San Francisco the next day and would be stopping by on his way up. I didn't need the intrusion and kept the news to myself, but it invariably leaked out. The priests all made a big thing of it. I thought I knew why. Hell, the old man was brought up in Jesuit schools and he was loaded, so the visit was a perfect opportunity to hit up an alumnus of the system for a hefty contribution to the latest fund-raising drive. That may have been part of it, but I'm sure they were also just looking forward to spending an hour with Father O'Malley in the flesh. They genuinely liked him, and he liked them too. He enjoyed hanging out with the priests, especially old Father Flynn, who was the closest Bellarmine had to offer to the character Barry Fitzgerald played in *Going My Way*.

I knew the word was out when the other kids started riding me.

"Hey, the big movie star's comin' up to see his sweet little boy."

"Yeah, have you been a good boy, little movie star's son?"

By the following morning the whole school was buzzing. Everybody wanted to see Bing Crosby. I thought they were all nuts.

To give Dad his due, he never wanted the attention. His ego wasn't in trouble. He didn't need to have people making a big fuss over him, and he ducked as much of it as he could, which was beneficial to both of us.

My friends tried to be cool, but they couldn't get over him. I suppose they expected some sort of demanding, larger-than-life egomaniac, the way they figured actors were supposed to be, and then this smallish man showed up in baggy pants and a rumpled shirt and put them immediately at ease. "Hi, Jim. Hey, Tom. How you doin'? What's goin' on?" He could talk with them just like any other guy—which, of course, was his whole act in life.

I'll never forget how shook up Norm became when he met the old man for the first time shortly after we began rooming together. We had just come back from a game of touch, and Norm was sitting on his bed with a towel around his waist, picking at his toes, when Dad sauntered into the room. At the first sight of him Norm shot up and stuck out his mitt to shake hands, then realized he'd been picking his toes with it a moment before and abruptly snapped it back. Then, to make matters worse, his towel fell off and he found himself standing there stark naked. His face turned the color of a tropical sunset, and he was so mixed up he couldn't figure out what to do next. But Dad calmed him right down.

"Hey, you must be Benedetti. Glad to meet you. Oh, come on now, Norm. For cryin' out loud, it's all right. Don't worry about nothin'."

I wasn't the least bit surprised when my friends came away with the impression he was the greatest guy in the world, and I didn't think any less of them for it. I was used to the fact that everyone on the planet loved him. I knew how slick he was. I knew the power of the persona. I'd seen it in action all my life. He could charm the pants off fifty-year-old intellectuals, so what did it take to fool a bunch of high school kids? He didn't fool them, really. He got a kick out of meeting them and shooting the breeze. He was the same way he always was in public.

Afterwards, when Norm or Tom carried on about the old man,

I kept quiet until the subject exhausted itself. Rather than saying something negative, I didn't say anything at all. I knew they wouldn't be able to understand my viewpoint. I still carried with me the commandment to keep the family skeletons in the closet, where they belonged. And I still bought the proposition that I was all wrong and he was all right. Deep down, underneath my tough guy defenses, I felt awfully bad about it, but I didn't know what to do to please the guy other than to become a whole different person, someone I could never be.

When Dad pulled into San Jose, the first thing he did was make the rounds of the priests to say hello and gather up whatever goods they had on me. While I sweated it out in my room, waiting for him to appear, kids were constantly running in with frontline reports of his itinerary.

The information was crucial. If I could find out who he talked to, I could pretty well piece together what I was in for. I knew that certain guys, like Costa and Byrne and Dodd, were good Joes and wouldn't bitch to him about my conduct just because I sneaked across the street to the firehouse. Other priests, like Pettit and Finch, went crazy if you didn't follow the book to the letter, so if he met with them the outlook wasn't that rosy. If he got together with Father Rooney, the prefect of discipline, he would give me hell about any recent trouble, but I wouldn't catch too much else because he'd be satisfied Rooney took care of it himself. For some reason Father Flynn liked me and was always talking me up to my father, so that would be one on the plus side. He'd be honest, but he'd try to put the best face on it and give me a boost. "Yes, he's doing his work. He could be working harder, but he's doing all right." With Father Shegrew, on the other hand, it could go either way. I had handicapped the whole lot of them and had my personal odds calculated down to the fraction by the time the old man finally got to me.

No matter how well it worked out, though, he was still sure to hear about something I was doing wrong: I had failed the last math test or my effort was down or my conduct left a lot to be desired. Whatever it was set the tone for the rest of the evening. We might start off talking a little about sports—the one common ground we had—but both of us only went through the motions and it didn't take long to run out of things to say. I have to admit he tried harder than I did.

"So how are you doing in football?"

"I'm doing okay. Made first string."

"That's good. Playing a lot of offense?"

"No, defense mostly."

"Uh-huh. How's the team making out?"

"Fine. Won the last three."

That's about as far as it went. From then on it was the usual lecture with the usual questions and answers.

"When are you gonna stop messing up in math?"

"I don't know."

"Why aren't you doing better in Latin?"

"I don't know."

"What do you mean, you don't know? What are you, an idiot?"

"I don't know."

Once the twins started Bellarmine, he'd put all three of us through the interrogation at the same time.

"Okay, Denny, what the hell's goin' on in geometry? Phil, how come you're still in trouble in physics? Gary . . ."

Eventually dinner was over, and he continued on to San Francisco or wherever he was headed.

Mom hardly ever traveled with my father, and she skipped the trips up to San Jose. Every so often, though, she made her presence felt. Once, in an uncharacteristic moment of candor, I confided to her that I had started dating a girl and would be taking her to the prom that Saturday night. Saturday morning Roberta called me at the dorm, so excited she could hardly get the words out of her mouth. A florist truck loaded down with every imaginable kind of corsage had just pulled up to her front door. The driver told her it was a gift from Mrs. Crosby in Los Angeles, and any or all of the flowers were hers for the taking.

I was mortified by the extravagance of the gesture and more than a little angry. The way I saw it, Mom had done me in by making me look like a smartass rich kid out to impress his girl by throwing a lot of bucks around. At the same time, I knew that was the farthest thought from her mind. Mom never gave a damn about impressing anyone. She was just being good-hearted and generous. A thousand dollars for flowers meant nothing to her. Money was to be used to give pleasure to the people she loved and help them out of trouble. The old man was suspicious of any girl I dated. He was convinced her mother was setting her up to sink her claws into the Crosby fortune. Why else would she be interested in me? But Mom was happy I had a girl friend and the fact that I liked her were all the credentials she needed. Without having set eyes on her, she was crazy about Roberta and became so involved she couldn't do enough.

Standing there in the dormitory hall with the phone dangling in my hand, I remembered the time she had pulled the same number on me in the third grade. Again, I had let it slip that there was a girl in class I kind of had a crush on. Before the words had cleared my lips, Mom had an expensive bottle of perfume wrapped up and in my hand. Pushing me out the door, she urged me to take it to this girl and tell her I liked her and wanted her to have it as a present. I died. I didn't want to do it, but she kept after me until I finally brought it into school, dropped it down on the girl's desk with a curt "Here," then whirled around and ran. I was so embarrassed I never spoke to her again.

Roberta could tell from my silence what I must have been feeling.

"Gee, what are you so upset about? This is a nice thing. I love it. Tell your mom thanks for me. And don't worry. I picked out a wrist corsage and sent the rest back."

"Yeah, yeah, yeah," I answered, hiding my relief.

The moment we hung up I put in a call to home.

"Mom, well, she got the flowers. Uh, thanks a lot."

I hoped she was reading between the lines and could hear me pleading, "God, don't ever do that again. Please. I'm begging you." But I guess the message didn't get through. From then on until Roberta and I stopped seeing each other, she kept on bombarding her with hand-knitted sweaters, silk scarves and every other kind of expensive little present the shops on Rodeo Drive had to offer.

In April 1950, the spring of my junior year, Dad took off to Europe for what was described as a bachelor vacation. On his way to try his luck at the British Amateur Golf Tournament, he stopped for a while in Paris, where he was promptly arrested for taking a nap on the grass near the Champs-Elysées. The gendarmes couldn't believe that this rather ordinary-looking guy with his shoes off and a newspaper over his face was the famous Bing Crosby rather than your run-of-the-mill Ugly American. Before they cut him loose, Dad had to change his line and con them with the routine that he was really an American cop on vacation. The story made great copy—it fit Dad's image to a tee—and was picked up by all the American papers. For me the main benefit was that it gave me something to write him about when it came time to sit down and knock off my obligatory letter.

"Dear Dad,

"Well, how is Gay Paree? I think maybe I'd better send this letter to the county pokey 'cause I read in the paper that you had been picked up for vagrancy. How do ya like that? A guy can't even take a nap without getting the soles of his feet rapped and then thrown in the jug. Must be a fine country! Nice piece of business . . ."

Whenever Dad was away, Mom made sure we wrote him weekly, even though we had nothing to say and were happy for the breathing space. When we were younger we tried to keep the chore to a minimum. Our standard letter read, "Dear Dad, I am fine. How are you? We are all having a good time. Hope you are having the same." But when Mom looked it over she'd say, "Okay, take it back and put something in it," and we'd have to dig for ways to fill up the page. By high school I had the rap down pat. The idea was to keep it light and breezy and humorous, kind of like my lines on the radio shows, and steer away from anything—my weight, my conduct, my grades, what I was doing on the weekends—that might cause problems when I saw him face-to-face. Sports were always a safe topic, especially when there was good news to report about the Pirates, a team that Dad owned a piece of, or my own accomplishments.

". . . The baseball team is doing pretty well. I was up to .571 and then someone broke my bat. Now I'm hitting .394, but I'm coming out of the slump, I think. I've hit every game the last three, and the last game I got another home run. I'm getting a lot of good experience on J.V.s that I wouldn't have got if I'd have stayed out for varsity. I'm getting so I can throw pretty well. Last game we were ahead 5–3 in the last inning, with bases loaded and one out. The batter topped the ball and it hit the pitcher in the leg. He picked it up, threw to me for the force, and I made the best throw of my life to first base for a double play. Speaking of hitting, the Pirates beat St. Louis yesterday 4–3. Hopp got a double and Kiner got a home run to win the ball game, scoring Hopp ahead of him. Big John Hopp got four for four. Beard got three for four and Murtaugh got a smashing double. Maybe the Pirates are going places this year.

"Well, that about does it for this time, Dad. Have fun over there. Be careful of those French cops; but when you get to England, be especially careful! Remember, England has Scotland Yard.

'Your friend,'
Gary"

"Your friend" was a playoff on how Linny had closed a letter to him a few years before. Dad had gotten a big kick out of it and was fond of repeating the story to his pals. So far as I was concerned, it kept me from having to say "Love."

Three weeks later Dad was still hanging out in Paris when another item hit the papers. This one made the front page and didn't do anything at all to further the Crosby image. "BING CROSBY AND WIFE BREAK UP," screamed the headline of the *Daily Mirror,* and the other tabloids around the country echoed it. The story on page three filled in the details:

"Bing Crosby and his wife, the former Dixie Lee, have separated, the crooner's attorney admitted yesterday in Hollywood. Crosby, now in Paris, will return here in June, and the family is hopeful there will be a reconciliation. 'There has been no property settlement of any kind,' attorney John O'Melveny announced. 'There are strained relations, but the whole matter is in abeyance until he returns from Europe.'"

I'd long since stopped believing anything I read in the press about the old man and figured this was just another exaggeration, though certainly not one calculated to do him much good. When the reporters tracked Dad down in his Paris hotel, he completely denied it. "I don't know anything about this," he said. "These reports crop up every four or five months. Some columnist must have started it." The next day Mom issued her own denial. "There is no separation, and we don't plan any; I am still very much in love with Bing." Still, O'Melveny had confirmed the break, and somehow Sheilah Graham had gotten my Uncle Larry to admit to the proposition that there had been a serious family battle. "I hope they make it a legal separation," he told her, "because Bing is a Catholic and the family would want it that way . . . They have these battles about every six months . . . There have always been rumblings between them . . . We've all tried to talk with Dixie, but it seems to be an impossible situation. Bing has been terribly upset about this for some time." I'm sure I must have winced a little for Larry's sake when I read his words. I don't know for certain, but I guarantee you he took a beating for them. The old man would never let that go by. My brothers and I weren't the only ones who were supposed to keep our mouths shut about what went on in the Crosby home when the front door was closed.

Larry went on to say, "This is a little tough on the boys. They know nothing of any separation." He was partly right. The story *was* news to me. The first I heard about it was what I read in the papers. But as for it being tough on the boys, well, I can't speak for my brothers, but my own reaction wasn't exactly troubled. "Hey, that's the way it goes," I told myself. "If they're battling, they're not gonna be looking at me, so the more the merrier. Maybe I can live here a little bit." In less cold-blooded moments my thoughts took a slightly different turn. "Well, if they do split up, I want to go with Mom. If they're gonna do that number where they divide up the kids, I hope I get to stay with her."

A few weeks later, when school let out for the summer, I went back to Los Angeles and hung around the house, waiting to see if Mom was going to talk about it. One didn't ask for information in my home. It was volunteered. And whatever you got, that's what you lived with. I knew if I asked her, "What about all this trouble you and Dad are supposed to be having?" she wouldn't tell me anything anyhow, and I'd probably get whacked upside the head for not minding my own business. When Mom was ready, she called my brothers and me into her room and said, "Don't worry about what you've been hearing. Everything will work out. It's nothing. It's not like they say in the papers." And that was the end of the discussion.

The reporters were waiting at the dock for the old man when

the *Queen Elizabeth* landed in New York in the middle of June. He told them the reports of the separation still mystified him and that, in fact, Mom would be flying in the next week to join him at the Waldorf-Astoria. Meanwhile, he hoped "to see a few ball games." Then the plan changed, and she was supposed to meet him in Hollywood. A week later the papers seemed to feel that another story was called for when Mom didn't show up at the train station when he pulled in on the Union Pacific and put an end to the rumors with a big public reconciliation.

Back at the house, nothing much seemed to have changed. There was the same feeling of unrest between them there had always been. They still lived in different rooms. They still kept up the same facade in front of the kids and the rest of the world. If Mom had planned to leave, she must have decided against it, because their lives settled right back down to normal.

About the only difference was that later that year Mom finally agreed, for the first and only time, to join the rest of us on the old man's Christmas show. Dad had been after her forever to do the thing with him, to sing a song or at least take part in a skit, but she never would. That surprised me a little, being that Dad's image was family and the Christmas program was family time with a vengeance. Yet whenever he tried to talk her into it, she put her back up. "Oh, come on, leave me alone," she'd say. "I'm out of the business." I'm not really sure what brought her around, but if they wanted to make a public statement that everything was fine between them, what better way was there than to go on the air together, when the home folks were gathered around the radio to ring in the Christmas holiday with Bing and family?

Dad was delighted when Mom consented to play in one of the sketches, and my brothers and I were also pleased. The only one who seemed unhappy about it was Mom herself. When she ran us through a rehearsal at home the night before the taping, I kept my eye on her to see if she was going to get stoned. To my relief, she didn't, and the next day the performance went off without a hitch. Mom's comic timing was as sharp as my father's. They were both great with lines. When I listen to the tape now, though, I can hear how uncomfortable she must have been.

There's a dead quality in her voice. It sounds lower than usual, and all the laughter has gone out of it.

The show itself was more of the usual fantasyland, with Dad dressing up as Santa Claus, then getting stuck in the window when he tried to sneak into the living room to deliver his Christmas presents to the kids. As the oldest of the bunch, I took part in the masquerade and helped him into his costume. My lines had me smartmouthing him the way I never could in real life, and I read them off with a certain amount of pleasure.

GARY: Gee, Dad, why do you have to go through this every year?

BING: Never mind, never mind giving me any beefs . . . Just hand me those red pants.

GARY: Dad, why do you insist on playing Santa Claus? What are you trying to prove?

BING: Gary, you're a big boy now . . . You're grown up. You're sophisticated. You're worldly . . . We've lost you . . . But your little brothers aren't. I wouldn't think of not playing Santa Claus for them . . . They love it. It's wonderful to see their little faces light up with amazement and happy surprise when I bounce into the room!

GARY: They could be acting, you know.

BING: Oh, no. I admit I don't convince you anymore, Gary, but your younger brothers aren't wise to me yet . . . And as long as I can make their little eyes dance with glee, I'm going to.

GARY: Okay, but I still can't understand why parents always insist upon stifling their kids' mental development at this time of the year.

BING: Don't argue with Santa Claus on Christmas Eve . . . that's all I can tell you. You're liable to wind up with an empty stocking . . . Now come here. Put my beard on me, if you please.

GARY: Yes sir . . . There you are.

BING: The beard doesn't go up there—pull it down over my chin.

GARY: I was just trying to make your disguise more convincing.

BING: Well, I'm about all set . . . Oh, wait a minute . . . Santa has to have a big fat tummy. Hand me those two pillows. I'll stuff 'em in my coat.

137

GARY: I think you can get by with just *one* pillow this year.

BING: No comments . . . Just shove those pillows in my coat.

Predictably, the running gag was that my brothers weren't the least bit fooled by the disguise but went along with it because they were so crazy about the old guy.

GARY: Gee, Santa Claus is certainly a wonderful man, isn't he?

PHIL: Yep, Pop is tops!

GARY: What d'ya mean "Pop"! That was Santa Claus.

DENNIS: Oh, Gary, let's act our age, shall we?

GARY: Oh, you guys were wise all the time, huh?

PHIL: Sure . . . But if he wants to put on that hot suit and wear that itchy old beard, it's all right with me. Let him live a little!

In between the shenanigans Dad sang "Adeste Fideles" and "Silent Night." I joined him for a couple of Yuletide duets. Linny sang "The Snowman." And the twins ripped through "I'd Like to Hitch a Ride with Santa Claus" like two little hoodlums the nuns caught in church with their hands on the poor box and made sing for them. All in all, it added up to a nice family picture. In the closing commercial Ken Carpenter advised the listeners that the current issue of *Quick Magazine* had a picture of Dad on the cover and a caption reading "Bing Plays Poppa Santa."

The magazine was still on the stands New Year's Day when he took my brothers and me to the Rose Bowl and we played out another little family comedy. Only this time he left his Poppa Santa suit home, and without the help of his writers all my easy smartmouth seemed to fail me.

To keep from being stuck in traffic after the game, Dad had parked the car on top of a high bluff maybe half a mile from the parking lot. Then we hoofed it down the side of the hill and cut through the brush over to the stadium. To beat the crowd, we left the game a little early and he had me run ahead with Linny and the twins to start up the car. On our way back up the hill I tripped on a rock, and as I went sprawling ass over teakettle, the keys flew out of my hand. The four of us were still down on our elbows and knees searching through the underbrush when he came puffing along ten minutes later. It was the end of the universe. He was furious.

"You dumb, stupid . . . ! You can't do anything right! Jesus Christ, give you the simplest task in the world and you'll still find a way to fuck it up!"

On and on he went, ranting and raving, while I continued sifting through the scrub, silently agonizing over my own ineptitude and praying that God would put an end to my torment either by swallowing me up or granting me sight of the vanished keys. By the time my prayer was answered, the damage had already been done. An endless stream of cars was crawling past us, and it took forever to get home. While we inched along in the traffic jam, Dad lapsed back into the stony silence that was even more terrifying than his rage. I figured he was saving up his strength for the beating to come later. There was no doubt in my mind that I would get it.

When Dad recounted the story to Tex McCrary and Jinx Falkenburg some months later, he made it sound like another funny sketch on his radio show. As usual, he cast himself as the lovable butt of the humor, and my brothers and I played the disrespectful scamps who put his patience to the test. According to his version, while he waited for me next to the car, a hostile dog took an instant dislike to him and chased him over a fence, where, to our great amusement, he tore his pants and lost his wallet.

"Took us six hours to get home through that traffic and that heat," he told them. "The kids were with me in the car, so I couldn't cuss or stop for a short beer to cool off. I saw red. It wasn't so much that I lost my pants, or the money, or all that time in traffic. It was just that in the moment of direst peril, running for my very life from a raging beast, I caught a glimpse of my four stalwart sons *all grinning—that's* what infuriated me!"

To make sure their readers weren't left with the wrong impression, the columnists went on: "Despite such days, Bing is as successful a father as he is a singer and businessman. His sons toe the mark on important things and get plenty of leeway on the rest."

The part about the dog may or may not have happened, but if it did I wasn't aware of it. Once I saw that I had blown it, I withdrew and blocked out everything else. But one thing I know for certain. I damn sure wasn't grinning.

Four days after Dad returned home from Europe he drove my brothers and me up to the ranch for the usual summer of building character. The night before we left, I was throwing my jeans and work shirts into a suitcase when he popped his head into the room and said, "Listen, we may do a record together tomorrow before we take off." The words barely registered. All I could think about was the two months of cows and haying machines that were staring me in the face. A record session with the old man wasn't going to get me out of that, so what difference did it make? By the time he reappeared early the next morning and rousted me out of bed, I had forgotten about it completely.

"Come on, get up. We're goin' over to Decca."

"What for?"

"We're gonna make a record."

"Oh, okay."

When I came downstairs he played the demos of the two tunes I was to sing with him, handed me the lyric sheets and ran me through them a few times. The first one was "Play a Simple Melody," an old ragtime duet by Irving Berlin he had done on the radio with various guests, including Groucho Marx, Dorothy Kirsten, and, I think, Peggy Lee. I had also sung it with him when he brought me on the show the previous March, so it wasn't that hard to get together. The second was a new number called "Sam's Song." ("Sam" was Sam Weiss, a song plugger who had just turned music publisher. This was the first tune he published himself, and the writer named it after him for good luck.) I had heard Dad playing the demo around the house but had never sung it before, so he had to work with me a bit longer.

"All right, listen to this now . . . Okay, let's sing it through and see how it goes. I'll do the part with the patter, and you do the straight part . . . Not too bad. Can you add a little harmony right in there? Let's try it . . . Well, no. Do this harmony instead . . . Okay, I think we got it now. Let's go."

I doubt if the entire rehearsal lasted more than fifteen minutes from start to finish. That's how Dad liked to work. The less time he spent rehearsing and the less time he left himself to concentrate on a record session and make a big deal out of it, the better he felt he did. He was never unprepared. He learned the songs by running the demos while he shaved in the morning and before he went to bed at night, and he knew approximately what he was going to do. But once he had that covered, he just knocked them off.

Dad had been over at Decca the previous two days laying down one side after another, I suppose to make up for the three months he'd been away. The songs ranged from four new tunes by Johnny Burke and Jimmy Van Heusen to "La Vie en Rose," "Rudolph the Red-Nosed Reindeer" and "The Teddy Bear's Picnic." The session this morning started off with three solos backed by the Jeff Alexander Chorus and a large orchestra led by Victor Young. That gave me a chance to find a spot out of the way and go over the words to "Sam's Song" and "Simple Melody" until I had them down. I'd been to recording sessions with him before, so I already had some idea of the procedure. While I waited for him to finish, I sat in the back of the control booth and stared up at the picture hanging there of an Indian with his hands raised to the skies in prayer. Someone had drawn a balloon next to his mouth and written in the words, "Where the hell is the melody?"

Finally that part of the session was over. The backup singers and most of the musicians waved good-bye to the old man. Then, after a short break, Matty Matlock, Manny Klein, Nick Fatool and four or five other good Dixieland players came back in and began rehearsing the chart of "Sam's Song." While they were getting it together, Dad took me off to one side, and each time they ran it down he took me through the song again, adding little details and changing the routine to make it play better. Originally he was slated to do the part with all the tricky patter, but after trying it out he decided to switch with me and sing the straight melody. "Jesus Christ, that's too many words," he laughed, handing me his part. "Here. You sing that. You talk fast anyhow. Don't worry. You'll be all right." He kept working in close with me like that while the engineers set up the balance, so by the time the producer was ready for a take I'd been through it enough to know where I was going and could start to loosen up and enjoy myself.

The hour and a half it took to record the two sides were one of the best times we ever had together. Once the music started, he stopped being my father and I stopped being afraid of him. It was like singing with just another guy. When I hit a leaky note on the first take, he didn't bring everything crashing to a halt and snarl, "Jesus Christ, what the hell are you doin', you dummy?" As long as he was Bing Crosby, it wasn't the end of the world if I made a mistake. And he was such a strong singer and laid in such a solid foundation for me to work off of that it was almost impossible not to do right. He was giving to me and that made me good enough to be able to give back to him, and the momentum of the give-and-take carried us along as if we were both riding the same wave. We were working together as a team, and for once in my life with him that made me feel useful. I looked for little ways to please him in my singing, and he seemed to like what I was doing and we both had fun. After the second take of "Simple Melody" he turned to me and said, "Hey, I got an idea. You know that T. Texas Tyler number you're always singing where you do that heavy rasp? Well, try it here when we go into the last chorus." I did, and when he heard it he broke up, which got me to laughing. The feeling between us was so good that that was the take Decca decided to issue.

But then it was over, and we were back to being father and son again. By noon we were in the car heading up to Elko, and I had already begun to put it out of my mind the way I was supposed to whenever I came off of one of my little forays into show business.

Later that summer Mom casually happened to mention on the telephone that the record was doing well back home and getting a good bit of airplay. That was news to me. The two stations the bunkhouse radio picked up only played country and western music, so if it wasn't Hank Williams or T. Texas Tyler I didn't know about it. And I can't say that I much cared. Singing together with the old man had been a pleasure, but when it was finished it was finished.

When I arrived back in Los Angeles that September I discovered for the first time how well the record had actually done. It had sold a million copies and was way up on the charts, and I was supposed to be some kind of hot new young singer. Mom promptly called me into her room and tried to put it into perspective.

"All right, Gary, you got a record. That's nice. But don't forget your father was on there too. So don't get the big head. Don't think it's you that's selling them because it isn't."

"Yes, ma'am."

I knew that was true. It never crossed my mind to think otherwise.

"Oh, you sing all right," she went on. "You sing okay for your age and where you are and the experience you've had. If you want it, you can probably be a good singer someday."

Dad was even more to the point.

"Sit down, boy. Just remember one thing. This doesn't make you the least bit better than anyone else. Don't get bigheaded about it. And I don't want to hear any arguments. You're going back to school and that's it. There's not gonna be any career until after you finish college and get a degree. Then, if you want show business, we'll see about it."

Since that's how he felt, I couldn't figure out why he had hustled me back to the studio, along with my brothers, immediately after we hit town to record a bunch of Christmas songs with him.

"Okay, Dad. Fine."

"And as for your share of the money, that's going into a bank account for your education. We'll save it up for you. You're not gonna touch it. So don't be thinking you're gonna have a lot of bucks to throw around, because you're not."

"Right, Dad. Whatever you say."

The success of the damn thing even seemed to unsettle my brothers a little. As soon as they found out about it, they made a beeline for me, socked me on the shoulder a few times, called me a couple of dirty names, then laid down the law that nothing had changed.

"Listen, fuckhead, this don't mean you get out of mowin' the lawn. That's still your job, and you gotta do it. We're not gonna do it for you."

"Okay, guys, okay. Take it easy."

All of them seemed so afraid I was about to come down with a terminal case of the bighead, but they needn't have worried. It had been hammered into me for so many years that I was no-body special that, for better or worse, the indoctrination had long since taken hold. I was happy Sam Weiss was so thrilled when he came by the house to thank me for helping make his song a hit because he was a nice man and his wife was a nice lady. But I downplayed all the rest of the praise. I walked over it and by it and around it as fast as I could and kept on moving. Decca had printed on the record label that the tunes were sung by "Gary Crosby and Friend," and when someone congratulated me, my stock answer was, "Hey, 'and Friend' had an awful lot to do with that, y'know."

Predictably enough, the music trades, newspapers and maga-zines had a field day with the fact that Bing Crosby's current hot record was a duet with his kid. Seeing my name in print made me just as uncomfortable as being on the receiving end of a com-pliment. Whenever I stumbled across one of the stories, I either threw it away or brushed by it fast to see what lies were being perpetrated this time around. I was getting to be a real hard case by now. As far as I was concerned, reporters, like most everyone else, were all full of shit. If a friend happened to mention that a writer said something nice about me in the morning paper, I was likely to snap back, "So what? That's his job. That's what he does for a living."

It wasn't until a few years ago that I could bring myself to read the stories through from beginning to end. Some of the things they reported were a revelation. Evidently, after the rec-ord hit, I was deluged with requests for interviews, offers of movie contracts, invitations to guest star on radio and television shows, as well as bags full of mail that, according to *Collier's* magazine, contained "marriage proposals, business propositions, insurance solicitations, gripes, gifts, samples, offers, pleas, pam-phlets and demands for autographed pictures." You could have fooled me. If people were beating down the doors, Dad made sure I never heard the racket. He turned down the jobs, had the mail routed to his office, where it was handled by his secretaries, and kept me from finding out about any of it. Which was just as well. I wouldn't have wanted to go on Bob Hope's show or be in a movie. What I wanted was to get back to my real life in San Jose. All the show business hoopla just got in the way. I was trying to survive in a certain society, and my survival depended on being known for what I was there, not for what I seemed to be to the outside world.

There was no way to hide what happened over the summer from the kids at school. The first couple of days back, they rode me a little to check out my reaction. But as long as the razzing came from my friends I didn't much mind, and when they saw I could take it, it soon ended. More than ever I tried to keep a low profile. Anytime I heard the record playing I considered it an invasion of my turf. If it came on while I was riding around with the guys, I automatically reached for the radio and switched to another station. The foremost thought in my head was, "Stay in the middle of the herd, man. Just stay where you belong, right in the middle of the herd."

That wasn't easy once I found myself on the cover of *Life* magazine. Tom Wilscam and I were browsing through the newsstand of the Park Avenue Drugstore, hunting down the new issue of *Esquire* to catch a peek of this month's Varga Girl, when he suddenly let out a yelp.

"God damn, Gary! Take a look at this! Fan-fuckin'-tastic!"

Instead of the airbrushed beauty I was expecting, he held up a full-cover photograph of my kisser. Tom seemed to think it was great, but I was devastated.

"Sonofabitch!" I muttered to myself, flinging the magazine back down on the pile. "There's gonna be a year of takin' shit for this one."

What happened the first day of football practice made all that unimportant. I was weighing myself in on the scale in the locker room when the athletic director walked over and steered me off to the corner. It seemed that during the summer the California Interscholastic Federation had come up with some new rulings about eligibility, and I was now suddenly disqualified from playing during my senior year.

The news rocked me back on my heels. I couldn't believe it. Three and a half years ago, before I had graduated from St.

John's and signed on at Bellarmine, I had asked whether I'd be eligible to play a full four seasons and had been assured that I would. I had raised the question myself because St. John's took me through the ninth grade and I wasn't clear about whether or not that was considered the first year of high school. If it was, I would have to rethink the whole way I had planned out my future. The way I had it figured, I needed four years of ball to make up for the year I skipped a grade and get back with the kids of my own size and experience. At the very least, I would have entered Bellarmine as a sophomore. The last year of high school ball was too important to miss. That's when the scouts from the colleges are looking you over, and the reports they send back have a lot to do with what happens when you try out for the college team the next fall. If you don't play your senior year, nobody knows what happened to you and you die. My game had been building right on schedule my first three seasons at Bellarmine. By my junior year I was getting a name, a reputation and even some press. Now, all because of a last-minute change in the rules, I would just disappear.

I headed straight for the coach to tell him what happened. The word had already reached him, and he felt terrible about it.

"What the hell can I say, man? It's lousy. It stinks. I wish to Christ I could stand here and tell you we're gonna fight it, but I can't. There's not a damn thing we can do. You're just gonna have to accept it."

There wasn't much conviction in his voice when he went on to say that life is full of crummy surprises and you have to learn to take the bad with the good. But that's what you said to a kid. That's what you were supposed to believe. The rules were the rules, and in those days you didn't question authority. But at least he was in my corner. And I knew he was going to miss me too.

The rest of the team was still going through the warmup exercises when Father Flynn called me into his office.

"Now, Gary, you had a bad break, but you know there are other things than football that are important. Football is good, but you're not just a football player. You're a bright young man and a fine young man, and you'll be all right, so don't you worry.

You just keep on with your studies and work hard, and next year you'll go on to college and play there."

"Okay, Father."

I knew he meant well, and my head understood what he was saying. But that didn't ease the pain and anger in my heart.

"And I've already seen to it," he went on. "The 130-pound team will be needing a new coach, and we want you to take over the job."

I thanked him for his offer and turned in my player's jersey for a gray sweatshirt. If I couldn't play, at least I could do that, and I tried my best to do it well. If it took me thirty times to teach someone a crossover step, that's what I gave it. When the kids were feeling lazy and put out less than their best, I rode them hard, just like Coach Prentice did with me when I was still part of the team. And that included the twins. Denny played halfback on the 130s and Phil was a guard. If they tried to take advantage of the fact that I was their brother by easing up on the exercises or not running the laps, I called them down the same as I would anyone else. I didn't expect more of them because they were my brothers, nor did I expect any less. And when they did well, I tried not to show the special pride I took in them. Phil was small for a guard but had plenty of guts, and Denny was a natural-born halfback.

After a while I could feel myself getting fairly good at the coaching and began to enjoy it. Still, when Friday and Saturday nights rolled around, I seemed to be hitting the six-packs a little harder than before and the fights at the drive-in seemed a little more intense. And that small voice inside me kept buzzing away in my ear, "They're not to be trusted. Everyone who lays down the rules is full of it. Anytime they get the chance, they're gonna do you in."

My best friend, Norm Benedetti, had also been ruled ineligible his senior year. We cried in each other's beer for a while, but eventually he adjusted to the disappointment and moved past it. I admired the way he handled it but just couldn't do the same. I kept feeling that any shot I had at life was over, that I was a born loser and no matter what I tried I was bound to fail.

Chapter Eight
Confrontations

All through football season the distrust I felt for authority continued to smolder away in silence. Then, when I came back home for the Christmas holidays, it suddenly flared up into a rage.

Dad had invited Jimmy Van Heusen, Buddy Cole and a couple other pals over to the house for the afternoon. I was sitting in the living room listening to them shoot the breeze while they waited for him to finish some business in his office upstairs. Like I always did around Dad's scene, I stayed well in the background and kept my mouth shut, and after a while they must have forgotten I was there. They were swapping yarns about the good old days, when one of them came up with a story that blew my head off.

"Anyone remember the one about Bing and the cutie in the big picture hat? They were slinking out of someone's house about seven-thirty in the morning, all bleary-eyed from the night before, and just as they hit the front gate they're spotted by a civilian on his way to work. Well, the guy couldn't believe his eyes. He did a double take, slammed on his brakes and yelped, 'Father O'Malley?' and then sped off like the devil himself was after him."

Everyone thought the anecdote was hilarious, but to my seventeen-year-old way of thinking it signaled the end of the universe. They were still laughing as I slipped from the room and beat it out the back door. My mind was racing a hundred miles a second, and I had to get out of there and fit the pieces together before Dad came downstairs.

Father O'Malley. That meant it was after *Going My Way*, and the good old days they were talking about weren't all that old. So my mother isn't crazy! Nothing crazy about her. The sonofa-bitch does fuck around! This pillar of Catholicism and moral rec-titude is no better than any other two-bit Hollywood phony out cheating on his wife.

I thought of all the years Mom had spent holed up in her room juiced out of her skull, and I wanted to kill him. Sometimes, when she was heavy into the booze, the names of certain ac-tresses in his pictures would slip out of her mouth and she'd get a funny look on her face, but I never believed her. When I was still too young to understand what she seemed to be saying, I thought, "Wow, what's goin' on here? She really doesn't like those women." Then later on I figured she must be making it up to give herself a reason to drink. It couldn't be possible. Not my father, not Mr. Perfect.

But it was. It wasn't just something that found its way into her head in a crazy, drunken mood one day and she kept throwing the scotch down on top of it, feeding her paranoia until the grain of doubt swelled up to the size of a mountain. It was real.

Sure, nobody keeps a secret in this town. She put two and two together from a blurb in a gossip column, or one of her drinking buddies just had to tell her. "Gee, Dixie, I wouldn't mention a word of this, except I'm your best friend . . ." And how many other people around the business also know? Must be all of them. But nobody writes about it. Nobody talks about it. They just cluck their tongues and shake their heads and ask each other, "Gosh, why the hell is Dixie drinking like that? She's got everything a person could hope for. She's got a wonderful hus-band and a big house and cars and kids and all the money in the world. What's her problem?"

What's her problem? *She knows*, that's what her problem is. No goddam wonder she won't go anywhere with him and won't set foot outside the house and sits up there in her room getting herself good and pissed every day.

I saved some of my rage for myself.

If he's no better than that, then where the hell does he get off laying down the law like he's Pope Pius XII and meting out punishment from on high when you don't live up to his impossible fuckin' expectations?

I understood I could never be what he wanted, but until this moment I had still bought the proposition that he was right and I was wrong. The way I saw it, the big problem between us was that he was so pure and faultless in his own life, he just didn't have it in him to comprehend the lesser ways of ordinary sinners like me. I still knew nothing about the years he spent carousing and messing up and chasing after the good times when he sang with Paul Whiteman early in his career. In all his lecturing and moralizing he never once opened up to them. "What the hell can you do after ten o'clock at night?" he would ask with utter seriousness if I tried to convince him to stretch my curfew, and I couldn't really answer him. I couldn't tell him, "Hey, you can look for girls. You can have laughs. You can go cruising with the guys." He wouldn't have known what I was talking about.

It never occurred to me before now that he didn't practice every syllable that he preached. Searching my memory for some kind of precedent that would make sense out of what I'd just heard, the only thing I could come up with was how he used to slug down that big cup of coffee before dragging me off to communion Sunday mornings. He constantly preached that we had to be perfect Catholics and follow our religious instructions to the letter, so there seemed to be a real contradiction. He knew better than I did that from the time you went to bed the night before, you weren't allowed to put a single thing in your mouth but water. One morning he read the bewilderment on my face as I stood there in the kitchen watching him stir in the cream and sugar, and he threw me a little wink and said half jokingly, "Special dispensation." Given how the nuns and priests loved him, this seemed entirely possible, and even though it didn't quite jibe with how he set himself up in my eyes, I had to be satisfied with it. But not this time. There was no special dispensation for the mortal sin of adultery, not even for Bing Crosby.

Well, that's it. That hypocritical bastard isn't any better than I am. And he ain't gonna play God with me no more.

Eventually I calmed down enough to go back inside, and I managed to poker-face my way through the rest of the vacation. I never did let on to the old man that I was in on his little secret, nor did I say anything about it to my brothers. I figured that if truth will out, like they teach you in Sunday school, they'd discover it for themselves soon enough. But a lifetime's worth of fear had turned into anger now, and it was only a matter of time before it erupted into the open.

It happened a few months later, the next time I came down from San Jose. I was on my way out of the house one morning when he materialized in the front hall and stopped me dead in my tracks. Maybe his kidney stones were acting up, because he was in an especially rotten mood.

"Where the hell do you think you're going?"

"Out. Gotta meet some guys."

"Uh-uh, not today you don't. You're not going anywhere. The garage is a stinkin' mess. I want it cleaned up, and I want it cleaned up now. Get cracking."

"Hey, they're waitin' on me. I already made some plans."

"I don't give a damn about your plans. You're not leaving here till you do what I tell you. That's it. Move it."

"Okay, okay. Jee-sus Christ!"

I don't think I bitched and moaned more than usual, but this time it pushed all his buttons.

"I told you not to give me that look! I told you never to give me that tone of voice! Goddamit, boy, when you gonna learn? I've had just about all the lip from you I'm gonna take!"

He snatched a walking stick from the cane stand and pointed at the couch in the hallway.

Oh, shit, here we go again. Will this never end? I was almost eighteen years old, a big galoot five feet ten inches tall, who tipped the scales at two hundred and ten pounds, and he was still laying on the whippings like I was a ten-year-old. About the only difference was that these days he used one of his canes instead of the belt.

I bent over and placed my hands on the couch like he told me, and he went to work, swinging the thing like a baseball bat so that I got it good and hard with the curved handle. At first I resigned myself to the licking like I always did and counted off the strokes to myself to keep from feeling the hurt. But then, just after he'd taken his thirteenth swing, I turned my head and saw him leaning into me for the next one, and I suddenly blew. For a split second I went blank. The next thing I knew the cane was in my hands, not his, and I was breaking it across my legs and flinging the pieces down the hall.

"That's it!" I heard myself scream. "If you ever hit me again, you motherfucker, I'll kill you! I'll go to jail. They can put me in the fuckin' gas chamber. But lay another hand on me and I swear to God I'll kill you!"

I was even more astonished than he was. In all the years he'd been dishing it out, I never once thought to make him stop. I never thought to run. I never thought to fight back. I just took it and took it and took it. He hadn't heard a single word out of me. But now all the anger and hate and frustration I'd kept pent up inside for so long burst loose like a pack of wild animals on a rampage, and for the first time in my life I was telling him exactly what I felt. I had no more control over my actions than a maniac loose on the street with murder in his heart.

He put up his fists and went into a boxer's crouch.

"Oh, you're gonna fight your father now, huh? You'd raise your hand against your old man?"

"Yeah, give me that fuckin' boxing stance! Come on, I want to see that shit! I ain't gonna *box* you. I'll take a fuckin' lamp and brain your ass if you touch me again. You don't believe me? You want to try it now? Go ahead. I'll do it right this minute."

I would have, too. That's how crazed I was. As I was saying it I looked over at him and saw a kind of small, older man who'd gone about as far as he could go, and I knew I had it in me. Nothing was standing between us. If I wanted to start on him now, I could do him in. The realization was terrifying, and I began telling myself to cool down. Still, if he had come after me, if he had uncorked a fist and taken a swing, I'd have jumped all over him, and God only knows where it would have ended.

But he had the good sense not to do that. He was still in control, really. I was a rabid dog, and he was smart enough just to dance around me and keep out of reach until I stopped frothing at the mouth.

Eventually I simmered down, and we stepped around each

other, then continued on our separate ways. The next day was as if nothing had ever happened. Life went on as usual. I wasn't sure whether he would try to whip me again—and what would happen if he did—but as it turned out he didn't. There were still plenty of other punishments when I failed to live up to his rules, and I went along with them, taking whatever he meted out with no more than my usual complaints. But that was the last time he laid a hand on me.

The summer couldn't have started out better.

The first thing to happen was that I got my own car. Mom and Dad came up to San Jose for my high school graduation, and when I met them back at the room, after dropping off my cap and gown, Dad threw me half a smile and said, "Okay, Gary, I have a little surprise for you." I knew that parents usually gave their kids some kind of gift for making it through high school, but I wasn't expecting much, not after the big blowout earlier that year. A few months afterwards Mom had asked me what I wanted for a graduation present, and I had told her, "Gee, I know there's not much chance of getting it, but I sure would like a car." When she backed off with an "Uh-huh, well, we'll have to see," I figured that was that and forgot about it. But now Dad pulled a set of keys from his pocket, placed it in my hand and told me to have a look outside.

I took the dormitory stairs four at a time, burst out the front door and there it was, parked by the curb, a brand-new, shiny white '51 Mercury, all molded and low and round, just aching to be thrown into gear. For the moment the anger still lurking in my heart was overwhelmed by gratitude, and I thanked him profusely, then hunted up a couple of the guys and whipped them off for a shakedown cruise around the block. It wasn't too much longer before Dad began using the car as a weapon by threatening to take it away if I didn't knuckle under, but right then that little white devil was my passport to freedom.

"I got my own wheels!" I kept telling myself, not quite believing it was true. "I don't have to ride with the chauffeur anymore. I don't have to wait for somebody to pick me up. I don't have to refuse to go places. I can get away! Just me! I can jump into that beauty and get the hell away from everyone whenever I have to."

And then, to top it all off, for the first time in eight years I didn't have to go to the ranch. I had separated my left shoulder a couple of years before when my own defensive backfield ran over me in spring practice. The doctor who snapped it back in had advised me to quit playing before I crippled myself for life, but I wasn't about to. Schmitty, our trainer, had rigged up a harness that held the shoulder in place, but as the doctor had warned, it kept popping out on me. I wanted to be whole for football tryouts when I started Stanford in the fall, so right after graduation I went into the hospital for corrective surgery. Since I wouldn't be much good chasing cows and mending fences in a body cast that ran from my shoulder to my waist, Dad granted me a reprieve and let me go off with my mother to the bungalow at Lake Tahoe.

It turned out to be the happiest summer of my life. Mom eased up on the rules and pretty much let me run free, and I was just another kid enjoying his vacation. Ronnie Marengo, a friend from Bellarmine, was also spending the summer at Tahoe, and the two of us took to hanging out together. During the day we'd go over to Bob Stack's house up on the lake, and he and his brother Jimmy let us use their motorboat and fed us lunch. Then, after Mom fell asleep at night, we punked around and even went out a few times with two chorus girls who worked the line at the Cal-Neva Lodge. They'd brush us off early in the evening so they could get to their main dates with the big guys, but I really liked them. They were kind, funny ladies who made us feel we were kings loved and adored by the female population of the world. Hey, we're dating showgirls, whoopee!

The best part of the summer was the unexpected new closeness with my mother. We were beginning to look at each other differently. Once I discovered the old man wasn't the pillar of virtue he pretended to be, and that her insinuations weren't the half-crazed ramblings of a drunk, I stopped being afraid of her. She became more of a person to me, and I started to feel some sympathy for her drinking. On her side, she was also beginning to take me more seriously. Now that just the two of us were living together, she was treating me like a reasonably responsible eighteen-year-old who could be let off the leash once in a while without making a mess. I showed up at night whatever hour I wanted, and there was no bitching and yelling the next morning. Over breakfast she talked to me like one adult to another. Her tone of voice was different, and she'd engage me in conversations about such grown-up topics as the cold war, the draft and what was happening in Korea. Then she'd listen to what I had to say, as though my opinions were worth considering. The love that I suppose had always been there began to rise to the surface now. I found myself touched by all the sadness in her life and began speculating about what I might do to help make it better.

"Well, since she doesn't seem to act like I'm a retarded child anymore," I told myself, "maybe she'll pay some attention if I try to talk to her about the booze." At first the idea sounded absurd, and I put it out of my mind. "Who do you think you're kidding? *She's* gonna listen to *you?*" But I kept coming back to it and gradually evolved a plan. I'd have to do it the right way. I couldn't just sit her down and say, "Now listen here," and then deliver a lecture like my father. She wouldn't tolerate that for a second. I'd have to pick a moment when she wasn't drinking but in a good mood, which was still scarce as hen's teeth. Then I'd have to find a humorous way to get into it and let it develop gently into something more serious. "Y'know, Mom, you're not just hurting yourself with this. You're killing us. You're driving him fruitcake." Maybe she wouldn't listen. By now maybe she thought that was the only way she could capture his attention. Maybe she'd rather have him climb the walls trying to find out what was wrong with her than ignore her altogether. But it was worth a shot.

Instead of taking off the first moment I could break loose, I began spending more and more time alone with her, looking for an opening, a slot, a place to get started. I never found it. Before I could work up the gumption, July had given way to August and we were off to Idaho to join Dad and my brothers at his place on Hayden Lake. I told myself, "Okay, there's still Christmas vacation. There's always next summer." But the opportunity had passed. By the following year she was dead of cancer.

Mom may have become more of a human being in my eyes, but Dad still looked the same. And as far as he was concerned,

155

so did I. The moment I pulled into Hayden Lake, he put me right back in the trunk and nailed the lid down tight. Only now I wasn't quite so willing to stay there.

The night of the party, for the very first time I flat out disobeyed him. The event was being held at the house of one of his old chums, a man he'd gone to school with back in Spokane. Since I'd be in safe hands, I figured he'd ease up on my usual ten-thirty curfew, so I went ahead and invited a girl. She was up there working as a housekeeper for the summer, and I'd developed an instant crush on her. After supper I'd help her wash the dishes, then keep her company on the front porch while she baby-sat. This was our first and only chance to actually go somewhere together.

The day before our date Dad told me he'd thought it over and decided that since this was a special occasion he'd make an exception in the rules. I could stay out an extra hour and a half until midnight. I felt like a fool for painting myself into a corner. This was the big party of the summer. It wouldn't get started until almost ten and was bound to last till two or three in the morning. Now I'd have to call the girl and run my usual cop-out. "Gee, I'm sorry. Something's come up. I can't make it." But I couldn't bring myself to reach for the telephone. I'd already done that too many times and had gotten to the point where I wasn't going to do it again. It took a while to work up the nerve, but once I made my decision that was it. I didn't care how much punishment he laid on me. "I know I'm gonna catch hell, but screw it, I'm hanging in there till it's over. If he doesn't try to whip me, he'll probably never let me go out again. But I ain't backing down this time." I didn't show up until 4 or 5 A.M., and, just as I figured, the next morning he was furious.

"Okay, boy, you're grounded for the summer. You're not setting foot outside this house the rest of the nights we're up here."

It didn't work out quite that way.

One evening, about a week before we were due to leave, I was stretched out on the bed in the basement room I shared with Denny, attempting to keep myself awake until he showed up. It was already past midnight and he hadn't come in yet, so I knew there was bound to be trouble. When the phone rang I lunged for it before the racket could stir the old man from his sleep. The voice on the other end belonged to Ed Keegan, the bartender at the beer joint downtown in Courdelaine.

"Gary, listen, I got a little problem. Denny's here and he's kinda drunk, and a couple guys want to fight him. I don't want to see that happen. What do you think I should do?"

"Well, just keep cool. I'll be right over."

I slipped out the basement door at the rear of the house, eased my Mercury into neutral, then pushed it down the driveway and through the front gate. When I felt certain the Great Bald Eagle couldn't hear the sound of the motor, I started it up and headed straight for the bar. By the time I reached it, the immediate crisis had blown over. The guys had come up with some better way to pass the evening and moved on. But Denny, half unconscious, was slouched over at a table in the corner. I laid him over my shoulder and carried him off to the car, then drove back to the house. When we hit the front gate I cut the lights and ignition, and we drifted silently down the driveway. Then I hoisted him back over my shoulder, steered him into the basement and put him to bed. Mission accomplished, and nobody was the wiser.

I was still sleeping the next morning when Dad burst into the room. He was crazed with anger. Ripping the covers off me, he screamed at the top of his lungs, "You sonofabitch you! You're no fuckin' good, and now you're leading your brother down the same garden path! Get the hell out of here! That's it! I don't want anything more to do with you!" Then he whipped around on his heels and was gone.

Denny was totally bewildered. He'd been so loaded the night before that he didn't remember anything. I was almost as confused. It took me a while to figure out that Dad had heard me come in but hadn't heard me go out, hadn't even realized I'd been home all evening. By then he was already off to the links for his morning round of golf. I suppose I could have chased after him and explained what happened, but I didn't. What was I going to tell him? You didn't fink on your brothers, and I'd long since given up trying to explain myself to him.

"Well, there go college and football. The hell with them. But what now? Well, he told you to get out of here, so that's what you'd better do. Get cracking. Looks like you're on your own.

You're gonna have to pay your own way from now on, so better start figuring out how to make some money."

After all the guest shots I'd done with the old man and the success of "Sam's Song" and "Simple Melody," show business might have seemed like a logical place to start looking. But I didn't want any part of the business. It was too close to him, and I was through riding on his coattails. Once that had been rejected, I wasn't left with much choice.

"There's only one thing you can do in life," I told myself, "and that's manual labor. You know how to punch cattle, string fence and mow hay, so you might as well head down to Elko and try to find a gig as a ranch hand." I had no intention of working at Dad's ranch, but since I knew some of the foremen at the neighboring spreads, that seemed my best bet.

I threw some work clothes into a suitcase, dug out the hundred dollars I'd squirreled away from my allowance and wages, then hopped into the car and headed south. My route took me right through the middle of the golf course where Dad was playing. If I'd looked to either side I might have seen him lacing into the ball or measuring off a putt. But I didn't look. All that was behind me now, and I kept my eyes fixed straight ahead on the road unwinding before me.

I pulled into Elko two or three days later, after blowing most of my money in the bars and whorehouses along the way, then tracked down the foremen I knew and hit them up for work. I was sitting in the lobby of the Commercial Hotel, biding my time until something came through, when Dad's foreman, Johnny Eacret, appeared.

"Damn, Gary, sure am glad I found you. Look, I heard what you're up to, and I think we oughta put in a call to your father."

Before I could finish objecting, he had the old man on the line.

"What in the world are you doing down there?" he asked, more gently than I expected. "What the hell's goin' on?"

"What do you mean, what am I doing? You kicked me out. I'm looking for a job."

"Oh, for God's sake, boy, I didn't mean all the way out. I just meant get out of my sight for the time being, until I cooled off. Didn't you hear me calling after you when you drove past the golf course? Your mother's worried sick."

It wasn't an apology exactly, but about as close to one as he'd ever come. I wanted to tell myself, "Aw, he's full of shit. He's just making it up now to look good." I was still so furious at him, I guess, that part of me was happy he had cut me loose and I'd be out of his face forever. But I knew he was telling the truth. I could hear it in his voice.

Christ, what a stupid mistake. I had taken him absolutely literally, the way I always did when he lashed out at me, without once even thinking to ask, "Does he really mean it? Is that what he's really saying?" As grown-up and streetwise as I liked to think I was, I'd acted like a child, not much different from the ten-year-old who had run away from home Christmas morning because he didn't get the present he wanted.

"Oh, okay," I answered, struggling to keep my voice as matter-of-fact as possible. "What do you want me to do?"

"Well, we're about to leave here, so go on home and we'll meet you there. If you need some money, Johnny'll give it to you."

I promised that I would and hung up. A few days later we were all back together at the house in Beverly Hills. The incident was immediately forgotten, never to be mentioned again, and I went on to college as planned.

I knew I was bucking the odds, but I took off for Stanford two weeks early for the pre-school football tryouts. Having been disqualified out of my last season at Bellarmine, I was still short on experience and lacked the advance notices that would make the coaches sit up and pay attention. And, as luck would have it, Stanford wasn't fielding a freshman team that year. That was a big disadvantage. You don't play many games in freshman ball, but you do learn a tremendous amount by scrimmaging constantly against the varsity and each other. I'd have to try out directly for the junior varsity, where my competition not only included the expected high school phenoms, with tons of press clips under their arms, but upperclassmen who had already played a couple of years, as well as older, bigger Korean vets coming back to school on the GI Bill. The coaches only had a few weeks to pull the team together and couldn't really try guys out to see what they could do. They pretty much had to go with the players they already knew and those who brought heavy reputations with them.

I realized I had only a very slight shot but still figured that if they let me stay out there and scrimmage enough, if they gave me a chance to look good, I might luck my way through. The idea was to make first-string junior varsity now, move on to second- or third-string varsity my sophomore year, then get on the starting team as a junior. Watching the varsity run plays, there was no question that they moved a whole lot better and faster than I did and reacted more quickly, but I was confident that with enough experience I'd be able to pick up momentum and play just as well. With two years of first-string varsity ball behind me, I'd have some kind of crack at the pros by the time I finished college.

But the first step was to make the starting lineup on the J.V.s. If that didn't happen, I wouldn't play enough to make someone look up, and then no matter how good I was there'd be no way to move on.

The first two weeks of workouts consisted mostly of skull sessions, blocking and hitting practice and holding the tackling dummies for the varsity. To keep injuries to a minimum, there was very little physical contact, nothing to sink your teeth into. Physical contact was my meat, so I figured that if I could only hang in there until the heavy scrimmaging began, I'd probably be all right. Once the fight was on and I was free to cut loose, I'd be able to show them I could get the job done.

By the afternoon of the first scrimmage against the varsity, over thirty of the fifty or so freshmen who had tried out for the squad had been told to clean out their lockers. I was still in the running but not there yet. A lot depended on what happened today. Whoever got chosen to work against the varsity was not only assured of a place on the team but would play first-string the rest of the year.

We were all clustered together on the sidelines, trying to hide our nervousness from each other, when the head coach strode up with his clipboard and began reading off the starting players. As he called out each position, the guy he named sprinted away from the pack and took his place on the field. It seemed like an

Lindsay, Philip, Dennis and Gary, 1943.

Gary, Philip, Dennis and Lindsay, 1946.

Dixie and Bing at Elko Ranch, 1948. (courtesy Wide World Photos)

Gary and Roberta Morgan at their junior prom, 1950. (courtesy Roberta Morgan Schaeffer)

Gary, Dennis, Grandpa Wyatt, Philip and Lindsay, 1959.

Barbara, Steve and Gary, 1961. (courtesy Globe Photos)

eternity before he finished with the offensive team and moved on to defense, which is where I came in. Finally he got there. If I'd ever faced a moment of truth in my life, this was it.

"All right, defensive linemen. Tackles, so-and-so and so-and-so. Ends . . . guards . . . Linebackers, Mack and Crosby."

I wanted to let loose a whoop that would rouse the whole world as I stepped out to take possession of the linebacker's spot that was now mine. I was about halfway there when a voice stopped me dead in my tracks. It belonged to the assistant coach. Up to now he had been standing quietly in the background, minding his own business, but the moment my name was called he suddenly sprang to life.

"Mack and *who?*" he jeered. "Mack and *who?*"

I saw it coming before the words cleared his throat. Oh, Christ, here we go again.

"Hey, we don't want no fuckin' Hollywood faggot playin' linebacker on this team! Crosby, you get the hell out of there!"

Then he pointed to another player and sent him in.

I looked over to the head coach and waited for him to straighten the guy out. He was the power. This other joker was only his assistant. But he didn't say a thing. He just turned his eyes from my gaze and faded into the grass. So that was that. Without any support, there was nothing to argue about. What was I going to do, let them see it bothered me? I spun around on my cleats and headed back to the sidelines.

For the rest of the season I stayed there, watching the starting team steadily improve as it moved from scrimmaging to playing actual games, still hoping that somehow I'd get a chance. Once in a while, when the score was seventy-two to zero and it didn't much matter, I might get in for three or four plays, only to be yanked out again before I could make the brilliant block or perfect tackle that would turn it all around for me. But I continued to hang in despite the feeling that even when the power was on my side, my life had turned to shit, and that's the way it was probably going to stay from here on out. "You can't quit, not when they're screwing you unfairly," I told myself. "That lets them win. You just keep at it. Something'll happen. You'll see." But it never did.

His voice on the telephone sounded even colder and more disapproving than usual. "I'm driving up to Palo Alto Saturday," he announced. "Wait for me in your room. I'll see you in the afternoon." Before I could ask him what was going on, he had hung up.

It was always bad news when Dad came around, but this felt especially ominous. I'd just been home for Thanksgiving and would be back again during Christmas vacation. Something must have happened to make him give up his Saturday on the links, something too urgent to wait another two weeks.

"Oh, Jesus Christ, what's it gonna be now?" I asked myself, less in anger than fear. "Why's he comin' here? What did I do wrong this time?" I felt the old panic well up but slammed the door on it fast before it had a chance to take over. "Hey, be cool. So he's coming. So what? Who the fuck cares? Somebody must have called him. He'll go talk to the asshole, and then, when he shows up ranting and raving, you'll find out soon enough." To keep from worrying about it, I dashed out to the seven o'clock movie, then headed over to Risotti's for a couple of beers.

When he appeared in my room a few days later, he skipped the preliminary small talk about sports and got right down to business.

"Well, I thought so. I knew it."

"Knew what?"

"The minute anybody lets up on you, you take advantage, you fuck up. I never should have listened to your mother and given you that goddam car. I never should have let you go off to Stanford. You haven't even been here one semester, and the dean of men tells me you're already flunking out."

Flunking out? The words rocked me back on my heels. I knew I wasn't exactly headed for Phi Beta Kappa but had absolutely no notion I was that far down the drain.

God knows I should have. I'd hardly cracked a book the whole four months I'd been there. Somewhere in the back of my mind it did occur to me that I'd have to get down to it eventually, but eventually meant tomorrow, not tonight, not right this minute. Before Stanford someone had always been sitting on my back telling me exactly what to do. First it was my mother and father, then in grade school it was the nuns, then in high school the priests. But now, for the first time in my life, the lid was off completely and I was out of the trunk. No bell rang to get me up in the morning. No prefect of discipline called me into his office if I missed a class during the day. No teacher took roll call to make sure I showed up at study hall at night. There was no such thing as study hall. "You're a man now," they told us at the orientation lecture the first day of college, "and it's time you started acting like one. Here's the knowledge. Do you want it or not? Come and get it or don't. It's up to you."

I was as dazzled by my new freedom as a con turned loose from his cell after eighteen years in the slammer. You want to go to the movies? Fine, go to the movies. Who's stopping you? You feel like staying up all night to see what it's like? Go ahead, check it out. You want to drink beer with the guys? That's okay too. Nobody's saying you can't. I'd seen kids living with that kind of independence for as long as I could remember, but it was new to me and I wanted to suck up every drop before someone took it away.

At the same time there was a nagging feeling that this glorious freedom wasn't exactly everything it was cracked up to be. Cut adrift, with no one to answer to but myself, part of me felt lost and more than a little frightened. I'd had so little experience being out there on my own that I couldn't even find the right classroom half the time. They stuck a map of the campus in your hand, but there were so many buildings that I couldn't make sense of it and had to latch onto someone who was taking the same course and follow him over. At Bellarmine, if you didn't understand something that went down in class, you tripped next door to the Father's room during study hall, and he sat you down and explained it on the spot. Here you were only one of hundreds of bodies in a huge amphitheater, and the teacher was a faceless ant talking into a microphone half a mile away. The priests may have been a pain in the ass, with their constant supervision and discipline, but at least they cared about you, and if you started to slide they stretched out a helping hand before it was too late. Here no one seemed to give a damn whether or not you flopped on your face.

To give the old man his due, he had tried to warn me. "You've had nine years of grade school with the Sisters and four years of

163

high school with the Jesuits," he argued when I was sending off requests for college applications. "Seems to me you better keep right on with the Jesuits and go to Santa Clara. If you change now, there's no telling what you're gonna run into." But by then I had turned so utterly against him, I was so completely negative about anything he had to say, that if he had told me it was day outside I would have sworn to Christ it was night. Even if the sunshine was pouring in through the windows, I'd have been certain the sonofabitch was lying just to mess me up. The more he pushed, the more I bulled my neck until he finally threw up his hands in digust. "All right, boy, go ahead, don't listen to me. But don't say I didn't warn you."

Now the chickens had come home to roost. It was payday, and Dad was delivering the check in person.

"Okay, Gary, the dean of men just gave me a look at your grades for the first quarter. Know what they are? You're flunking Biology. You're flunking Western Civilization. You're flunking your language course. There's not a goddam thing you're not flunking. Boy, if you don't get your ass in gear this very minute, you're not gonna be around here long enough to flunk the finals."

I couldn't let him see he was getting to me, so I sat there stone-faced while he raved on. On the inside, though, it was panic city. I didn't want to flunk out. It was part of the picture of everything I didn't want to be: a rich man's no-good son, a wastrel who bums his way through college until he blows it out his ass, then squanders the rest of his life pissing away his father's money. I wanted to make something of myself. I wanted to be able to hold my head up high and be respected for what *I* was, for what *I* did. It didn't have to be anything big. I didn't have to make a lot of bucks. By the time I was thirteen or fourteen I already knew that money wasn't the answer to anything. I'd seen too many happy people without a quarter in their jeans and too many miserable bastards with huge mansions, fancy cars and million-dollar bank accounts. You didn't have to be a genius to understand that if you wanted to be happy you had to find your own groove, whatever it is, get in the sonofabitch and work hard at it, so that when you went to bed at night you could tell yourself, "Well, I did pretty good today. I accomplished something." Hanging out with the guys at Risotti's wasn't going to do it. Searching out every movie in town wasn't going to do it. Busting out of school wasn't going to do it.

"Okay, Gary, give me the keys to the car," he finished up. "That's it. I'm driving it straight to the garage, and that's where it's gonna stay until you show me you got enough sense to be trusted with it. It was a mistake to give it to you in the first place, but maybe now that you can't go joyriding around you'll stay in your room and hit the books like you're supposed to. And if you don't knuckle down, well, the goddam thing can just sit up on the blocks until it rots."

"Right, Dad. Whatever you say."

Trying hard to keep the slightest flicker of emotion from showing, I pulled the keys from my pocket and handed them over. I reminded myself that I'd known from the start that little white beauty was just one more way for the old man to keep a hold on me and I shouldn't get too attached to it. Chances are it wouldn't be around for long. I'd been proven right, but somehow it still smarted, and that made me even angrier. The bastard still knew how to get through my defenses and find my weak spot.

My mother played it differently when she followed up Dad's visit with a phone call from home the next night. There were no lectures from on high, no angry threats, no punishments, just a simple declaration of how I was making her feel by acting like such an asshole.

"Aw, hon, I'm so disappointed you're not doing well. I know you could if you wanted to, but evidently you don't and that makes me sad."

Mom had gotten real smart with me by now. Toward the end she was able to read me like an open book. She knew that yelling and beating on me didn't do any good. She knew that the only way to get to me was to make me feel I was letting down someone else, someone I cared about. Maybe she finally figured that out because that's how *she* was, and she came to recognize that, as much as I looked like my father, she and I both had the same insides. You could never get anywhere with her by ranting and raving. All that did was make her put her back up. You had to come at her more indirectly, show her what she'd be doing for those she loved if she straightened up, and then she just might listen.

In any case, the guilt did its work. Two minutes into the conversation and the ice around my heart had turned to water. I didn't want to add to her hurt. She was already hurting enough. And I told her what she was waiting to hear.

"All right, Mom, I'll try to do better. I'll try to get it together. You'll see."

And I did. I dusted off the textbooks, stopped cutting so many classes and got some tutoring help from Malcolm McHenry, the brother of one of my friends from Bellarmine. Malcolm never cracked a book either, as far as I could see, but he pulled straight A's and was a natural born teacher. He took me and four other dumb-cluck jocks who were also in trouble, sat us down in his room and patiently explained how each of the subjects worked and how all the separate parts dovetailed neatly together. Then, with the additional help of a lot of bennies and black coffee, I crammed my head with as many facts as it could hold until it was time to recite them back on the finals. It did absolutely nothing for my education. A week later I couldn't even remember where the courses were held. But I just did manage to scrape by. Two points less on my grade point average and I would have been out on my ass, but as it worked out they allowed me to stick around in the vain hope they were teaching me something.

Mom was relieved. Dad felt vindicated that he had handled me the right way and let me hold on to the car keys until the next time I messed up. But I was still the same guy. The rest of my quarters at Stanford followed exactly the same pattern. The first week of school I'd tell myself, "Hey, dummy, you may not be a mastermind, but you're not stupid either. If you show up for the classes and take notes and do some work, you could get through here with a *C* average and have some fun on the side." But I was too full of hate and revenge to listen. "Fuck it, fun on the side's not enough. I've been doing what everybody else wants all my life. Now I'm gonna do what I want for a change. And if I flunk out, well, I flunk out." I could see the error of my ways, but there was always that fight in there. It was as if they were going to close the door tomorrow and I wouldn't have that freedom any longer, so it was more important to screw around first than to study. And pretty soon I'd be screwing around all the time and not studying at all. Then, three or four weeks before finals, my conscience and the guilt would take over and I'd find myself starting in again with the coffee and the bennies and the cram sessions.

Four months after Dad blew up at me he came back up north to transcribe his radio show in San Francisco and brought me on as a guest. When I read through the script the day before the broadcast I was appalled. It made me uncomfortable enough to see the jokes that cast me as some kind of teenage heartthrob. I'd cut two more duets with him by now—"Moonlight Bay" and "Maggie Blues"—and they'd done all right, but I sure as hell wasn't a heartthrob to any teenagers I knew. It was Dad's fans who were buying the records, and if I did have a few of my own, they certainly weren't enough to justify the heavy hype. The main thing that got me, though, was the fact that the script made my humiliation at Stanford public. "Oh, Christ," I groaned when I saw the dialogue, "now he's gonna be broadcasting over national radio that I'm damn near flunking out of college so everyone in the country can hear about it." But I did what he wanted and read my lines as written.

I suppose Dad had mentioned to Bill Morrow, his head writer and fishing partner, that I'd been having a lot of trouble at school, and Bill must have said, "Well, let's do something funny on it. Let's use it for a routine." With a new show to get out every week, they pulled their ideas wherever they could find them. As usual, all the dark, gritty parts of the reality that was mirrored in the script—his bitter disappointment and rage, my anger and guilt—were neatly edited out, and the situation was transformed into another jolly installment of Crosby family life. Dad played the concerned but loving father who rolls up his sleeves and helps the kids with their homework. I was the devil-may-care chip off the old block. We might be going through a little problem right now about my grades, but, gosh, folks, we get along so well that it's bound to work out.

After a few opening gags about how he had locked me in the car downstairs to force me to work, he brought me on for some humorous repartee about my study habits. The way the script had me talking back to him, I gave every bit as much as I took.

BING: Now, folks, it's time to present the student from Stanford . . . just arrived from the parking lot downstairs. Here he is—Gary Crosby!

APPLAUSE

GARY: Thanks, Dad.

BING: Got your studying done?

GARY: Yeah, but when you were my age, did your dad lock you in the car and make you study?

BING: (*dramatically*) Son, we didn't have a car . . . I just can't understand your lethargy, though, Gary . . . your lack of interest in your studies . . . your aversion to opening a book.

GARY: It must be hereditary, Dad.

BING: Oh no . . . no, I'm not gonna hold still for that. You don't get it from me *or* your mother . . . Let me tell you something . . . when I was in college, I had such a desire—such a feverish, burning *hunger* for knowledge—I was known as the "Gonzaga Glutton."

GARY: You really went for higher learning in a big way?

BING: I tell you, I just don't know what to do with you . . . You and your brothers are all old enough to take care of yourselves, but what happens? Every night I have to sit down, and I do arithmetic with Lindsay . . . I have to corner Dennis, and I do the history with him . . . I have to hogtie Philip, and I study physics with him . . . It's a little annoying.

GARY: Yes, but think of the education you're getting.

BING: Let's just think about *your* education . . . Right now, the most important thing in your life is your studies.

GARY: What about athletics?

BING: Fine . . . Athletics are fine, but I still say your schoolwork should be your major concern.

GARY: What about girls?

BING: Yeah, what about them?

GARY: Well, Dad, you gotta admit it . . . a poodle-cut coed is more attractive than a dog-eared book.

APPLAUSE

BING: Now get out! . . . Poodle-cut coed.

GARY: I don't mean to upset you, Dad, but I guess I'm different than you were when you were in school.

BING: Now I don't want you to get me wrong—I was no angel when I went to college.

GARY: Gee, did you once like to stay up late and ride around in open cars and go to parties?

BING: Did I?! . . . But that's all in the past . . . It's early to bed for me now . . . I've seen the light and I've heard the music.

GARY: Yeah, Dad, but when I see the light and hear the music, I wanna *go!*

What I really wanted to do was puke. Except for the embarrassing fact that I was messing up in school, the bit had about as much reality as the duet that followed, a piece of special material called "Fatherly Advice" that had me seeking him out for a heart-to-heart chat about my problems with girls.

The sound of his voice spooked me immediately. It was full of emotion, wavering around the edges as if he were about to burst into tears. I'd never heard him so vulnerable, so overwhelmed by human feeling, and didn't know what to make of it.

"Gary, listen, I got bad news for you," he said. "Your mom is dying. It's cancer. She's in a coma, and the doctors don't think she's gonna pull out of it. You better come home right away."

And then he started to cry.

I put down the phone, walked out to the car and drove straight to the nearest bar. I stayed there, getting myself good and whacked until I ran out of money, then climbed back in and headed south.

The old man's news came as a complete shock. I had no idea Mom was sick with cancer, much less that she was so far gone. Three months ago, just a few weeks after I'd finished my first year at Stanford, she'd been taken to St. John's Hospital in Santa Monica for stomach surgery, but it hadn't sounded all that serious. When Dad told us about it at the ranch, he just casually mentioned out of the side of his mouth, "Well, your mother went to the hospital today for a little operation, but don't worry about it. It'll be all right. She'll be up at Hayden Lake the end of the summer." He didn't seem especially worried or concerned, so we weren't either. To the extent I thought about it at all, I assumed it was because of the booze. I figured it had finally caught up with her and she needed the surgery for ulcers or a damaged liver or whatever it was that years of constant juicing do to you, and once they patched her up she'd be okay.

When she flew up to Hayden Lake in a chartered plane in the middle of August, she hadn't seemed any worse than usual. She was terribly thin—you could see the bones sticking through her hands and shoulders, and the skin around her face was drawn tight—but she'd looked like that for a while now. I was used to her being a semi-invalid. Even before the operation she hardly ever got out of her bathrobe or left the house, and her routine now was just about the same. As always, she moved very slowly, with her back hunched over, yet with a certain grace. About the only difference was that she didn't seem to be drinking, and even that wasn't all that extraordinary. Over the years I'd seen her stay off the booze for weeks and even months at a time, only to climb right back in the jug again once the pressure got to be more than she could handle.

I suppose if I hadn't been in such a rush to split out of the house I might have sensed how ill she was, or she might have told me herself. We had gotten so much closer the previous year, when just the two of us were together at Lake Tahoe. But once that ended and I no longer had her all to myself, we picked up the old roles pretty much where we had left off. While she was recuperating from the operation, she'd pad out to the living room every now and then and drop a hint on the old man that if she had a vote in the matter she'd just as soon ease up on the discipline and let us run a little more free. But since she didn't seem to feel she had a vote, she couldn't fight him about his rules— nobody did that—and continued to go along with whatever he said. For my part, although I tried to behave myself so as not to add to her aggravation, my first priority continued to be to get away from the two of them every chance I got. I figured, "Well, I can always hang out with her later," but of course later never came.

I whipped the automobile down through the valleys and

finally braked in front of the house. It was morning now, and the place felt even more like a mausoleum than ever. It was already as quiet as the grave. Mom was still in a coma upstairs. Dad and Grandpa Wyatt were keeping a vigil by her bedside. Grandma Crosby sat in her room with her rosary beads, maintaining her own counsel. Linny and the twins were off in their wing of the house, each lost in his own thoughts. About the only sound of life was Georgie's sobs as she shuffled along the corridors doing whatever had to be done to keep the place running.

"Your mom's going to be fine," she sniffled, trying hard to pull herself together as she joined me at the kitchen table while I downed one cup of black coffee after another. "She's not suffering now. Whatever happens is the will of God, and that's how we have to take it. We'll miss her, but—" And then she broke off and started blubbering again. For all her faith, she was losing the one person in the world she loved, and the grief was more than she could bear.

Between bouts of crying, Georgie filled me in on what had happened. The previous Saturday Dad was on his way back from shooting his latest picture, *Little Boy Lost*, in Paris, and Mom took herself out of bed to welcome him home. The doctors had tried to keep her from leaving the house, but her mind was made up and she was waiting at the station when his train pulled in from New York. The next morning she suffered a relapse, then two days later slipped into a coma and had remained unconscious ever since. There was nothing more to be done. The cancer had gone too far, and it was just a matter of hours or days until she passed away.

"And before your mother lost consciousness," Georgie went on, "she asked to be baptized. I called Monsignor Concannon and he rushed over from Good Shepherd and brought her into the Church and then he gave her extreme unction."

She clasped her hands together in a kind of prayer and began crying again. Despite my own distress I almost smiled. Yeah, Georgie was gonna get her into heaven no matter what. Whether Mom wanted it or not, she was gonna make absolutely sure she went straight upstairs.

But she most likely did want it. I thought about how, during that summer we spent together, she'd taken to dropping questions on me every so often that indicated some kind of interest was brewing.

"You really believe that stuff?" I remember her asking at the dinner table. "You really believe in God? He's really there, huh?"

"Uh, well, yeah, Mom, I guess I do."

"Well, it must be nice to have a faith like that," she had answered, almost speaking to herself. "It must feel good to believe in something."

It was all quite off the cuff, and she quickly moved on to some other topic. But a week or so later she came back to it.

"So there's three persons in God, but God is still one, right? So how does that work? And tell me about confession. You can be bad all week, but then you go in the box and say you're sorry and the priest says it's okay and then you come out and go right back to being bad again, is that it? Can you explain that to me so it makes sense?"

"Well, I don't know, Mom," I had answered. "That's what they tell us."

I'd logged in enough years with the priests and nuns to quote her chapter and verse about what she was waiting to hear, but I kept the explanations to myself. However much she had loosened up with me, I was still reluctant to get into any kind of verbal fencing with her. She'd had a few drinks by then, and there was always the possibility I might say the wrong thing and touch off her rage. It was still safer not to battle her on anything.

"Oh, come on," she had insisted. "You have to do better than that."

"Well, I don't know. That's it."

"Mr. I Don't Know again," she had laughed. "Here we go again with the I Don't Know Kids."

Sitting there with Georgie, I tried to conjure up how Mom might have undertaken her conversion. It wouldn't have been out of cowardice or fear. If she was lucid enough and the pain wasn't too great, she probably took the step with a certain amount of skepticism and even humor.

It had been decided that my brothers and I weren't to see Mom in the coma, so we were kept out of her bedroom. We were hardly kids anymore but were still looked on as babies. For the next three days we drifted aimlessly around the house, waiting for the inevitable to happen as she gradually slid downhill into the arms of God.

Every few hours Georgie or Dad or the doctor would walk downstairs and issue a report on her progress. Often there were tears running down Dad's face, and he didn't seem to care who saw them. The display of emotion coming out of the old man was so totally foreign that it put me on edge. I didn't know how to handle it. Over the years I'd come to think about him tough and hard and deal with him tough and hard like a convict does with the warden, and now suddenly the warden was doing something so human that I wanted to put my arms around him—and that scared me. I didn't trust the feeling, didn't dare lower my guard, so I held myself in check and made sure I stayed as mean and hostile as ever.

"Well, what do you know," I thought to myself, "so he cries just like the rest of us. He feels things. He must have really loved this woman all this time. Why the hell couldn't he show it? Why couldn't he act like it?"

I tried hard to be just as callous about my mother. I'd long since come to believe that if you show any feelings, the first thing someone's going to do is cut you up with them, so if you don't want to be hurt you have to stay hard.

When I caught myself about to break down, I fought back the tears by forcing myself to remember the very worst moments I'd had with her as a kid—the whippings, the crazy alcoholic rages, the whole accumulated history of punishment and terror. I kept working on my head that way until I was actually glad she was dying and I could say to myself, "Well, that's it, she's going. Hey, man, we all go sometime. It's just one more sonofabitch off my back."

Anger was so much easier to handle than sorrow.

No one had to tell me my mother had died. The third morning home I was heading downstairs when Georgie burst out of Mom's bedroom blubbering with grief. One look at her face and I knew it was over. Spinning on my heels, I ran back to my part of the house and began slamming my fist against the sitting room wall.

"God Almighty, why her?" I demanded in an agony of self-centered rage, letting the tears flow freely now. "Why not him? Why couldn't it have been him? What's fair about that, God? Show me where the fairness is. She was so good. She tried. He doesn't give a shit about us. Why did she have to go just when we were starting to get along? And he's still here with all his bullshit!"

I stared out the window, looking for an answer, but no answer came.

I stayed furious at him even after the shock began to fade.

"Aw, come off it, Georgie," I lashed out over the breakfast table the next morning as she launched into a weepy reminiscence about how much Mom and Dad loved each other. "What the hell did he care about her? For Chrisake, he wasn't even around when she was dying! He was off in Paris making a goddam movie!"

Georgie sat bolt upright and cut me off in the middle of my assault.

"Now you listen, Gary, you just shut your mouth about your father. This is why he wasn't here. He knew how sick she was and he wanted to stay home with her, but the doctor wouldn't let him. That's right. The doctor told him that your mother would have fallen apart if she found out he knew how bad off she really was, and if he cared about her peace of mind he wasn't to let on. So he had to go ahead and pretend that nothing was wrong. He had to do that picture. And don't you think it was easy for him, you hear."

That made sense, and I backed off. Sure, Mom would never want everything to turn around and suddenly change because she was ill. She couldn't stand to be pitied. It would have made her crazy to have everyone sitting around her bedroom watching her die. The old man was lanced by his own blade. He had to keep up the same indifferent, cold-ass attitude he'd always shown her. If he had stepped out of character and had suddenly begun pampering her with a lot of affection and concern, it would have been a sure tipoff that he was onto her secret.

Years later, when I finally got around to catching *Little Boy Lost*, I saw for myself that Georgie had told me the truth. There's a scene with his son where Dad breaks down and cries, and it's so convincing, so full of anguish and pain, that he could only have been working off sense memories of what was happening in his own life at the moment. It must have been a terribly sad time for him. I didn't know it then, of course. The letters he sent back from Paris were full of the usual light, breezy anecdotes, followed by the usual lectures. "Keep your grades up. Keep your weight down. And watch your drinking. Saint Augustine cautions moderation in all things . . ." If he had something out of the ordinary to communicate between the lines, I threw the letters away too fast to notice.

The funeral was a three-ring circus, the media event of the season, and we stumbled through it as best we could. The entire Crosby clan and some six hundred of Mom and Dad's friends showed up for the requiem mass at Good Shepherd. There was Bob Hope, Dorothy Lamour, William Gargan, Johnny Mercer and God knows who else. But they were far outnumbered by all the newsmen. There seemed to be a million of them, and they were everywhere—dogging our footsteps at the church, dodging in front of us on the way to the limos, pushing and shoving each other at the graveyard to secure the best positions as Mom was lowered into the ground.

"Hey, Bing, look this way," they shouted at him, popping off one shot after another as he slumped in the back of the limousine after the funeral service. "C'mon, Bing, give us a picture." He held his head down, but his shoulders were shaking from the sobs. He looked so small and defenseless that I wanted to draw a circle around him and knock the shit out of any intruder who dared to cross it. We may have been at war inside the house, but it was our war and he was still my father. When a photographer forced his camera in through the window, I rammed the heel of my hand into his lens and smashed it back in his face.

They pursued us up the hill to the grave site like a plague of locusts, running along backwards six inches in front of us to make us slow down, stumbling into each other when we bumped into them, then bouncing right back again. There was no way to escape them or the microphones they jammed in our faces as they jabbered away with their endless questions. "Hey, Gary, how do you feel? Are you gonna miss your mother? Anything wrong between your mother and your dad?" I kept on moving in a straight line, whacking them with my shoulders when they wouldn't get out of the way, trying to keep myself under control when they shoved back. They wouldn't have minded if I had uncorked a swing. They'd have loved to have gotten a picture of that too. From the middle of the frenzy, just as the priest was preparing to deliver the final words, I heard a sudden loud clang, then a scream. A cameraman had climbed on top of the tombstone next to Mom's grave so he could get a hot shot of her coffin going into the hole, and Uncle Everett had picked up a shovel and sent him flying.

Finally it was over and we had her safely in the ground. The date was November 3, 1952, one day before her forty-first birthday.

Back at the house the mail sacks of condolence letters were already piling up in the front hall. Grandma Crosby and my uncles sat quietly with my father off to one side of the den. Through her sniffles Georgie kept herself busy making sure the coffee and cake were ready for the visitors who'd be coming to pay their respects. Denny was more devastated than any of us and couldn't seem to stop crying.

My own grief didn't last long. I just stood there and nodded mechanically while the people passed through and told me how sorry they were. Meanwhile I thought to myself, "Well, she's so much better off where she is now. Thank God. Thank God she doesn't have to go through the tortures of the damned anymore— falling on her face and spilling makeup all over the joint, puking on her clothes and fucking herself up with all the agony that must have been seething inside her to make her end up like that. The pain and the aggravation and the sadness are over now. They're over, and she's with God. That's where everyone wants to be. The greatest people in the world all want to be where she is, for Chrisake, and she's there. We're still here. So in a way she's better off than we are." Maybe I was just copping out to keep the feelings buried, but it worked for me.

Life returned to normal a couple of days later when Dad called my brothers and me into his office for a lecture and pep talk.

"Well, your mother's gone now," he announced from his customary place behind the desk, "and now we have to go on with our lives. I still have to get you kids educated and out in the world. You know how important that was to her. The best thing we can do for her memory is move on and succeed like we should. So do your schoolwork and try to stay out of trouble."

I ignored him just like I always did. Back at Stanford, I showed up for a few classes and made a vague pass at the books, but I spent most of my afternoons and evenings getting whacked.

When I came home for Thanksgiving vacation, the old man took me along to the studio to transcribe his Christmas show. On the drive over he seemed kind of sad and down, but once he stepped in front of the microphone he perked right up and was back to being his old warm, charming, breezy self again. There was no mention of Mom's death. Someone who'd passed the last weeks living in a cave would never have known it had happened. Like a lot of performers, Dad felt the audience wasn't interested in your personal problems. All they wanted was the show, and that's what he gave them. With the help of his scriptwriters, I dusted off my own wisecracking persona and we went at each other with the standard good-natured give-and-take.

BING: Thank you . . . Thank you very much. Well, guest time has arrived, and our guest is a husky college lad who has been encouraged into the belief that he has a flair for singing . . . We shall see. Here then is Mr. Gary Crosby!
APPLAUSE

GARY: Thanks, Dad.

BING: Gary, Mr. John Scott Trotter and Tom Adair have come up with a flashy new arrangement of that old song "Jingle Bells," with parts for you and me and the Rhythmaires. You got your part there? Have you? Been studying? You got it down?

GARY: I am ready.

BING: That's what I like to hear . . . When I do a number with somebody, I like to have them on the ball . . . Anything you'd like to say to the folks before we launch into this thing?

GARY: Well, yes . . . yes, I would. I'd like to wish everybody a very Merry Christmas.

BING: That's nice of you.

177

GARY: And I'd also like to say that when we sing "Jingle Bells," *I* only assume responsibility for *half* of it.

BING: Now wait a minute . . . Let's not be cutting anything in half here . . . We are committed to do this song as a team, and joint responsibility will be shared.

GARY: All right, Dad . . . that's all right with me . . . But if *I* flop, you flop with me.

BING: Thank you for the note of false modesty . . . Great, great comfort to me . . . Now, Gary, shall we jingle those bells?

GARY: Sure.

BING: Then we're away!

Chapter Nine
Getting Out of It

Dad was even more withdrawn than usual after Mom died. When he wasn't busy cutting records over at Decca and doing his radio show, he kept to himself or took off for some fishing with Phil Harris or one of his other pals. If he happened to be home when the twins and I came down on vacation, he pretty much stayed in his end of the house and we stayed in ours. That suited me just fine. Since I was such a pain in the ass to him, I wasn't looking to be around him either.

After the funeral he had gone right back to being the same way he'd been with me before. He was still on my case about the weight, the drinking, the bad grades and all the other things that had him climbing the walls. For my part, I was still ignoring him, still wasting most of my days at Stanford screwing around, then barely managing to scrape through with the help of last-minute cram sessions. I wasn't consciously trying to upset him. I didn't want to challenge him or argue with him or fight him. The fact that my very life-style drove him nuts, well, that's how it was. If anything, the gap between us had grown even wider, so it was better for both of us if he went his way and I went mine.

The nights we were both home and the cook was making dinner, we might catch a glimpse of each other over the dining room table and exchange a couple of lines between bites before beating it back to our rooms. As always, the dialogue shied away from anything important. We never talked about my mother.

"Did you hear the show last night?" he might ask if he were in an especially good mood.

"Yeah," I would answer, "I heard it."

"How'd you like Rosie? Wasn't she great?"

"Yeah, she sang great."

"Which song did you like best?"

"Oh, I liked the way she did the first one."

"Uh-huh. Well, who else do you like? What other singers?"

"Well, I like Como . . . I like Ella Fitzgerald, Louis, Sinatra . . ."

I'd reel off a list of his favorites—people I liked too—but would steer clear of the rhythm and blues shouters and down home country wailers who meant just as much to me. The old man could be devastating about singers who didn't come up to his standards—I remember how he used to make fun of Vaughan Monroe for bleating through his nose—and I didn't want to get into any long, drawn-out arguments about why this one was good and that one was bad.

Mostly, though, I avoided even these brief encounters by making sure I wouldn't run into him. I geared my own coming and going to his hours, and when I knew he'd be staying home I'd find myself some reason to hit the streets. As far as I was concerned, we were just two strangers living in the same house.

Mom's death seemed to hit Denny harder than the rest of us. Linny was Dad's favorite, and the old man made a point of spending time with him to ease the pain of her passing. A few months after the funeral he pulled Lin out of high school before the semester ended and whisked him off to Europe for a three-month vacation. I was a real hard case by now and didn't let anything get to me. From what I could tell, Phil was pretty much the same. But Mom had been Denny's whole support system, constantly boosting his ego to make sure he realized he was as good as he really was, and once she died he seemed to feel that everyone on his side was gone. I suppose he figured that all that was left were people who didn't think he was much good, so therefore he wasn't much good. After the funeral he went back to Washington State to study animal husbandry and continued playing sports for a while, but he didn't really knuckle down. His incentive was gone, and it didn't much matter if he flunked a course or failed to make the team. All he wanted to do was get juiced. Nothing else interested him. He missed his mother a lot.

When the assistant coach had bawled out, "We don't want no Hollywood faggot playin' on this team!" and had yanked me from the starting lineup, there wasn't much doubt that my football career at Stanford was over before it had even begun. But I continued to hang in, hoping that somehow I'd find a chance to execute the hot play that would draw some kind of attention and turn it around for me. That's what had to happen if I was going to achieve my plan and make it all the way to the pros. I knew the odds were terrible, but I had to take the shot. There was too much riding on it to just throw up my hands and quit.

I kept at it all through my freshman season, and when April rolled around, instead of switching over to baseball I went out for spring practice. I could see that the baseball lineups were more or less set and they were going to stay with the excellent catcher they already had, so I figured I'd do myself more good by just concentrating on football. The following September I came back again and continued plugging away, but the big breakthrough I kept working and praying for still eluded me. I spent most practice sessions during the week holding the tackling dummies for the varsity and most Saturday afternoons warming the bench. And then, as the surgeon who had fixed my left shoulder had warned would happen if I didn't stop banging it around, it kept popping out on me again. To compensate for the injuries, I tried favoring my right side when I made a tackle, but you can't really get away with that, and after a while that shoulder started to go too.

When I showed up for spring practice the next April, a few months after Mom died, the coach announced he was switching me over from linebacker to offensive guard. I tried it for a couple of weeks even though the change didn't make much sense. I had never played offensive guard before, and it takes a special mentality to work that position. You have to be able to let a guy hammer your head in and just keep coming at him cold and cool until you get the job done, and I knew by now that if there was going to be a hitter and a "hit-ee" I had better be the hitter.

It was becoming crystal clear that ball playing just wasn't going to work out. I'd done everything I could, but I was fighting my way up a glass hill and couldn't get a foothold anywhere. The realization was devastating. I was so full of frustration, anger and hostility that for the first time in my life I stopped showing up for practice. After I missed a couple of sessions I had to tell myself, "What the hell, if I'm goin' to be like this, ain't no sense goin' out there." So, without saying anything to anyone, I went down to the clubhouse when I was sure it was empty, opened up my locker for the last time, turned in my gear and took a walk. I wasn't really quitting, I told myself. I was just facing reality.

I waited awhile before breaking the news to the old man. It would only give him one more reason to ride me about being a failure and a quitter and a fuckup. Eventually, though, I did have to tell him, and a few weeks later I casually dropped it on him when he called me from home.

"By the way, Dad, I'm not playing anymore."

"Oh, okay, yeah," was about all he had to say, and we never discussed it further. I was thankful that the expected lecture didn't come pouring out of the telephone, but at the same time I took his silence to mean he didn't really care. I figured he thought I could have made it if I had tried harder, but since he knew I was a quitter anyhow, it didn't make much difference. When I look at it now, I suspect he was relieved I was done with it and wouldn't be getting hurt anymore. After my shoulder operation the doctor had told him that I shouldn't be playing ball, and he had tried to talk me out of it, but of course I wouldn't listen to either of them.

Ball had been everything to me, and now that it had ended there was a big, aching hole in my life. For so many years I had been following exactly the same routine every autumn and spring afternoon. When it got to be three o'clock I'd hustle down to the clubhouse and start putting on the tape and my jock and the pads, then go out and practice, then come back and shower and hang out with the guys for a while before taking off to my room. It was the one part of my life I really enjoyed, and now all of a sudden I wasn't doing it anymore, and I just didn't know what else to do to fill in the spaces. Three o'clock would come. That old feeling would be there. But there was no place to go. It was over. It was over, and that hurt.

The guys I had played with were still my friends whenever I saw them, only now I didn't see them that much. They had different interests. They were down on the practice field. They were working out. They were going to games on weekends. The common ground where we used to meet wasn't there anymore. A few times I drifted over to the field and sat in the bleachers in my civilian clothes to watch them do what I would have loved to be out there doing with them. But it was too painful to have the loss of it parading in front of my face, and I soon gave it up. It was better to divorce myself from it altogether.

There were half a dozen other jocks in my fraternity in the same boat—they'd been injured or had busted out of the program or had gotten tired of fighting the odds—and we took to hanging out with each other. Three or four afternoons a week we'd get together and go out to a bar and sit around and juice, telling each other lies and laughing and joking while we waited for dark. We all missed it. An important part of our lives was gone, and nothing was there to take its place. We were so choked up with frustration that after a while we were ready to rip shit and tear ass out of everyone in sight. And that would happen. We would run into town guys or kids from other schools or other fraternities and get to arguing about nothing, or maybe they'd start in on the Crosby name and we'd answer them back with any nasty badmouth we could think of until they were angry enough to take the first swing and off we would go. I didn't give a damn if I won or lost. I just wanted to get it on, to rap somebody. It wasn't hard to arrange. Half the time all I had to do was not back down.

From what my buddies would tell me the next day, I was a happy, funny drunk for about an hour, and then I'd move into one of those black Irish moods and just sit there waiting to explode. I was a walking time bomb. I hated everything and everyone, most of all myself. Busting out of sports kind of made Dad's little prophecies about my future come true, and I bought the whole bill of goods he'd been selling me all those years. Yeah, I guess maybe he was right. I *was* stupid. I *was* fat and unattractive. I *couldn't* do anything right and *never would* amount to anything. Yet I can't say I much cared. Once in a while I'd think about how I was going to end up, and I'd tell myself, "Well, somebody will probably stick a knife in me or shoot me in some dumb brawl. Either that or I'll drink myself to death. But who gives a fuck? I'm nothing anyway. I don't matter."

Often, what started out as an afternoon of drinking with the guys wouldn't wind up until two in the morning, when they closed the bar down on us and threw us out into the street. The afternoons we broke up early I'd head back to the fraternity house and either hit the bottle I kept stashed in my desk or dig up a couple of other buddies who felt like going out to hoist a few. The next night they might have to study, but I'd find a couple of others to take their place. Then, the night after that, when it was their turn to hit the books, I'd scrounge up two more. On the weekends everybody drank, so finding company was no problem. Friday afternoons would start with the T.G.I.F. happy hours, where between five and seven you could slosh down all the double gibsons, manhattans and martinis you could handle for fifty cents apiece. Saturday night there were plenty of parties and dances, and even the nonalcoholic kids got fractured. Then on Sunday afternoon there were brunches with pitchers full of bloody marys that were supposed to fix you up and return you safely to real life. The normal kids would laugh about how drunk they got the night before, then they'd go back to work. Guys like me, though, were still out there boozing.

If nobody wanted to drink with me, I just hopped in my car and went out alone. There are always guys who want to drink in bars. Why else are they there? I'd hit certain joints all the time and run into the same people, and after a while I was enough of a habitué to pretty much call the shots as to who would be there what night. Or I'd meet up with someone who was looking for the same kind of action I was, and we'd run together for as long as the evening lasted.

There was a whole world of bars out there just waiting to be explored, and I made a pass over into all of them—from classy little piano bars in San Francisco to workingmen's joints in San Jose filled with tough dudes looking to get plotsed and start a riot, to shitkicker country bars where the most fun you could have in life was to get ripped, fight your best friend for an hour, then laugh like hell, sit back down together and get drunk some more. Most of the guys from Stanford were lovers, not fighters, and didn't much care to be around that kind of action. They liked to put on the neckties and sport coats and head for the nice places with the mai tais and pretty young ladies. That was cool too, but as long as I had a glass in my hand I could fit in anywhere. I didn't care what happened to me, so I had no fear about where the night might take me. In fact, the further down the social scale I traveled, the more comfortable I felt.

I thought I was ready for anything, but sometimes the surprises turned out to be even more than I could handle. That's what happened one night in San Francisco when I staggered to the back of the bar in search of the men's room. Somehow I went through the wrong door and found myself out in the alley. Through the darkness I made out another door in the building across the way, and without thinking too much about what I was doing I stepped around the garbage cans, opened it up and walked through. It was another joint, even sleazier than the one I had just left, but a bar was a bar and I flopped down on an empty stool and ordered up a double vodka. The next thing I knew a soft, feminine voice was whispering hello and a black net stocking with a leg in it was draped across my lap. I traced it back to its source and saw it belonged to a rather fine-looking woman who was waiting for me to light her cigarette. We got to talking about this and that, and before long it was closing time. But the night was still young.

"Listen, why don't we get some breakfast?" she asked. "There's a terrific after-hours joint in town where everyone goes to eat. Let me show it to you."

That sounded good to me.

"Sure. Great. Let's do it."

We necked a little out in the car. Then, after the ham and eggs, we headed over to her apartment to complete the scenario. She was already undressed and lying on the bed by the time I got my shirt off. When I looked over to catch a peek, I saw she was a guy, and I went crazy. This was 1953, and I carried with me all the fear and loathing of homosexuals that were part of that dumb decade. More than anything, I was furious that he thought he was going to fool me. I belted him a few times, working him over pretty good, then grabbed my shirt, raced outside to the car and sped away. The poor bastard didn't know what hit him. He must have assumed that since I was hanging out in a female impersonator bar I had to be there for a reason.

For the next six months I couldn't stop thinking about it. All the Hollywood faggot lines I'd been hearing forever now took on an added meaning, and I began to question whether or not they were true. Maybe I was a homosexual. Why else did he try to hustle me into bed? Something sure as hell was wrong with me. Maybe it was that. I kept the thought to myself—I was too closed in to talk about anything personal to anyone, much less something this shameful—but I kept brooding and sweating over the possibility. I didn't get past it until I was back up in San Francisco again for another night of boozing and wound up in the men's room in the bus terminal. I was standing at the urinal taking a leak when I tuned in on the two sailors peeing next to me.

"So what'd you do last night, man?" one asked the other.

"Aw, shit," he answered, breaking into a sheepish grin. "Don't you know I got juiced and went into one of them fag bars, and I thought she was a broad till I got to her room and then I found out it was a fuckin' guy. Jesus Christ, what an asshole I am. I was so stinkin' drunk I didn't even know where I was."

They were both still howling with laughter as they headed off to their bus. I must have stood there for ten minutes shaking with relief. The thought that it was no big deal, just a normal dopey thing that could happen to anyone instead of the earth-shaking trauma I had made of it gave me my whole life back.

Bar hopping gets to be expensive, and my sixty-dollar-a-month allowance didn't take me very far. But necessity is the mother, and one way or another I scratched up the money. I'd borrow it from friends, pay them back when my check came in, then borrow it again the next day. Certain joints knew a steady customer when they saw one and would run a tab on me for a while. I'd sell whatever came my way—jewelry, a watch or typewriter I was given for my birthday, even my clothes if anyone wanted them. When I was back home on vacation, I'd steal the odd twenty from Dad's wallet, never so much that he'd notice but enough to get me through another night of booze.

As to the larger problem of the booze itself, well, I didn't think I had a problem. I wasn't drinking more than anyone else I hung around with. Of course, I wasn't hanging around with anyone but drunks, but that little detail could be overlooked. It was the old story: Hey, I can quit whenever I want to . . . I just didn't want to. The old man and his friends and a few of my own pals would try to talk some sense into me, but I was such a jarhead by now that all you had to do was tell me to do something and I headed straight in the opposite direction. I suppose it should have been obvious that I was following in my mother's footsteps, but the connection never dawned on me, not even when I saw Denny and Phil falling into the same pattern. Sure, *she* had a problem. But not me. I'm just a drinker and a swinger and, whoopee, the life of the party. Well, after a while there isn't any party going on. You're just partying by yourself.

To protect myself against the secret fear that somebody might discover the real me, which I knew was nothing, I cooked up a fast-talking wiseguy personality that didn't give a damn about anything but having a good time.

Everything was hip and flip and cynical and delivered out of the side of my mouth at a hundred miles a minute. It was a good defense. Anytime people tried to get inside and ask a serious question, I just fluffed it off with a joke or sarcastic line.

"How does it feel to be Bing Crosby's son?"

"I don't know. How does it feel to be your father's son? . . . It feels blue. Orange, it feels."

"What do you mean?"

"I don't know what I mean. What do you think I mean?"

"Do you ever feel scared? Does anything ever worry you?"

"Ah, who cares how I feel? I feel like a banana, all right? How's that? Good enough for you? Now let's talk about something else."

A couple of months after I quit sports the initial shock began to wear off and I started playing a little intramural and outlaw ball once or twice a week with the other bustups, the guys with the bad knees and elbow braces. We'd play for the fraternity or a local tavern for a case of beer, and that wasn't too bad. Once I moved into the rhythm of the game, it meant just as much to me as if I were competing in the Rose Bowl. It didn't matter if you were hung over while playing those games. Some guys came out half whacked and played.

I was too out of shape to be much good. The boozing and lack of exercise had taken their toll, and I had blown up to over 225 pounds. When I saw myself in the mirror, I looked like a basketball with arms. I wanted to lose the weight but wasn't about to quit drinking, so I figured I'd quit eating. Well, the way to quit eating was to get some diet pills. I made an appointment with a doctor and pitched him in my most sincere manner.

"Gosh, Doc, I'm trying to thin down, y'know, but I can't stop eating. I'm so frustrated, it's just too much for me. I don't know what to do."

Sure enough, five minutes later I was back on the street with a prescription for a month's worth of uppers clutched in my hot little fist.

At first I took them one at a time like he told me, and they did the job just fine. I never ate and, Jesus, I felt terrific. I was wide awake and my mind was racing on all cylinders and my mouth didn't stop moving. A couple of weeks later, though, one at a time wasn't doing it for me anymore, so I started popping two at a shot, then three, then four. I was determined to climb back up there again no matter what it took. I didn't care if I had to swallow a whole barrel of them. Pretty soon I was talking like a tape recorder on fast forward and my teeth were clenched so tight my jaws ached and my eyeballs were popping out of my skull. But everything was still wonderful, wonderful, wonderful until it got to be come down time. Then the paranoia, hostility and depression took over, and the snakes invaded my brain. Just going to the bathroom was a three-act play, and it was impossible to sleep without getting drunk and popping some downers. They weren't that hard to come by either. All I had to do was dig up another doctor and lay the same kind of riff on him. "Gosh, Doc, I have a lot of trouble sleeping . . ."

After a while my upper connection began to back off on me.

"Gee, I don't know," he answered when I came in for a new prescription. "I've been giving you a lot of these things the last couple of months. You've got to start tapering off. This stuff is for dieting. You're supposed to kill your appetite and then you come off the pills, see, and your appetite is down. That's how you lose the weight."

"Oh, right, Doc. I get it. Thanks a lot."

I headed straight for another doctor. By the time he started to catch on, I knew my way around well enough to be able to score whatever I needed off the street. It was always better to cop from the doctors because then the bill went home to the old man. He didn't realize uppers were bad for you and thought I was trying to do something about my weight. But one way or another I got by.

If I managed to pull myself out of bed before afternoon, I might still make it to class, even though it was a complete waste of time. The uppers and downers and boozing were the main focus of my life now, and that's all I could think about. While the instructor droned on about the importance of D. W. Griffith or the rise of English culture in the sixteenth century, my head was too filled with other things to even hear him. Where am I gonna get the money to get drunk tonight? What bar will I hit? Will I see this chick there? Have I got enough pills to last me for the weekend? Should I make a call? Should I not? As far as I was concerned, everything else was bullshit. All I wanted to do was get high, get out of it, get away—from myself mostly.

The closest I came to cleaning up was the three-week period before finals. Then I'd cut off the booze, double up on the bennies and get the crash marathons going with the smart guys. After a while I had it down to a science, and it became kind of a personal challenge to see if I could blast a term's worth of work into my head in a couple of weeks. "Wonder if I'm gonna be able to do it again," I'd ask myself, "fool these assholes and make them think they're educating me." However it ended, whether I passed by the skin of my teeth or failed miserably, I celebrated by getting uproariously drunk throughout the holidays.

The vacation juicing always had to be done in a rush. I may have been twenty years old now, but I was still due back at the house by ten-thirty during the week and midnight Friday and Saturday. If there was a party, I'd be the first one to show up and the first one to leave, but in between I'd belt down enough doubles to float a battleship. Or I'd run off to one of the joints in town that would slip me drinks if they weren't too crowded and no one was around checking IDs. The nights the heat was on and the bartender shook his head when I dashed in, I'd turn on my heels and double-time it down the road to the next bar that would serve me.

If the old man was away, the twins and I might buy our own jug and get wasted at home. We never went near his liquor cabinet. Georgie could read the bottle levels like a clock, and the last thing we wanted was to get caught tapping his private stash. Every now and then he'd surprise us by coming back early, but no matter how smashed we were we straightened up the instant he walked into the room.

"Hi, Dad, how are ya? How's everything? Good."

We might be practically in a coma, but we'd hold up our end of the small talk without fluffing a word, making perfect sense until he took off upstairs. Then we'd collapse like somebody had just cut the string in our necks.

Sometimes he'd throw us a funny look and ask if we'd had a few. We'd flat out deny it and tell him what he wanted to hear.

"Nah, we're just waitin' around to go out to a party."

"Well, okay, but don't you be drinking."

Our answers seemed to satisfy him, but I doubt if he was fooled for a second. He seemed to know every detail of everything we did, almost as if he had hired a private detective to dog our footsteps. Maybe he did. To this day I don't know for sure. When I was younger that used to amaze me. While he was laying into me, I'd think to myself, "Goddam, the sonofabitch sure has it down cold. How the hell does he know what went on?" By now, though, it didn't make any difference how he knew, and that was liberating in a way. I didn't flaunt the drinking at him. I didn't get stoned in front of him. But neither did I worry much about hiding what I was up to once I left the house. He was sure to find out anyhow.

Some nights my carryings-on were so outrageous he'd have to have been deaf and blind not to know about them. There was so much anger bubbling inside me that after a few drinks almost anything could bring it boiling to the surface. That's what happened the evening I wandered into Ciro's and found myself sitting across from one of Dad's fans. The man took one look at me and immediately started in on what a great guy my father was and how proud I ought to be that I was his son, and how his father was a great guy too and how proud he was to be his father's son. On and on he went with his fathers and sons, sons and fathers, until I had just about all I could stomach.

"Tell you what," I said to him. "Tonight let's take your father and my father and shove 'em both up your ass, all right?"

He was an older, gray-haired man who looked fat in a suit, but he was built like a block of granite and his right hand moved so fast I didn't see it coming until it whacked me in the middle of the forehead and sent me flying backwards. I skidded across the dance floor on my shoulder blades, then sprung up and started to go for him, but the waiters and bouncers jumped all over me and enveloped me with weight until I had cooled off enough to be hustled peacefully outside. I don't know if the story made the gossip columns the next morning, but there were enough high rollers in the audience to guarantee it would be all over Beverly Hills by breakfast.

Georgie loved me in her way, and when she caught me moping around the house nursing my hangover she did what she could to get me to straighten up.

"Now, Gary," she'd implore, "you shouldn't be running out like that every night. You shouldn't be drinking so much."

"Oh, Georgie, come on," I'd answer, trying to hold on to my patience but not doing a very good job of it. "Would you shut up? Leave me alone, will ya? You're not my mother and you're not my father and you're not my nurse anymore. You know, I'm grown now. There's nothing you can do to me now, so just relax. I'll be all right."

"Well, I hope so."

The tears would be streaming down her face, but they didn't get to me. She had beat on me too much when I was small. I didn't want to hurt the woman, but I wasn't about to let her interfere with my life.

I was the same way with the old man whenever he decided it was time for another lecture about my fighting.

"You can't get down to their level," he'd intone from behind his desk. "If somebody gives you trouble, you rise above it and walk away."

That's what he had always said, and it didn't make any more sense now than when I was a ten-year-old scrapping in the school yard.

"How the hell can you rise above anything by walking away from it?" I wanted to ask him. "If you don't confront it, it's gonna ride right up your ass. Walk away from some guy in a bar and he'll just follow you out to the car. He'll follow you home. He'll be looking for you the next night and the night after that. Because now he knows he's got a pigeon. He's got a guy he can look good in front of. He's got a guy he can insult and push around and do whatever he wants to, so it's a license to steal. Guys that want to fight all the time, they don't look on walking away as any sign of superiority. They look on that as if you're a chickenshit. And that's their meat. And the sonsofbitches ain't never gonna back off until you turn around and confront them. So why not do it right off the bat and get it out of the way? 'You can't get down to their level' my ass. Man, you're playing in their ball park. You gotta get down to their level. You can't just sit back and be reasonable and charming and civilized. You'll get tromped on."

But of course I couldn't tell him that. I could only repeat what I always told him whenever he called me on the carpet.

"Yeah, you're right. You're right, Dad. I shouldn't do that. Okay, I won't do it anymore."

Meanwhile I'd be sneaking a look at the clock to see how late he was making me for going off to do it again.

I must have been paying more attention than I realized. One afternoon I found myself reaching for the telephone to dial Dr. Sturdevant, Mom's old shrink. Not that I could admit it to my father or even, really, to myself, but underneath all the self-justifications I knew something was wrong with me and I could use some help. Dr. Sturdevant seemed to have been able to help my mother, at least temporarily. Even if he couldn't get her off the bottle for good, she did manage to stay straight during those five- or six-week periods when she saw him every day. Eventually she always went back to it, but, who knows, I reminded myself, without him she might not even have had those times of hope.

About eight or nine years ago, when Sturdevant had been at the house for her session, he had told me I ought to see him. I had been chasing after Denny for socking me on the arm when I wasn't looking, and as usual the little bastard ran me around in circles until I was exploding with rage. Sturdevant had witnessed the scene from Mom's window, and on the way to the car he stopped to talk with me for a minute while I was still doubled over trying to catch my breath. "I think you should start seeing me," he said, "because you get too angry. I don't like that kind of anger. You're going to kill somebody for sure someday." At the time I thought he was full of shit, like every other adult I knew, and brushed him off, but now it seemed to me it might not be such a bad idea to dust off the old invitation and hear what he had to say.

He didn't say much. He just sat there at his desk, with his yellow pad in front of him, his pipe in his mouth and his foot hooked over a drawer, and when I asked him a question he asked me one back.

"What's wrong with me, Doc? Why am I like I am?"

"Well, what do you think? Why do you think you are like you are?"

"Well, hell, Doc, I don't know what to think. If I knew I wouldn't have to ask you."

His only answer was a meaningful silence that kept him well out of arm's reach.

We went on and on like that for the full fifty minutes. It was almost as if I were back trying to catch Denny again, and by the end of the session I was just as choked up with frustration and anger. I was looking for instant help but was too ignorant to understand that Freudian therapy doesn't work that way. I thought I was wasting my time, but for a while, anyway, I kept on seeing him whenever I came home on vacation. There was nowhere else to turn, and at least it allowed me to spew out a lot of venom at the old man, though even that didn't seem to get me anywhere.

"How do you feel today?"

"I feel okay. A bit hung over . . . and, oh, mad."

"Well, what are you mad at?"

"Oh, I don't know. Just mad at everything and everybody."

"Uh-huh. Well, why are you mad?"

"I don't know, Doc. Why *am* I mad?"

"Well, I don't know either. Give me an example. What are you mad at?"

"Okay. Well, I'm mad at the old man."

"I see. Why are you mad at your father? Can you give me a reason?"

"I'm mad at him because he's bugging me about the fighting and drinking. I'm mad at him because he's driving me fucking nuts with all his rules and regulations. I'm mad at him because I'm such a pain in the ass to him. Okay?"

"Oh? . . . Well, what do you think you ought to do about it?"

"Goddamit, what kind of shit question is that? That's why I'm here!"

"No, you're not here for that. You're here to try to find out about yourself."

"Yes, Doctor. Wonderful. Well, obviously I have no answers. Now could you possibly give me some?"

"No, I'm not in the business of giving answers. I'm in the business of helping you find out about yourself."

"Okay, Doctor. Fine."

"So why do you think you can't get along with your father?"

"Hey, I can't get along with him because he's too fucking strict! That's why I can't get along with him."

"Well, so don't you think you might tell him that?"

"Tell *him* that? What? I'm not gonna tell him anything! The man's God! *He's* gonna listen to *me* tell him what I think's wrong with him? Are you fuckin' crazy?"

At the end of the hour I'd usually go steaming out of his office and head straight for the nearest bar.

Chapter Ten
The Magic Age

From the time I was a small kid I could hardly wait until I reached the magic age of twenty-one. I counted off the months and years like a con sweating out his jail sentence. Every time the old man laid some shitty job on me, every time I was disappointed, every time I couldn't get to do what I wanted, all I could think was, "Man, twenty-one. When I'm twenty-one nobody ever again tells me what to do." I had it all planned out. I made lists in my head.

To my way of thinking, whatever the old man wanted was bullshit and whatever I wanted was how it was going to be, and neither he nor anyone else better fuck with me or tell me no. "Once I'm twenty-one I'm through paying dues," I'd say to myself. "From that moment on everybody else is gonna have to pay. If you leave me alone I won't bother you, but if you get in my way I'll stomp all over your ass." Which was a terrific attitude. Walk around like that with a chip on your shoulder the size of a two-by-four and you're sure to get mangled.

By the spring of 1954 the magic day was almost at hand. Not that I had breathed a word of my intentions to the old man, but I guess he read them clear enough. At the very least he knew he wasn't about to ship me off to the ranch again when school let out in June, and I suppose he figured he had to come up with something to keep me out of trouble for the summer. One evening during Easter vacation he just casually dropped it on me over dinner.

"Listen, Gary, I'm gonna go on my summer vacation from the show in a few months, and we want you to take it over. It'll be for thirteen weeks, and then we'll see what happens from there, after you graduate from college."

The way he delivered the last line, there was no doubt in his mind that I *would* go back to Stanford and keep plugging away till I graduated, but I let that pass. If I had been capable of gratitude I would have thanked him profusely. As it was, I just mumbled my usual, "Oh, okay, Dad. Fine. Whatever you say," almost as if nothing had happened.

It was a huge break, and I knew it. Now that sports had given me up, I still had to do something with my life, and the way I saw it I only had two choices: manual labor or show business. The more I thought about putting in ten hours a day busting my butt on someone's ranch the better show business began to look. And the truth of the matter is, even if I didn't think I was much good, I was beginning to enjoy it. Over the last few years there had been more "Gary Crosby and Friend" records, and during the past season Dad had brought me on the radio more than a dozen times. I knew I still had a long way to go before I could stand on my own two feet, but at least I was starting to get comfortable with the idea of becoming a professional.

"Okay, so you got a break," I told myself later that night when I began beating myself up for accepting the old man's generosity. "Hey, a lot of guys out there would gladly give their left nut for that kind of shot, but they never get it. So go on and do it and do the best you can, and maybe if you hold it together you can move on from there to springboard out on your own."

Looking at it now, it seems pretty clear that in turning over his show the old man was also putting out a hand and trying to reach me. My drinking and fighting and temper were really starting to concern him. It just wasn't his style to come right out and say so. The gift of the show was supposed to tell me what he meant. Every now and then I'd catch myself thinking, "Hey, he wouldn't be handing this thing over to a guy he believed was gonna fuck it up, so maybe he does have *some* faith in you." But before I could follow the thought down to its logical conclusion I'd tell myself, "Yeah, well, maybe he's fixing it so you *do* fuck up, so you'll be humbled enough to do things his way." By now any gestures of friendship he offered were automatically ignored. "Want to go out for dinner tomorrow night?" he might ask, and I'd rebuff him with a fast "No, I don't think so" before he even finished the question. As far as I was concerned, it *was* too late. I was too far gone in my anger and hatred to wipe the slate clean and start up a new relationship with him.

The CBS press release proclaimed that this was my first venture into show business strictly on my own, but about the only thing I did strictly on my own was open my mouth. The shows followed exactly the same format as the old man's and were put together by the same bunch of top people. Bill Morrow and Tom Adair still did the writing, Murdo McKenzie directed, Bill Thompson looked after the vocals, and Ken Carpenter was the announcer and straight man. The guys had been working with Dad forever and had the thing down pat, so it was like slipping into the old man's rocking chair for the summer. All I had to do was go along with the routine—sing the songs they handed me and say the lines—and if I did get something wrong we could always stop the tape and start over again. I had a lot of help, especially from Bill Thompson, who showed me how to sing from the diaphragm, the right way to support a note and all the other basic techniques you're supposed to know before you get to the point of headlining your own series.

There was no way for me to lose unless I failed to show up or started a fight with someone, and I wasn't about to do that. I had known Murdo and Morrow and the others since I was a kid. They were like my uncles, and I could see how they were knocking themselves out to give me the support I needed. When you feel that kind of goodness coming at you, you'd have to be a complete idiot not to give it back. More than anything, I was determined to show the old man I wasn't a fuckup. These guys were all his friends, and the last thing I wanted was to create any problems or ugly scenes that would get back to him. Even when I read through my lines and saw that the language and rhythms were constructed so like my father's that I couldn't help but talk like him, I kept my mouth shut, though it made me a little hinky.

"If that's how you have to start, then that's how you have to start," I reminded myself. "Ain't no sense denying you're his son. People are going to expect a certain amount of that from you anyway, and it is his show, so don't make waves. Just do what they tell you. Someday—next year, the year after that—you'll have the chance to be yourself. Don't get cocky. Remember, there are a lot of hungry guys out there with a lot more talent than you who ain't getting anywhere near these breaks, so you better not waste them. You better make them pay off."

The day-to-day working atmosphere on the show was loose and happy and funny. Bill Morrow even had fun with the fact that Dad and I weren't getting along. From all the hours he had spent hunting and fishing with the old man, he knew we were battling, so when it came time to write the script that would be aired on Father's Day, the temptation to slip in a little reality was too great to resist.

KEN: Okay, Gary! . . . Nice lively beginning!

GARY: Thank you, Ken! Thank you.

KEN: But say, tell me—what made you select an *old* song like that for your opener?

GARY: Well, Ken, I'm just following some advice I read in the paper last week.

KEN: Yeah?

GARY: It said that young singers should use material that they know is good. They shouldn't try to sing a lot of new songs.

KEN: Well, the old ones are usually surefire.

GARY: That's what this fellow said . . . and I intend to go right along with his recommendation.

KEN: Well, I guess you should . . . that is, if this fellow knows anything about show business.

GARY: Oh, this fellow's pretty active in the business.

KEN: Who is it?

GARY: My poppa!

KEN: Oh, *him!*

GARY: That's the guy!

KEN: Well, Gary, I'm sure your dad will be very pleased—very happy to know that you read—and are *taking* his advice.

GARY: Well, Ken, it's the least I could do today . . . After all, it is Father's Day!

KEN: Proper timing, I'd say.

GARY: Buying dear old Dad a necktie is one thing, but taking his advice—that's what *really* makes him happy!

KEN: My boy—as a father of long standing, I must say you've made a very neat point there . . . If you kids would only listen to us!

GARY: Oh, Ken, I think most young people *listen* . . . They just don't *hear* anything—that's all.

KEN: Well, that's the trouble. It doesn't even go in one ear and out the other . . . If only advice could be, well, *injected* into you kids like penicillin.

GARY: Gulping it down in candy-coated tablet form might be pleasant.

KEN: Yeah—Or if it could only be rubbed in like liniment.

GARY: I've had quite a bit of it *thumped* into me!

KEN: Well, a little thumping doesn't seem to have hurt you any. You know the old saying, Gary—"Spare the rod and spoil the child."

GARY: Yeah yeah, "Spare the rod and spoil the child" and "This hurts me more than it does you"—How often have I heard that corn while I was down on my knees begging for mercy!

KEN: Yeah—I'll bet!

GARY: Just trying to have a little fun, Ken . . . And in order to clean this whole matter up, I wish to state that my reason for singing "Row Row Row" tonight had nothing to do with the fact that my father paddled my canoe now and then!

KEN: That's for the record, is it?

GARY: That's for the record!

When I rehearsed the lines for the first time, I threw a look over at the control booth, and Bill was cackling away like a maniac. He loved to write that kind of cheeky, inside dialogue. If he could tip into what was really happening but put humor around it so it wouldn't inflame the Great Bald Eagle, and if the people out there still found it funny even if they didn't actually know what we were talking about, he considered it quite a feather in his cap.

If Dad thought handing over the show for the summer would get me to straighten up he was half right. From the start of rehearsals Monday afternoon to the taping Thursday evening, I cut way back on the booze. I had work to look forward to. I was doing something positive and creative. For the first time since I stopped playing ball, I felt that all my energies were flowing in the right direction. After work the cast and production staff would head across the street to the Villa Capri for dinner and a couple drinks and I'd tag along with them, but we all had business to take care of the next day so no one got really wasted. Once we finished taping, though, I had nothing to do with myself until Monday and slid right back into my old habits.

The low point was Sunday night, when the show was aired. Then I'd tote a jug up to my room, close the door behind me, turn on the radio and listen for all my mistakes. Just one and the rest of the show was ruined for me and I'd get myself thoroughly whacked. It didn't matter if everything else went fine. I wasn't looking to take any bows for not messing up. Some nights I'd be able to rise above the frustration and disappointment by telling myself, "Well, maybe you'll do better next week." Other nights I was so despondent I'd think about quitting. "What the fuck am I doing? I don't belong in this business. Man, if you can't sing better than that you ought to fold it up."

When I came back to the studio the next day, I'd head straight for Bill Thompson and itemize each and every flat note I hit.

"Will you stop, for Chrisake!" he'd answer. "You think anybody in the world heard that but you? I was listening. I didn't even hear it."

"Bullshit, you didn't hear it. Your ears are better than that."

"Well, so you bent a note a little. What the hell is that? That's no crime."

To me it was. If it wasn't perfect it was worthless. It didn't even cross my mind that I was playing in a league with top professionals who weren't in the business of putting out bad shows, and if they okayed my songs they couldn't have been too awful. I simply figured, "Hell, they're just being nice to me. They think maybe it's cute that a guy twenty-one years old still sings flat, Dad's son and all that shit."

I got myself so crazy that by the middle of the season I broke my vow not to make waves and started pestering Bill to let me do a song over again as soon as I heard the slightest flaw on the playback.

"No, it's all right," he'd try to tell me. "So it's not exactly right on the button, but, my God, you're not singing flat. You're not singing flat enough to notice."

"Well, I can notice. It's driving me nuts. Let's do it again."

Dad was out of town for the summer, and I had very little direct feedback from him. Every now and then Morrow or Murdo might drop a casual line to let me know he'd been listening, but for the most part that was it.

"By the way, talked to your dad the other day. He called in to say that, geeze, you're doing a terrific job. He liked what he heard a lot."

"Well, that's good. Wonderful," I'd answer, not quite believing it was true, and then try to move on to another subject.

According to a review of the opening show in *Time* magazine that I didn't read till years later, he kept his hand in a lot more than it seemed.

". . . And to top off the talent, Gary had his father coaching him from the sidelines. Bing, according to Morrow, 'is overseeing —not as a stage mother, but as an interested, proud parent who wants everything proper and in good taste. He doesn't tell Gary what to do, but he suggests things or changes, and Gary and I had better do it!' Among the changes before the premiere: A veto on 'I Get So Lonely' and 'Make Love to Me'—fine for adults to sing but not for Gary. Considered more appropriate for a Stanford University student were 'Oh, Baby Mine,' 'You Were Meant for Me,' 'No Teardrops Tonight' and 'Crystal Ball.' . . . 'Bing throws out anything he feels is too sexy for Gary,' says Morrow, and the father does not even want the son's dialogue 'too flip or too hep.'"

With one large exception, all that may be true. It sounds like the old man. It was always important to him that his show maintain a certain wholesome, clean-cut air, and even a pop song of the day that had a slight sexual connotation could cause him trouble. When it came to his work, he had very pristine attitudes. I remember him telling me how he had been approached several times to play Vegas for huge amounts of money but wouldn't do it because he didn't want it on his conscience that one guy came there to see him and in the process lost his house and car and all his money at the tables. It seemed to me a pretty long shot that something like that might happen, but that's how he was. That wasn't just a line he handed the press. In his later years, when the movies loosened up in the way they treated sex, he had a hell of a time finding a script that met his moral standards.

But if he was coaching me from the sidelines that summer, I wasn't aware of it. Whatever supervising he did was strictly from around the corner, quietly passed on through Murdo or Morrow so I couldn't see where it was coming from. And that was smart of him. He knew he was losing his grip on me. He knew how I felt about him. I was twenty-one now. Don't tell me nothing. I don't give a damn if it is good for me, I don't want to hear it. But whatever Murdo and Morrow told me I went along with. Why not? Hell, they'd been around show business since before I was born. They weren't out to screw me. Of course I was going to take the benefit of their experience, just like I did with my coaches when I played ball. Bill was one of the best comedy writers on radio. Murdo had been producing a hit show for years.

Dad did his best to give me breathing room, but old habits die hard. Every few weeks there'd be a letter from him in the mail full of criticism and admonitions. They always took the same form: "The show was good *but . . .*" *But* the ballad was a little leaky. *But* you should talk slower. *But* you need to do more practice work.

If part of his motivation was to keep me from coming down with the dreaded Big Head, I'm sure he was also trying to help me become a better performer. Looking at the letters now, I can see that the disparagements really aren't all that severe. At the time, though, I only saw more faultfinding, more reinforcement of the negative. I already had so much full-blown negativity working on me from inside and so little self-confidence that the smallest grain of criticism from him was transformed into a huge mountain of disapproval, one more thing he was on my ass about that I wasn't going to listen to. "Sure," I'd tell him in my imagination, "you never sang a bad note in your life. How do you know what it's like?"

Had I uttered the words out loud, he probably wouldn't have understood why I was kicking up such a fuss. It wasn't as if he said I was doing terribly and the show was bad. He never was too handy with a compliment, not with anyone. "True, I'm not very effusive," he told an interviewer toward the end of his life. "I'm not very demonstrative. I just never have been. My mother was that way—my father was just the opposite. I don't know why, it's just something I inherited. I may think a lot of a person, but I seldom tell them so."

In any case, it soon got so that the moment I took one of his letters out of the envelope my eyes darted straight for the "but," and when I found it I threw the damn thing in the garbage without reading any further. So far as I was concerned, I didn't have to. It was just more of his usual bullshit, and I was tired of hearing it.

By the third week in August the series was over and my brothers were back from Elko.

"Shit, you get to stay home and we had to go up to the ranch and work like slaves."

"Yeah, assholes. Well, I was up there a year ahead of you, so this just evens it out."

"Yeah, but you got a summer off when you were seventeen and hurt your shoulder."

"I'll go break the other shoulder. Will that be all right? Will that make it even?"

"Aw, bullshit, you get away with murder. Did you have a nice summer sitting on your ass?"

"I didn't sit on my ass. I worked the radio show."

"Yeah, yeah, we know how much work that is."

The best thing about the summer was Betty Clooney, Rosie's kid sister. Rosie was one of the old man's favorite singing partners, and I had known her so long she was almost like family. The first time I met Betty was when she turned up at the studio that June afternoon to rehearse the guest spot for the second show. I think I must have loved her right from the start.

I loved her looks: the long, thick brown hair; the warm, wide, generous mouth; the bright brown eyes that always seemed to be smiling; the friendly, open face that showed everything and would suddenly explode into laughter. I loved her talent: the deep, warm voice that sounded so much like her sister's but still had its own personality; the wonderful sense of rhythm and phrasing. Most of all, I loved the way she enjoyed life. She was up and bright and positive—everything I wasn't. She loved her mother and her brother and sister, and she loved her work. Not that she hadn't had her share of hard career knocks, but she was happy with what she was doing and looked forward to doing better. She and Rosie had been on the road together since they were kids singing with Tony Pastor's band, but the same experiences that made Rosie hip and sharp and aware of how the game was played didn't seem to have touched Betty at all. She wasn't naive. She didn't deny the rotten things that can happen to a young woman in the business. She just didn't dwell on them and let them get to her.

The first afternoon of rehearsals I played Charlie Host—"Hey, how are ya? Glad to have ya on the show!"—and spent my breaks fooling around with Bill Morrow. But the next day we started talking, and all my bullshit Mr. Cool persona just quietly melted away. Before I even knew what happened, she had disarmed me completely. I didn't feel like she'd hurt me. I didn't feel like I had to throw up a front. She put me immediately at ease. It was like I had known her all my life. By the time we played the broadcast on Thursday I was so hung up standing six inches away from her at the microphone that I damn near forgot to say my lines.

For the lead-in to her solo Morrow had put together some mildly flirtatious college boy dialogue—the same kind of stuff he wrote whenever there was a good-looking girl on the show—and I made a point of reading it very straight and off the cuff. I meant it about ten times more than he intended and wasn't about to let anyone see how I really felt.

After her solo we moved on to the duet. The key we sang in was completely compatible. There was no stretching, no problems of any kind, and our voices blended together like we'd been singing harmony forever. The feeling between us was so good I didn't want the duet to ever stop.

The way she got to me scared the hell out of me at first, and I tried to stay away from her. Other than hookers, the only women I felt comfortable with were wild, funny, hip, semitragic pill takers and boozers, crazy people like myself. At least you knew where you stood with them. If they liked you they went to bed with you, and there was no big deal about it—no guilt, no remorse, no heavy emotional commitment. Everything stayed right on the surface exactly where it belonged. You popped some pills and split a jug. You laughed and talked and cried together. You made love. Then you both moved on to someone else. Neither of you expected any more than what you got, and that was fine. Having someone to share the load with for a while wasn't too bad. But this other thing was too confusing.

There had been times in college when I'd gone with nice, square girls for a few weeks or months, but I always reached the point where I had to cut it off. "Okay, this is about due to end," I would tell myself. "This is not the kind of girl you just fuck and laugh and giggle with, and when it's over it's over. This is the kind of girl you fall in love with, the kind of girl you marry. And that's not for you, man. You can't handle that shit." It wasn't that I didn't like them. Maybe I was afraid I liked them too much.

Rather than saying, "Okay, I'll stop using and boozing, I'll straighten up," I'd just walk away. I'd disappear on them or act like such an asshole that it would be easy for them to drop me. I'd make a date and not show up or pick a lot of stupid fights, and if that didn't work I'd go out with someone else and make sure the word got back.

I tried running the same tape with Betty, but it didn't play. "I'm no good for her," I'd tell myself. "This will never work. She's good and I'm bad." But then I'd answer, "Yeah, well, I'll change, that's all. I'll live straight." And that really scared the bejesus out of me. But I wasn't all that much in love with what I was doing anyway—fucking up, fighting, juicing, wrestling around. You get the style and then you get the rep and pretty soon that's what you're living every day, even more than you want to. I suppose I was ready for a change.

Still, it was amazing to find myself acting like a gentleman whenever I came near her. I was a nice guy again, doing all the square, jerky things I used to put down. I'd call her up and ask for a date, then take her to a movie or out to dinner, someplace nice where I didn't go to juice and nobody knew me. Maybe I'd even put on a necktie. I'd still drink, but I wouldn't get crazy. Or we'd go for long walks and talk for hours about whatever was on our minds. She'd tell me stories about living in Kentucky and Cincinnati, her parents' divorce, and her brother Nick, who was a songwriter, and what it was like singing on the road with Rosie. I'd talk about my brothers and the old man and how different it was at home from what people thought. Mostly, though, I told her about how much I loved her. I don't think I'd ever told anyone that before. I'd always kept myself from feeling it. But once I felt it it wasn't hard to say. The words just tumbled out of my mouth.

Betty was based in New York, where she worked with Jack Paar and Arthur Godfrey. When she flew home I called her almost every day. Luckily, though, she had been booked for three more guest shots on the show, so she kept coming back to L.A. Whenever she was in town she stayed with Rosie and her husband, Joe Ferrer, and I spent as much time as I could hanging out at the house with all three of them.

Joe wasn't landing much movie work then, but he refused to let it get him down. He decided he would return to Broadway to do musical comedy, and the fact that he wasn't a singer didn't deter him for a minute. He was such a fierce worker and had such guts and incredible self-confidence—the word "can't" wasn't even in his vocabulary—that once he made up his mind he just threw himself into learning how. He hired a singing coach and spent hours every day practicing, banging the walls down with his huge voice. At first he was terrible. I may have sung a little flat, but this joker seemed hopeless. Rosie would throw me a look and go "M-m-m," and I'd think to myself, "Oh boy, you're gonna sing on Broadway with that?" But he kept right on running scales, giving it everything he had. He wasn't the least bit shy about it. He'd sing flat notes dead in your face and damn near make you believe them. "I'm gonna get it yet," he'd laugh. "Some fucking way I'm gonna get it." And he did. By the end of the summer he was a good singer, and when he eventually went on to play *Man of La Mancha* he did a hell of a job. If there was a lesson to be learned from that kind of optimism, I didn't see it.

I think Betty loved me a little. I think she might have loved me a lot more if I hadn't scared her off. But the drinking and the cynicism and the hard-ass attitude finally got to her. She just wasn't that way. I wasn't that way with her either, but that's how she saw me with other people. Even though I was in love, my anger at life still seethed just below the surface, and once I had a few drinks in me and got to feeling half mean it didn't take much to set it off. A stranger might throw me a funny look across a restaurant or ask, "How's your father?" in the wrong tone of voice, and I'd be scraping my chair away from the table ready to do battle. The moment I remembered she was with me I immediately calmed myself down, but when I glanced over she'd still be looking all nervous and concerned.

"Hey, don't worry," I'd reassure her. "It's all right."

"Yeah, but it upsets me," she'd answer. "I don't like to see you so angry. It's not that big a thing."

"Well, yeah, to you it isn't. And maybe not to someone else. But I don't know, to me it is."

Then I'd spend the rest of the night apologizing for acting like such an asshole.

After a while she would seem to relax and get back to her old cheerful self. But that kind of rage takes its toll. When you see it flaring up again and again, it gets to be frightening. And she saw things. I was not above banging walls and doors and punching my fists through closets. I think she probably loved the part of me that was with her when we were alone. But as soon as we stepped into the world I turned into someone else, and she didn't care for that guy at all. If there were other people around I automatically went on the defensive, and that included becoming a wiseguy, giving and taking with my mouth, and being ready at a moment's notice to back it up with my fists.

When the summer ended I went back to Stanford and Betty went back to her work in New York. I missed her so much I called her constantly all hours of the day and night just to hear the sound of her voice. We'd shoot the breeze about the business and talk about our lives and families—how her brother was doing in Kentucky and what was happening with her mother, who shared an apartment with her in the city. As always, she would be full of enthusiasm, looking at the up side of everything, and I'd be just the opposite.

"Hey, I got a new job today!" she'd announce, all bright and bubbly. "Isn't that great?"

"Yeah, that really is," I'd answer, trying to match her mood. "Congratulations!"

I loved the happiness in her and never wanted to bring her down with my own doom and gloom, but that was me and there was no way to get around it.

"Uh, they're talkin' about some kind of contract with CBS when I finish school, but I don't know. Jesus, Betty, I want to get jobs and do things because they want me for myself, not for the name."

"Well, that's why you are getting them. You're not getting them because of the name. You're getting them because you're good."

"Yeah, well, I don't know. I'm not that good yet. I haven't had that much experience at it. I haven't been around long enough to be gettin' that kind of deal."

Often I'd be loaded when we talked, and that put her off as much as the negativity and anger. She was listening to a guy slowly killing himself one shot glass at a time, and that was so far away from her own experience she didn't know how to handle it.

I guess I was so much in love I wouldn't let myself see the danger signals. All I could think about was how, when I finally put school behind me, either I'd move to New York or she'd come out to Los Angeles and we'd get married and live happily ever after. As the months went by, though, it became hard to overlook the fact that she was starting to be out a lot when I called and sometimes she didn't call back. Finally one night when she wasn't home I just had to ask her mother about it.

"Fran, what the hell's going on? What's wrong?"

Gary, Bing and John Scott Trotter, 1963. (courtesy American Broadcasting Company, Inc.)

Kathryn, Bing, Barbara and Gary, 1971.

Gary and Barbara, Dennis, Peggy Crosby and Philip, Sandy Crosby and Lindsay, 1973.

Gary and Andrea, 1981.

There was a long pause, then she said, "Well, dammit, I guess I have to tell you. She's seeing somebody else."

From the feeling in the pit of my stomach, the ground under my feet must have opened up and I was plummeting down to the bowels of the earth.

"Really? . . . Uh, well, what's happening?"

"Oh, Christ, Gary, he tried to date her a few times and she turned him down because he was married. So he went home and kissed off his wife, and now he's saying, 'Hey, I did this for you,' and that's making her so damn guilty she's going out with him."

A couple of unanswered phone calls later and it was over.

"She's marrying him," Fran announced, not at all happy about it. "Jesus Christ, I'd like to stop her, but I can't tell her what to do. She'll only bull her neck and go do exactly the opposite."

"Well, don't do that . . . Just tell her good luck."

The door had slammed closed, and that was that. I'm sure Betty called me later to tell me about the marriage. It would have been hard for her, but she never would have ducked it. But I must have been so drunk I don't even remember the conversation. I suppose I could have picked myself up and tried to win her back. I didn't. Her love for me had been so fragile to begin with that once it had ripped I couldn't see any way to repair it.

"Hell," I reminded myself, "that's probably the way it should happen. I'm such a bum, she's probably better off for getting rid of me."

It wasn't until almost thirty years later that I found out from Rosie what made her break it off. Betty was working at the Waldorf-Astoria in New York, and I had flown in to see her. By the time I reached the hotel I was so drunk that the only thing I can remember is watching the blue-white haze of the spotlight on her face while she sang "My Man." But according to Rosie, after the show I went back to Betty's suite with her mother. Betty started telling me how the drinking and violence were wrecking my career and life, and I got so angry at myself—because I knew she was right—that I ran into the bathroom. A moment later they heard this terrific crash. When I stumbled out they saw I had ripped the sink from the wall. Tearing up sinks was no big thing to me. I'd been doing that kind of nonsense since the drive-ins in high school. But it scared Betty to death. I didn't realize it, but my temper scared everybody who crossed paths with me in those days, and now Betty saw for herself that my reputation was more than justified. Later that night she told Rosie on the telephone that she'd had it; I was too much of a wild man for her. I don't suppose it helped my case that their father was also an alcoholic.

It wasn't that easy getting Betty out of my system. Not a day or night went by that I didn't think of her. Especially the nights. I spent a lot of them sitting in front of my stereo, with just the jug in my hand for company, listening to Sinatra's "Only the Lonely" over and over again, crying like a fool, then crying harder because I was so angry that she still got to me and I was being so maudlin. The more I cried, the angrier I became and the drunker I got, until I finally passed out in the chair. I'd still be sitting there when I woke up the next morning, and the record would still be spinning around the turntable. I'd suck it up, go out and do whatever I had to do, then come back with another jug and sit down again. Some mornings I'd have a vague memory of what happened the night before and want the earth to swallow me up. "Oh, my God, did you really call her last night? Idiot! Asshole! You got to let it go!"

It took some years before I could. She was back in town visiting Rosie with her children, and I drove over to see her. By then I was married myself and very much in love with my wife, but I had to have one last look to make sure it was really over and done with. It was, and that was a blessing. I still liked her. I still enjoyed being with her. But the passion had burned itself out and, thank God, I could finally put it to rest.

Chapter Eleven
On the Loose

After working the old man's show for the summer, college seemed more pointless than ever. All things considered, the work had been a good experience. I may have been too full of self-doubts to live off the high of it, but at least while I was doing it I felt like I was involved in something positive and productive that kept me reasonably straight. Stanford meant nothing to me by now. I had no business there. I was just taking up space that could have been used by some guy who really wanted to study, who needed that seat to become a doctor or a lawyer, and here I was, an asshole screwing around in speech and drama and just barely scuffling through. With all my incompletes, I was looking at another year and a half before I graduated, assuming I ever could con my way through Biology 1 after already flunking it three times.

It wasn't easy breaking the news to the old man. I knew it would be a bitter, bitter disappointment. Maybe because he had dropped out of college himself just a year or so short of becoming a lawyer, he was absolutely determined that his sons would go on to graduate. Maybe he figured he had made a mistake and didn't want to see us repeat it, but being the way he was he couldn't sit down and tell us that. He simply said, "Everything else can wait. The first thing you guys are gonna do is finish school." As it turned out, none of us did. After a couple of years of partying, the twins dropped out of Washington State, and when it got to be Linny's turn he lasted less than a semester at Williams. Lin was a great passive resister. He wanted to go to school in L.A., where all his friends were, but Dad said one of us had to graduate from an Ivy League college and he was the last one left. Lin nodded his head, said okay, then went off to Williams and promptly flunked out. I know he did it on purpose. He's probably the smartest of all of us. That was his way of sticking it to the old man. But as the oldest of the bunch I was the first to leave school, and it took some doing to work up the nerve.

It wasn't until January, after I had already packed up my bags, that I was able to make the phone call.

"Uh, hello, Dad. Look, I got something to tell you. I'm quitting school. I'm coming home."

He went bananas just like I knew he would.

"Jesus Christ! Goddamit, boy, what the hell are you talking about? After three and a half years you're gonna throw away all your education! Jesus Christ! . . ."

I let him go on ranting and raving, and when he finished I said, "Well, like I told you, I'm quitting and coming home."

The silence at the other end of the line was frosty enough to freeze an Eskimo.

"Uh-huh, I see. Well, what now? What do you think you're gonna do? What *can* you do?"

"I'm gonna go to work."

"Go to work, huh? Okay, fine. I'll see you later."

He slammed down the receiver, and I stood there for a minute listening to the dial tone buzz on and off.

He was so angry that for the next few months he refused to talk to me. Whenever he passed me in the hall he lowered his head and kept right on moving. I can't say it bothered me much. It was almost a relief that he wasn't calling me into his office for a lecture and laying all his bullshit on me. I figured it was only a matter of time before he threw me out of the house altogether, but until then, hey, I had free rent, free food, free laundry, and he wasn't causing me that much headache. Most days he was gone, and when he did come home the joint was big enough to keep out of each other's way. We were living in an armed truce, and that suited me just fine.

The silence didn't end until I got my first job singing in a nightclub somewhere in town. Then he saw that I wasn't going to sit on my ass and hold my head forever. He still wasn't pleased I had quit college, but at least I was doing something. The gig had gone fairly well, and one morning he stopped me on the way out the door and said, "Well, I hear you did a pretty good job." I would have bet every cent in my pocket on what the next word was going to be—and I would have won. "*But* don't forget to practice your vocalizing and work on your ballads." In any case, we were now back to normal.

If I was going to be in the business, I needed someone to find me work, so I went to see Dad's agent, George Rosenberg. The fact that Rosey represented the old man was a little too close to home for comfort, but I had known him all my life and he was almost like an uncle to me. Rosey was a real Damon Runyon character. He spoke out of the side of his mouth in a deep, gravelly voice, and he used worse language than I did. He'd call up the head of the biggest studio in town and yell at him, "Hey, you cocksucker, when are you gonna use my man? What do you mean? Don't bullshit me. You owed me this a long time, and I want him in this picture." It was said that when he was talking business with Joe Glaser, his counterpart in New York, you could hear them going at each other like that two floors away.

"Sure, kid. What the fuck. I'll get you something," Rosey answered, then stuck out his mitt to shake hands. That was all the contract he ever needed.

A month later he had me signed with CBS to do guest spots on radio and television. I started right at the top with people like Tennessee Ernie Ford and Edgar Bergen. I knew it was because of the name, but it still amazed me that a guy of my modest talents was allowed in their company. The Bergen show was populated with great radio actors like Hans Conried, Jack Kirkwood and Ray Noble, and it was a privilege just to be in the same studio and watch them trade off their crazy zingers and one-liners with Charlie McCarthy and Mortimer Snerd. The shows were so funny that if you play the tapes today they'll still make you fall on the floor. When I did Ernie's show I'd find myself a seat in the corner during rehearsals and practice getting my voice down as deep and low as he did and still stay in key. They were all terrific, happy people, never nasty or short-tempered with anyone, and going to work each day was a joy. It was like being part of a family or team. I added my one or two songs to their much more substantial contributions, and the parts added up to a successful whole.

As the months went by, Rosey began to find me bookings on television. I worked the Ed Sullivan and Jack Benny shows and did a stint with my Uncle Bob on his daytime series. Television was completely new to me, but because I was Dad's son everyone seemed to assume he had sat me down and made me all-knowing and all-wise about everything in the business. He hadn't done anything of the sort, partly because he realized by now I wouldn't listen to him and partly because he was such a natural he made all the right moves out of instinct and probably couldn't teach them to you any more than O. J. Simpson could tell you how he makes his moves. The directors would quickly run down the way they were shooting my scenes, as if I were perfectly at home with the terms that came flying out of their mouths, but even basic things like "camera right," "long shot" and "close-up" were still a mystery to me. Being the defensive guy I was, I would just nod my head and say, "Yeah, right," like I knew, then scurry around in a panic to find out what the hell they were talking about before I had to do it.

The same thing would happen when I began making my own records over at Decca. If the musicians played the song through a couple times in front, then I'd have it, but when the producer started getting technical on me I was lost. I didn't know about counting bars and modulating from this key to that and coming in at A tacit. I only knew what it felt like when I was supposed to come in, and when we went to a second take I'd be terrified that I wouldn't get the same feeling again in the same spot because that's all I had to go on. On the outside I'd be Mr. Cool —"Oh, great. Yeah, let's try it like that"—but underneath I'd be chewing a ton of rug.

Because I had no real training behind me, I didn't know what I was doing and felt like I was fooling everyone. All through my schooling with the nuns and Jesuits and all through sports I had been made to learn everything step by step so that I got it right. And that's the way guys like me have to learn. We don't have enough natural talent to skip over the fundamentals. But now I was just jumping in without the learning and having to operate on the natch. I started feeling guilty about getting the jobs when other singers who had studied and worked at it and learned their craft were backed up at the unemployment line. I knew I had an unfair advantage and shouldn't be getting those breaks, so there was no joy in any success I had. If I had success it was only because I was lucky, only because I had pulled the wool over everyone's eyes.

Of course I kept this to myself. When Rosey gave me the news that CBS wanted me to take over the old man's radio spot for the second summer, I simply answered, "Terrific," even though it made me a little hinky when he went on to say the name of the thing had been changed from "The Summer Show" to "The Gary Crosby Show." I didn't want star billing. I didn't want the star parts until I put enough good work behind me to deserve them. I wanted small parts in out-of-the-way things with good people so I could watch them and learn from them and begin to grow. But because of the Crosby name, that wasn't how it worked. I had to start at the top, and that meant I had to be perfect the first time out.

Rosey must have been thinking the same thoughts. That fall he called me into his office and said he wanted me to go out with Les Brown's band as the boy singer. "It'll be great experience, kid, great training. That's how your pop started out in the old days." The way he said it made me suspect the idea might have come from the old man himself. But even if it did, I had to agree with him for once.

I hopped on the bus and we headed east, where for the next five months we played one-nighter after one-nighter in every small town large enough to have a dance floor. It was a freezing-cold winter, with so much snow that some nights we'd play to the owner, the waiters and maybe five or six brave souls who must have skied down to see us. But the conditions didn't matter. Whether you were sick or well, rested or exhausted, working before ten people or a crowd of three thousand, you just went ahead and did what they were paying you to do. Most of the night I sat in a chair off to one side of the bandstand with Lucy Ann Polk, the girl singer. Maybe twice a set Les would call me up to the microphone and I'd do my number, then sit down again. I was just part of the show. Les Brown's name was up on the marquee, not mine. I wasn't the one dragging the customers in, so the pressure was off and I could work and learn and try things out without being afraid to fall on my face.

More than anything, I wanted to stand on my own two feet and be accepted for *what* I was, not *who* I was. I wanted to be called in just like any other singer and get the job because of my talent, not because the producer was my old man's pal. I made a big point of keeping away from all Dad's friends in the business who might do me some good, even though I'd known a lot of them most of my life. When they asked me to dinner or invited me over to a party, I always concocted some kind of excuse and turned the invitations down. I tried to duck everything that linked me up with him. If I was rehearsing a show and saw that the script had me sounding exactly like him—and that happened often—I automatically rephrased the lines to my own way of talking. I'd throw a look at the writers in the control booth, and they usually wouldn't say a word. They knew what was happening and realized there wasn't much point arguing about it.

I understood I was starting off in a business where my father was lord and master, but for that very reason I figured that anyone with a brain in his head wouldn't compare me with him. We were on completely different levels. He was way up *there*, and I was down *here*. And to me, I didn't sing like him any more than I looked like him. I was a time singer, a rhythm singer, an emotion singer. I was not a technical singer. I didn't have that pure tone and beautiful quality he had. I was just a scatter and a shouter and a jazz-and-blues type guy, because that's the kind of music I was into by now. I was listening to Joe Williams, Dinah Washington and Al Hibbler on the black radio stations. That and some country, because I could find soul in country music too. And that's what I was after. I was after those guys who were screaming, "I'm hurtin', I'm hurtin', man." Most straight pop music just put me to sleep. And more sophisticated songwriters like Cole Porter were musically and lyrically way too intellectual for me. I didn't hear those blues in them, and there had to be some kind of protest or wail in there somewhere. I was coming at the music from a totally different angle than the old man, so how the hell could anyone compare me with him? Or so I thought.

"Well, Gary, how do you feel about following in your father's footsteps?" the reporters kept asking.

"Follow him?" I'd answer. "I don't want to follow him. How are you gonna follow the number one cat of all time? You'll break your stones trying to do that. I'm just trying to get out there and make a living. I don't want to follow anybody."

It was easier said than done. When I signed with Decca records they kept handing me songs, arrangements and formats that were carbon copies of what they used for the old man. They put me with Sammy Davis, Jr., and we did records like Bing and Louis Armstrong. They put me with the DeCastro Sisters, and we did records like Bing and the Andrews Sisters. It was all the same kind of material, the same voicings, the same everything. I certainly wasn't about to go storming off to Milt Gabler, the head of Decca, to complain. I was lucky to have a record contract in the first place. But it didn't make any sense to me, and I tried talking to some of the producers about it.

"I don't sing like him, for Chrisake. Why would people want to hear me do him? Why would they buy a poor copy when they can have the original? C'mon, give me a way to go here."

They would nod sympathetically, but they only worked for the company and there wasn't a whole lot they could do. Finally someone sneaked through a compromise. When they called a record session together for six sides, four would be what they wanted—songs that Bing would sound good doing—and I'd get to choose the last two. I headed straight for Buddy Bregman, who had arranged and conducted the music on the summer radio show my second time out. We picked a couple of good raunchy Jerry Leiber–Mike Stoller R & B tunes, and he went to work on the charts. Buddy wrote outstanding funk, and it seemed to me they came out fine. I was almost happy with the sound of my own voice. But when it got to be release time, only the four sides they chose showed up in the stores. The same thing happened at the next session and the one after that. Predictably, the sides they released headed straight down the tubes. And for all I know, the things Buddy and I did together are still sitting in the Decca basement somewhere.

I wanted to work, work, work all the time. I couldn't get enough of it. It was the only thing that kept me halfway sane. I still juiced when I worked. I knew I was nothing and only fooling everybody for a while until the name value wore off, so I always had to slug down a couple of belts before I went on. I'd rationalize it by saying, "Well, I'm too tight. Gotta loosen up here, gotta get relaxed." I felt like such a fraud I needed two drinks just to say hello to someone. Later on, when I started playing the clubs, a couple of belts before showtime turned into four, five, a half dozen belts then another half dozen between shows, which meant I was so loaded by the last set I was lucky if I even made it. But I wasn't messing up like that yet. I still took care of business whenever I had work to do. When I didn't have work, though, I stayed stoned constantly. Even if I was playing "The Tennessee Ernie Ford Show" three days a week, that still left four days with nothing to do, no way to justify my existence, and I had to fill up the hours somehow.

The main piece of advice Dad gave me about the business was, "Just show up on time and say the lines, then get the money and go home." That was his way of telling me not to carry on, carouse, or burn myself out with partying. But I didn't feel for an instant that I was carrying on more than anyone else. I certainly didn't think I had a problem. The business was filled with performers, like Sinatra and Dean Martin, who were players and swingers and fun guys. Hell, even one of the old man's closest friends fit that description. I remember overhearing Dad talk about how, when he went backstage to visit him a half hour before curtain, he found him passed out at his dressing table with just his shorts on and his face flopped down in a bowl of chili. But when the music started he headed straight for the stage and hit every cue perfectly. He did a sensational show just working by rote. And then, when it was over, he staggered back to the dressing room, his head went right back down on the table and he was out again. As straight as the old man kept his professional life, there was as much admiration as wonder in his voice when he told the story.

The way I saw it, everybody drank. Maybe I was having two to their one, but we were all out there. We were all sitting in the bars with a glass of something in front of us. Hey, I was just hanging out and being hip and sharp and a rounder like everyone else. I didn't think it would hurt my work. A lot of guys screwed around and got away with it. Nor did it dawn on me that because I was who I was, people didn't want me to be like that. They wanted me to be more like their image of the old man, eating my Wheaties and going to bed by ten o'clock. And if it did dawn on me I said, "Well, the hell with them. That's not me, and I'm gonna be me. If they like me the way I am, fine. If they don't, too bad, because I ain't gonna be no phony."

The nights I didn't have a job the next morning I'd hang around the house until ten o'clock, when the action started, then jump in my car and take off for the joints. I'd hit the Cloister, the Crescendo, Ciro's, the London House, Ye Little Club and three or four other spots before the evening ended. Maybe I'd run into a girl or find some guys who knew about a party, but mostly I stayed in motion and kept moving. I don't know what I was looking for, but it had to be truly spectacular to hold my attention. A lot of nights nothing was shaking anywhere, and when the bars closed at 2 A.M. I wound up alone with the newspaper. Then I'd just go home to my room, get out the jug and sit there drinking till dawn and watching old movies. When the light started to come through the window I'd pop some sleeping pills and hope to God I'd be able to crap out for a few hours.

Other nights I'd end up at the after-hours bar in the Garden of Allah apartments, along with the other show business "swingers" like myself—musicians, comics, agents—who didn't want to go home either. A number of big stars kept bungalows in the back where they could shack up, and when the bar finally closed down, whoever was left standing usually ended up in one of them. There would be plenty of booze, plenty of drugs, plenty of ladies, and whatever happened happened. I watched the action more than I took part in it.

Yet other nights I'd wake up passed out someplace and not even know where I was. When I checked the other bodies still crapped out on the couches and chairs, I'd be lucky if I recognized one of them. I'd pat my pocket for my wallet, find a mirror to see if I was banged up anywhere, then hit the front door and start searching up and down the street for my car. The next day Dad might ask, "Say, what time did you get in?" and I'd answer, "Two, probably." If he knew I was lying, he didn't bust me on it.

The class show business scene made me nervous, and I kept away from it. I was much more comfortable with people on the edges of the business who were struggling to gain a foothold. Some of them had done good work and were known, but their careers weren't lighting any fires. I hung out a lot with Huntz Hall from the old Bowery Boys movies. Huntz was a funny, bitter guy, full of frustration because Leo Gorcey had somehow walked away with all the money from those pictures. Now, even though he was a good actor, Huntz was having trouble making a living. His bitterness didn't bother me in the least. It went right along with my own. Everybody I hung out with was bitter and cynical and down. We all had troubles—girl troubles, work troubles, money troubles, family troubles—and we all dealt with them in the same way: boozing and partying and getting out of it. We were so caught up in our own miseries that the Russians could have invaded and we'd have just offered them a drink.

The twins and I had covered a lot of ground since the days we were the media's darlings, the fair-haired sons of the beloved Bing Crosby. I had dropped out of Stanford and turned into a boozer and pillhead and all-night carouser. Denny and Phil had quit Washington State and knocked around until they were grabbed by the draft. All three of us had gotten into our share of trouble. The same week CBS announced I'd be taking over Dad's show for the first summer I had crashed my Mercury into a car full of Mexican farm workers speeding across an intersection up in San Jose. God must have been looking after the fool because the fool couldn't look after himself; for some reason I still don't understand, I hadn't touched a drink that night and their car smelled like the inside of a wine vat. Still, a man was killed. Denny was arrested for drunkenness the day before his induction into the Army. Phil banged himself up in an automobile accident on his way back to Fort Lewis, and was later arrested for drunken driving and hitting a pedestrian. All the cases were thrown out of court, but the signs were clear enough that the wonderful clan named Crosby wasn't exactly what it had been cracked up to be.

Even the old man had gotten himself into a bad scrape. Almost a year to the day after Mom died he had an automobile collision that sent three people to the hospital, and he was charged with reckless and drunken driving. The charges were dismissed, but the injured passengers in the other car sued him for a million dollars. Following his principle that it was always better to pay up and shut up rather than get involved in a long, drawn-out legal hassle, he settled with them for a hundred thousand and the case was forgotten.

Each incident was duly reported in the daily press, but it took the feature writers a while to let go of the old Crosby family fantasy. They still churned out heartwarming pieces like "My Four Sons—and Me," "The Role Bing Likes Best Is Playing Dad" and "My Pop, Bing Crosby." Dad played along with the game, of course, as did the rest of us. Talking to *McCall's Magazine*, he credited Mom with molding his boys into "the well-adjusted young men they are today," then went on to enthuse, "I can say quite frankly that were it not for these sons of ours I would be completely lost. Their affection and respect, their spirit, good humor and companionship have filled a void that seemed bottomless when Dixie died two years ago."

Eventually, though, reality had to catch up with us. After a while other, darker stories began to appear with titles like "Can Crosby Cure His Four Little Headaches?" As if to make up for lost time, the scandal sheets went to work titillating their readers with details of juicy escapades that may not even have happened. One of them told about how the old man had walked into a nightclub and discovered me so drunk and disorderly that he chewed me out on the spot before all the ringsiders. Something like that may have gone down. I don't really remember. I never did remember much of what happened once I got juiced. The drunk and disorderly part sounds right, but not the part about Dad reaming me out in public. He would have paid the check and made a beeline for the door, saving whatever he had to tell me for the privacy of the next morning.

I may have been over twenty-one, but when he got hot and bothered the old man still laid into me like a fourteen-year-old, especially when it had to do with Denny and Phil.

". . . and your goddam brother; he's out there knocking people down with that fucking car. Juiced to the eyeballs, probably . . . They're just copying you, that's all. They just want to go along like you do, drinking and fighting and fucking up."

Maybe that was true, but if it was I couldn't begin to understand why. They're trying to copy *me*? What the hell for? Do they dig disaster or what? I suppose I figured I could handle trouble and they couldn't, but I never sat them down and lectured them about it. I was on their side. The way I saw it, if your name was Crosby they were going to nail you for everything anyhow, so they already had enough heat on them.

I liked to think I was way past the point where the old man could get to me, but sometimes after the bars closed I'd be feeling so bugged and down I just had to talk to somebody about him. When I was sober I wouldn't crack to anyone, certainly not any men, but once I was half sizzed and got with one of the few women I trusted, someone I knew wouldn't be blabbing all over town or going back to my father, the words came tumbling out of my mouth.

I trusted Nancy Sinatra, Frank's ex-wife. We had been close since the days the two families started socializing together in Palm Springs. When Sinatra first got hot the press tried to create a rivalry with the old man, but neither of them would go for it. When asked, "What do you think about Sinatra?" Dad would answer them, "Oh, Frank's the greatest singer I ever heard." And Frank would say the same when they asked him about Bing. There were never any problems between them. Nancy was a warm, good-hearted woman—a lot like my mother—and sometimes at two in the morning I'd find myself phoning her from the street asking to come over. If I woke her up—and I must have—she pretended I didn't. The coffeepot would be perking by the time I knocked on her front door, and she'd sit there at the kitchen table trying to sober me up while I rattled on and on with my complaints.

She'd listen sympathetically, nodding in all the right places, then give me the usual arguments any sane person would make to a crazy man.

"Well, he's doing that because he loves you."

"Ah, horseshit. He doesn't love anybody. He just wants everyone to knuckle under to his fucking rules and his way of life. Anything else he doesn't recognize. You never have any reasons for doing something different other than you're stupid or a rebel or just plain anti. Only his way makes sense."

"Well, that's your opinion. I guess you're entitled to it, but I don't think you're right."

"Yeah, okay. Different opinions are what make the world go round."

On and on we would go like that all through the night. Sometimes I'd sit there bending her ear till eight or nine in the morning, and the sun would be shining when I finally climbed back in my car.

I received more good advice than you could shake a stick at and never listened to a word of it. I'd be up at Rosey's office talking to him about the next job when he'd throw a long, hard look in my direction and start in on me.

"Jesus Christ, kid, what the fuck you doin' with yourself? C'mon, c'mon, you want to be a success in show business, for Chrisake, you gotta take care of yourself. You gotta lose the weight and you gotta . . . Look, you're great. You're great like you are. But you could be ten times better if you lost a few pounds and quit drinkin' so the voice cleared up."

"Voice cleared up? Man, I've had this hoarse, fuckin' voice all my life. Drinking's got nothing to do with it . . . Hell, Rosey, there's a lot of guys in the business doing what I do. I'm not out there alone. I run into them every night. You know it isn't just me."

Other days he'd find a way to bring up the old man, trying to get across to me that he was really interested in how I was coming along.

"Hey, heard from your father this morning. He caught you on the Sullivan show last week. Thought you did terrific."

"Yeah, wonderful, okay, fine."

"Well, what the hell's the matter with you now? You gonna stay mad at him the rest of your fuckin' life or what?"

"So far as I can see, I probably will."

"Aren't you ever gonna change?"

"Nope."

Phil Harris was another one constantly knocking himself out to get us together. He loved us both, and it saddened him that we were so far apart. Whenever I ran into him he'd tell me, "Y'know, Gary, your old man's a great guy. And, Jesus, he loves you. I know it don't seem like it sometimes, but he really does, and you ought to start talking to him again." Then he'd go to my father and lay in the same line about me. Harris really knows how to tell a story, and sometimes he'd regale me with anecdotes about the old man aimed at getting me to see him as a human being: funny things that happened on the golf course; how, when they went hunting geese up in Canada, they looked like such derelicts the hotel clerk wouldn't rent them a room until Dad proved he was Bing Crosby by singing the guy a song. I'd laugh at his punch lines and keep myself from arguing with him. I knew he meant well. He was acting out of love. But I can't say I paid him much attention.

I was the same way with Jack E. Leonard. I'd be sitting in the Stage Delicatessen in New York or some other late-night hangout in Chicago or Las Vegas when Fat Jack would cruise in and begin nailing everyone in sight. He was a great insult comic and instinctively knew where to hit a person. "Boy are you fat. If you were any fatter you could wear *my* pants. It would sweat a mouse to run around you . . . That's a clever outfit. Don't worry, it'll be back soon . . . Nice suit. Salvation Army? . . . Hey, skinny, how much you weigh? That much? I had more than you for breakfast . . ."

Jack was my kind of comic. "Everybody's full of shit," he seemed to be saying. "We're all assholes, so we might as well realize it." But that was just his humor. That wasn't him. When he finished leveling the room and the place simmered down, he would take me aside and, suddenly turning very serious and quiet, begin to lecture me like an uncle.

"Jesus, come on, Gary. You got a lot of talent. You got a lot of ability. You know, just don't be such a bad-ass. Don't hate everybody. Use your talent. Don't let the fact that you're your father's son ruin you."

While he was trying to straighten me out I'd mimic him, back to himself. I'd stick my stomach way out, put my hand on my side and say real fast out of the corner of my mouth, "Right, Jack, right. Certainly, certainly. Fine, fine, fine." Or I'd throw up some other smoke screen, anything to keep from talking seriously about it. But he was a sweet, kindhearted man, and he kept trying to make me see the light. They all tried. But I was through listening. I was agile, mobile and hostile, and that's how I planned to stay.

Everyone else could see the handwriting on the wall in large, clear letters, but I thought they were worrying themselves over nothing. I took care of business, didn't I? I showed up on time and did what I was supposed to. And that was true. I still did. It wasn't until I toured Australia with Louis Armstrong that I began to get the message.

Louis Armstrong was one of the finest, most genuine human beings God ever put on the face of the earth. Louis was Louis twenty-four hours a day. Whether he was sitting in his dressing room in just his shorts and a rag around his head, playing before three thousand people in a tuxedo or forced to deal with the low, tight situations every black person in America has to endure, he was always the same. He loved everyone and he loved what he was doing, and he never let anything or anyone change him.

I loved Louis' music from the time I was a kid and heard his records being played around the house. Later on I even began to imitate the way he sang. Louis' gravelly voice couldn't sustain long notes, so he backphrased, holding the lyric until the last bar of the line and putting it all in there, which worked magnificently. I was having my own trouble holding long notes, and Louis' example showed me there was a whole other way to go from the kind of singing my father did. Then, in June 1955, when I was given the privilege of playing on the same bill with him for two weeks at the Chicago Theater, I came to know and love the man himself.

For a performer, working with Louis Armstrong was like going to finishing school. We were doing five shows a day, which meant we started off at eleven in the morning and didn't finish up until one o'clock at night. Now, when you walk out on stage at eleven in the morning the house is empty except for a few winos and stiffs and horseplayers waiting for the track to open. It is not exactly the most responsive audience in the world. Jack E. Leonard had worked the same theater the week before us, and his opening line for the first show was, "Good morning, opponents." But that didn't matter to Louis. He put out the same amount of energy and enthusiasm whether two people were sitting there or the joint was packed to the rafters. When I'd be out there on stage with him for the first show finale, he'd be swinging and wailing away and jacking me up with all kinds of asides and gags and funny takes that made me feel better and work harder. It was an invaluable lesson. A lot of performers will slough off and trim numbers when the house is empty or the audience is down because they know they're not going anywhere anyhow. I had been guilty of that myself. But not Louis. He was such a professional and had so much love and joy in him that he gave 110 percent of himself every time out.

Like everybody else in the world, Louis loved my father. Between shows he'd tell me endless stories about him. "Your old man is the greatest singer," he'd say. "Really, he's got the chops, daddy. He can wail." Then he'd go on to reminisce about all the funny things that happened when they crossed paths in the old days and how much he enjoyed working Dad's radio show and being in his movies. "Well, Dad loves you too, Louis," I'd answer, and that was so. Louis was always one of his favorites. I don't know if Louis could tell how I felt about working in the old man's shadow, but when the reporter from *Time* magazine came backstage and, inevitably, asked him to compare our two voices, he gave him a response that helped raise my ego a couple of notches. "Bing's voice has a mellow quality that only Bing's got. It's like gold being poured out of a cup. But Gary has qualities that Bing doesn't have . . . And no one can imitate *my* singing like Gary."

Later that year we recorded a few duets—"Ko Ko Mo—I Love You So," "Struttin' with Some Barbecue," and his theme song,

"When It's Sleepy Time Down South"—and off of that came an offer to do a foreign tour together the following spring. The itinerary took us to Australia for two and a half weeks, back to L.A. long enough to change clothes, then on to England. It couldn't have sounded better. Louis was a pleasure to be around, a pleasure to talk to, a pleasure to work with, and so were his sidemen. Billy Kyle, Trummy Young, Arvell Shaw—they were all a ball. They loved to work. They loved to laugh. They loved to have fun.

Life on the road isn't easy, and you pick up your kicks wherever you can. For Louis it was eating his red beans and rice, smoking his joints and hanging out with the people. For his drummer Barrett Deems it was searching out the jewelry stores in every town we played for some new kind of wristwatch he didn't already have strapped to his arms. For the other guys—including myself—it was hitting the local bars.

Louis wasn't much for juicing. Thirty years of one-nighters had taught him how to take care of himself. His dressing table was crowded with ointments and salves to keep his lips in shape, and he followed his own special health diet. He had the thing printed up and would press a copy on anyone who evinced the slightest interest. The main point was to take two heaping tablespoons of Swiss-Kriss, a laxative, before you went to bed at night. Down at the bottom of the page he had written "Louis' Motto: The more you shit the thinner you git!" But Louis knew how it was with the rest of the guys, and as long as you showed up on time and held it together he didn't care what you did on your own time.

The drinkers in the band understood that. No matter how stoned they got, they never missed a show, never threw out anything less than great performances. I understood it too, and although I had my first taste the moment I climbed out of bed and kept sipping all through the afternoon, I made sure to wait until work was over before getting myself seriously wasted. But the day we were leaving Adelaide to fly back to L.A. I blew it. Louis was at the airport waiting to take off on the chartered plane, and I was still fast asleep in my hotel room, passed out from the night before. I was in such a stupor that neither the alarm clock nor the telephone calls nor the knocks on the door had been able to wake me. Billy and Trummy raced back from the airport and eventually tracked me down, but they couldn't rouse me either. They tried to shake me awake, but all that did was make me clutch the mattress with both hands. Finally they had to roll me up in the damn thing and deposit me on the plane like a piece of luggage. By the time we got off the ground we were hours behind schedule.

When I finally came to and pieced together what had happened, I was devastated. Louis was the last person in the world I wanted to let down. I made my way to his seat and blurted out my apologies.

"Jesus Christ, Louis, I sure am sorry. I really didn't mean to fuck up like that. And it'll never happen again, I promise you."

He was less angry than hurt. "Mm-m, okay, Gate," he mumbled, then turned away and fixed his gaze out the window.

It was a long ride home, and my guilt kept me company all the way. The one consolation was that I still had a chance to redeem myself. After a forty-eight-hour layover in L.A. we'd be taking off for England to continue the tour for another seventeen days. I would make it up to him by staying straight the entire time and not screwing up anywhere. I would do a magnificent job, and then he'd be happy with me again.

That's not how it worked out.

Rosey was waiting at the airport when we landed, wearing a somber look on his face.

"Got some bad news for you, kid."

"What's that?"

"Looks like you're not going to England."

"Why not?"

"Because you just been drafted."

"*Drafted?* . . . But what about my C Profile, the limited motion in my arm? I thought they're not taking guys like me."

"Well, I guess they are now."

". . . But you got that six-month extension for me, didn't you?"

"I tried."

"What happened?"

"They wouldn't give it to you."

"Well, would they give me three weeks?"

"No."

"How much would they give me?"

"Two weeks."

"Two weeks? . . . Sonofabitch, then that means I can't go to England with Louis and I can't . . ."

"That's right."

"Why is this, Rosey? How come?"

"Well, the way I get it, kid, the draft board just got busted for favoritism. Some asshole down there buried some Beverly Hills hotshot's file and got caught at it. Now they gotta straighten up their game, and you were the next one in line. Those are the breaks."

It might have gone down just like Rosey said. I reminded myself that I *had* dropped out of school, I *had* quit ROTC, and for those reasons alone I was likely to get nailed. But it didn't add up. Even if they drafted you, they still gave you a one-month extension at the very least, usually more. I couldn't think of anyone in show business who got less than six months. You needed that kind of time to build up a backlog of work so people would know you're still alive while you were gone. That was standard. Without it, especially if you were just getting started, your career slammed to a halt and you died.

It seemed to me that somebody was in an awful hurry to get me in there right away. I didn't have to think very hard to figure out who that might be. Who else but the old man? The instant I flashed on the possibility I knew I was right. Sure, he was displeased with me for leaving school. He was displeased with my drinking and my wild, carousing way of life. Undoubtedly he had heard every detail about how I fucked up in Australia five minutes after it happened.

Maybe I had it all wrong. Maybe it was just the booze and amphetamine paranoia talking. Maybe I was only rerunning an ancient tape from my childhood: I had been bad. I had been caught. And now the lord high executioner was going to make me pay for my sins by stuffing me back in the trunk. On the other hand, maybe I had it exactly right. To this day I don't know for sure. But at that moment, while I was standing there with Rosey watching Louis and the guys disappear into the limos, there wasn't a single solitary doubt in my mind.

Chapter Twelve
Back in the Trunk

A drinking buddy kept me company on the drive over to the induction station. As we pulled up in front of the place, I gave him my car.

"Here, man, it's yours now. I won't be needing it anymore."

"Really? Gee, okay, thanks . . . Well, we'll hear from you."

"Nah, you ain't hearing from me."

"Aren't you gonna write any letters?"

"No."

"Why not?"

"Just look at it this way. I'm dead. I just died."

That's how I felt. A more rational person with a normal amount of self-confidence would have told himself, "Okay, this is only a temporary setback. The time will pass before you know it, and then you'll come back and pick up the old career where you left off. No big deal." But the way I saw it, for someone in my doubtful position a two-year absence from show business without any backlog of work meant that I no longer had a career. And without that to justify my existence, for all intents and purposes my life was over.

Because I had messed up in Australia and been punished, I was back in the trunk again, back to doing what everybody else wanted, and as far as I was concerned it didn't much matter what happened from here on out. Standing in the haircut line the first day of basic, I watched the two cocky hoods in front of me with the tattoos and turned-up collars melt into jelly the second the barbers handed them a mirror and they saw what had been done to their long, fancy hairdos. One moment they were popping wise and talking tough, the next they were pussycats. The barbers had been watching the line for me, and the first one to spot me laid in her claim. "I want him!" she called out, then went to work with her electric razor, cutting off every hair on my head in about twenty seconds. I suppose she figured she'd have me bawling like those two kids, but I didn't give a damn. I didn't have that much ego built up anyhow. "Great haircut," I told her and tipped her a buck. The same thing happened when I went to draw my uniforms. The supply clerks were overjoyed at the opportunity to make Bing's boy look like an idiot and handed me all the wrong sizes. The pants were too big, the jacket too small, the hat fell down around my ears. I could see from their smirks they were thinking, "Hey, watch this turkey. He's really gonna get uptight and have to go to the tailor." But I took whatever they gave me and wore it exactly the way it came off the shelf. What did I care? The dopier and weirder I looked the better I liked it.

On the way to the billets I was warned that someone was gunning for me. A tough guy had been spouting off how he was going to cancel my ticket real good. "That's nice," I answered. "Well, we'll see what happens." He started glowering at me as soon as I walked through the door, but I pretended not to notice. I threw my duffel bag down on a bunk, then went back outside and took my place on the chow line. Five minutes later I caught him out of the side of my eye striding straight for me with his fists clenched. I set my right foot, waited until he was within arm's reach, then wheeled around to face him.

"You Crosby?" he demanded, as if I'd be too terrified to admit it.

"That's right. What the fuck do you want to do about it?"

He blinked a few times, then faded right into the woodwork.

"Oh, nothing."

"What do you mean, nothing?"

"I was just . . . Hey, it must be great to have an old man like yours. Gee, he's such a terrific singer and a terrific—"

"Yeah? Is that all you got to say?"

"Yeah."

"Okay," I answered, then turned away as he moved off to the back of the line.

Now that the old man had me where he wanted, he was free to lay in the advice just like when I was a kid. The day before I left he sat me down for one of his customary lectures.

"You have to hew the line and do what they tell you . . . This could be a very constructive time in your life . . ."

"Yeah, Dad, hew the line . . . Right, Dad, it sure could."

As usual, I yessed him to death while keeping all my real thoughts to myself. I was so convinced he had put me in there I didn't need to call him on it. There certainly wasn't any reason to listen to him. What the hell did he know about the Army? He was never in it. But by now I had become so adept at bullshitting him that he was able to persuade himself I was hanging onto every word.

A few weeks later a letter arrived offering more of the same salutary counsel. Without his presence to go along with it, his advice made me hit the roof. "Jesus Christ, you think I'm gonna shape up? You think this is gonna turn me into a good boy? You asshole, that shows how little you know me! And now that you've got me in here, for Chrisake, don't be trying to make it easy for me."

His letter had gone on to recommend that I get in touch with some of his high-ranking friends on the post who could be "helpful." That was the last thing I needed. "Fuck you and your friends and everyone else," I raged. "I'm just US 56278269, and that's how I want to stay. All I gotta do is start getting special favors and special attention, and they'll kill me in here. They'll draw and quarter my ass for sure."

I was already having enough trouble from the press. A photographer had been waiting at the induction station the morning I went down, and the first weeks of basic had been interrupted by a constant flow of picture sessions. It seemed that every newspaper in the country wanted a shot of Bing Crosby's son doing his part, and the post's public information office was happy to oblige. Finally my commanding officer, a big, tough-looking professional soldier who'd had half his face paralyzed in Korea, got fed up with the foolishness and ordered me into his office.

"All right, Private, you can have it one of two ways. I can let the press in whenever they call for you, and you'll have to repeat all the time you missed. Or I can bar 'em. I can make you go through it just like any other guy, and then you'll be done and out of here."

The choice was easy.

"I don't want no press at all, Captain. Just put me through it like everybody else."

"Okay, you got it."

The next time I turned around the whole post was buzzing that Bing Crosby was about to arrive at Fort Lewis for a little visit. I got the news when one of the guys in my squad rushed up to me all excited and out of breath.

"Hey, Crosby, your old man's gonna be here tomorrow!"

"Oh, no-o-o. Please be lying. Don't tell me that."

"Yeah, it's true. He's really gonna be here. They're getting all ready for it."

"Getting ready? What do they have to get ready for?"

"Oh, man, it's a star coming to the base and the generals are gonna . . . and the colonels are gonna . . . and everybody's gonna . . ."

I was mortified. It was just the kind of attention I'd been doing everything in my power to avoid. Tomorrow we'd be crawling through the infiltration course with live machine gun bullets whizzing over our heads, and I could just picture how the photographers would go about staging the scene. "Okay, Gary, now you get down on the ground there and crawl along. And, Bing, would you stand over him and point in that direction? That's it. Thanks very much. Could we try just one more?"

I wasn't far off. The next morning I caught a glimpse of him perched on top of the hill overlooking the course, surrounded by the generals, public information officers and other high mucky-mucks who'd been able to wedge their way into the golden circle. I tried to block him out and stay connected with the other guys, but in the middle of the sergeant's instructions I was pulled out of ranks to stand next to him.

"Well, hi, Gary, how are ya?"

"Fine, Dad, great."

"And what are you gonna do today?"

"Well, Mr. Crosby," one of the officers chimed in, seizing the opportunity to engage in a bit of direct dialogue with the great man, "today they're crawling the infiltration course."

"Oh, good. Okay, well, go on down there and do it."

"Okay, sure will. See you later, Dad."

While the photographers clicked away, I watched the guys at the bottom of the hill glaring up at me, just waiting for me to be handed some kind of break. It wasn't long in coming. At lunchtime I was singled out to join him at the special table in the mess hall reserved for officers, and then that night I was given a pass to have dinner with him off base. All through the meal the only thing I could think about was, "Jesus Christ, everybody else is in the fuckin' chow hall eating that grease and I'm out here in this fancy restaurant with dear old Dad trying not to choke on my steak. Don't he realize this does nothing but make more aggravation for me with the guys I'm going through the shit with, and if I don't have them I don't have anybody? Can't he see it only gives them an opening to start in with the dialogue and the bullshit after he leaves? Why don't he have the sense to just stay the hell away?" But of course I knew he wouldn't see it that way, and I didn't bring it up. Our conversation kept to the same superficialities it always did.

"So how are you doing in the Army, Gary?"

"Just fine, Dad. I'm a squad leader now."

"Well, that's good. How'd you get that?"

"Well, St. John's and Black Foxe really helped me there. I knew the manual of arms and how to dress right dress and all that kind of stuff, and that was more than anybody else knew, so they made me a squad leader."

"Uh-huh. Well, that's fine."

It seemed to take hours before we finished dessert and I could get back where I belonged.

"Well, got a big march in the morning, Dad, so I better hit the sack. Have to get up early."

"Yes, I guess you better. Well, take care of yourself. See you later."

"Okay. Terrific. So long."

Predictably, the guys were waiting for me back at the barracks.

"Hey, Crosby, how's it feel to be a star?"

"Yeah, did you have a nice dinner?"

"What ya eat?"

"Oh, get off my fucking back," I answered. "Just leave me the hell alone."

When I finished up at Fort Lewis they sent me on to clerk-typist school at Fort Ord, but the general kept pulling me out to do shows and I was finally transferred to special services and shipped off to Germany. Up to then I had stayed fairly straight. I was too busy to get drunk. But as soon as I boarded the plane to Frankfurt I uncorked one of the jugs I had brought along for company, and by the time we got there I was thoroughly wasted.

For the next year and a half I stayed that way. I more or less did my job, but I was whacked nearly every second of the day. I started with a couple of glugs the minute I woke up in the morning and kept at it until my head hit the pillow at night or I passed out in some alley. Booze was cheap, and I had bottles stashed everywhere—in my footlocker and duffel bag, hanging by strings out of windows, hidden in bushes. And if I ran out I could always get more at the enlisted men's club or one of the soldier bars in town. With no future in sight and not much of a present, I needed some way to get through the days, and juicing did the job just fine. Other guys used being stationed in Europe as an opportunity to travel and learn and see things they'd read about in history books. But not me. I didn't want to see anything but the bars and nightlife and hookers and musicians and funny people. I was just passing the time. I had drawn up a little calendar with 730 squares, one for each day I had to be in the Army, and every morning I'd cross another one off.

I was not a pleasant drunk. There was no hide left on me by

now. All someone had to do was make me hurt by smarting off wise or saying the wrong thing and I automatically reached out and started whacking. It didn't take much to get me going. I lashed out at everybody and everything and had absolutely no self-control. I wouldn't know who I was fighting or why I was fighting, and I didn't much care. I'd care the next morning when I woke up in my bunk, still wearing the same clothes from the night before. I couldn't remember how I got there, much less what had happened, so I'd have to search out a witness to find out what had gone down.

"Well, you were a beauty last night."

"Yeah? . . . Well, did I kill anybody or anything?"

"No, but some GI came up to you and gave you shit about being Crosby's kid, and you didn't take it. You went after him, and there was a helluva brawl."

"Jesus . . . Well, is it all right? Is everything cleaned up or what?"

"Yeah, it's okay. We apologized for you."

Sometimes it wasn't okay, and the stories would make my flesh crawl. A scandal sheet titled its account of one of my barroom escapades "When Gary Crosby Blackened the Eye of the Gorgeous Nude: The Blond Babe Was Willing to Play, but the Groaner's Son Slugged Her Instead." I don't know if that actually happened, but it might have. Things just as bad did.

When the booze didn't make me hostile it made me loose-mouthed, and I'd parade the family secrets before anyone who showed the slightest interest. "You think he's a great guy, huh?" I'd ask some GI I never saw before who was standing next to me at the bar, and then I'd go on to straighten him out. "Shit, that fucker's on my ass night and day. He never lets up with his rules and regulations and bullshit. There's no way to please him, nothing you can do to make him happy. *Here's* your great guy!"

Naturally, word got back to the old man with the speed of light, and in his cool, dispassionate way he did what he could to get me to button up. A few weeks after I hit Frankfurt he sent me a letter full of advice about keeping the Crosby family business to myself. I have a tendency, he wrote, to shoot my mouth off when I'm feeling "bugged"—by which, I suppose, he meant "drunk." I should try to avoid quick friendships and just stand there discreetly while the other fellows do the talking. If I needed any more motivation than I already had to keep popping off, that kind of lecture gave it to me.

My army assignments left me plenty of opportunities to carouse, and I took advantage of every one of them. In Frankfurt I was a disc jockey on the Armed Forces Network. All I had to do was play dinner music—Morton Gould, André Kostelanetz—one or two hours a day for the brass. After I got the hang of it I could work the damn thing three-quarters stoned. Then I was transferred down to Stuttgart to the Seventh Army Symphony and Soldier Show Company, where there were so many maniacs and fuckups like myself they wouldn't even let us stand inspection or draw firearms.

For the next year I was the boy singer in a touring soldier-show troupe that included a comic, a tap dancer, a bass player who had worked with Olsen and Johnson and could do comedy shtick, and sometimes a black vocal quartet. The sergeant in charge of us was a black WAC singer who looked and sounded like Nancy Wilson. Sophie—which is what I'll call her—was making the Army her career and took it seriously, but she had come from show business and didn't pull her rank as long as we did what we were supposed to. That wasn't asking for much, but a lot of the time it was more than I could give her.

We worked the service clubs, where our only audiences were GIs who had been restricted to post or didn't have the money to go into town and get drunk. They weren't happy to be there in the first place and just wanted to be left alone to shoot pool and play Ping-Pong. They sure as hell weren't interested in being entertained by a bunch of half-assed bastards who had it so soft they didn't have to pull KP or guard duty or freeze their butts off out in the field. I didn't blame them for hating us. I'd have hated us too if I was sitting where they were. But working in front of them was like going out to be devoured by a pack of hungry lions. Everything was "Boo!" Comedy—"Boo!" Dancing—"Boo!" Singing—"Boo!" We would go through the motions of putting on a show, then run for our lives.

The other guys could see the humor in the situation and took it in stride, but I had to get myself half blind to go out there. "All right, show time!" Sophie would announce, rousting us from

237

the tiny office that served as our dressing room. "Wait a minute," I'd answer as I tossed down one more slug from my jug. "Hold it, hold it. I'm not drunk enough yet."

Some nights, when I was sufficiently whacked, I could thrive on the hostility and fight them back.

"And here he is, Gary Crosby!"

"Boo! Fuck you, you creep."

"Oh, my public awaits. Wonderful. Hey, if this'll get me fired, terrific. Come on, fellas, boo some more."

"Ah-h-h, get out of here, you cocksucker!"

"Well, thank you very much. All right, here's a song you're probably gonna hate . . . And here's another one you won't like either . . . Okay, I'd like to thank you for your inattention. It's been my pleasure to work before a great many wonderful audiences. Too bad this isn't one of them."

Other nights, though, it would get to me. In the middle of a song I would tune in on all the anger and disdain, then just stop cold and walk off the stage. "Hey, if that's how you guys feel, fuck you too. You don't like me, so maybe you'll like the next act. See you assholes later." Or I wouldn't show up at all. I'd go out drinking in the afternoon and get myself so wasted I'd pass out somewhere. Then Sophie and the others would have to search out every bar and gutter in town to find me and try to sober me up in time to go on. And when I couldn't be found, she'd make up a cover story to keep me out of trouble, telling everyone I was back in the billets sick with the flu or some other lie. I'd try to apologize the next morning, but she'd say, "Hey, don't. Forget about it. No sweat."

Sophie didn't have to put herself out on a limb like that. She had a lot of stripes to protect, a whole career, and each time I messed up on her I was jeopardizing everything she'd worked years for. She would have been well within her rights to report me back to the colonel, who without a doubt would have thrown me into the Crowbar Hotel. But she never did. Out of pity or compassion or whatever it was, she dealt with all the hassles I caused her less like my sergeant than my friend. She saved my life more times than I can remember.

Like Nancy Sinatra and Jack E. Leonard and the other people who somehow saw some good in me, Sophie did what she could to straighten me out. She was not a rounder of any kind, but she hung with me in the bars to try to keep me from losing it totally. She tried to get me to answer the old man's letters. She gave me little pep talks about my future.

"Man, you're a talented cat. You got a lot on the ball. You can make it good in the business and not just because of the name. You're a fine singer, you really are."

I'd listen to her and tell myself, "Ah, it's only because she's my friend that she says that shit."

As the months went by, friendship evolved into love, and we began living together, staying in hotel rooms instead of the billets when we went on tour. Then I proposed to her, and we planned to get married after my discharge. Sophie was older and more experienced than I, and she had some doubts about it.

"Hey, Gary, Bing Crosby's son marrying a black woman, that's heavy. You don't know what you're letting yourself in for. Man, they're gonna hang our ass."

I wouldn't buy it. I was full of piss and vinegar and thought I could lick the whole world, and I didn't care what anyone thought. My mother and my grandfather had taught me all human beings were created equal, and that's what I believed. If some people got upset because my wife was black, well, they were dealing from bigotry and we were dealing from truth, so how could they win?

"Fuck 'em," I told her. "They can't hang our ass. You know we love each other. What are you gonna do, stop seeing me because of them?"

"I should. I really should, but I can't."

"Well, I ain't gonna stop either. If we stop seeing each other it'll be because *we* decide to, and that's it."

I didn't tell Dad about Sophie. I didn't have to. He got the news straight from my commanding general. Some GI must have seen us coming out of a hotel with our arms around each other and started the gossip flying. When it reached the top, the general sat himself down and wrote the old man directly. From the way he reacted, it must have flipped that mucket on his head around, but he never once breathed a word to me that he knew anything about it. Instead of firing off one of his usual lectures and forcing a confrontation, he went over my head and engaged

239

the general in a little back-and-forth correspondence on what could be done to get me out of the relationship.

It wasn't until many years later, long after I had made my peace with him, that I came to read his words for the first time, but they still stung. Too bad he couldn't have told the general to mind his own business and stay out of my life. Too bad the color of Sophie's skin wasn't less important than the fact we loved each other. Too bad he didn't give a damn what people might think and the possible consequences to my career—and his. But then I reminded myself that that just wasn't him. I flashed back to the afternoons I watched him and his cronies shaking their heads over Lennie Hayton. "Poor Lennie," they would say, almost as though they were sitting at his wake. "He was a genius, one of the greatest arrangers of all time. It's such a shame what happened to him, such a pity." I knew that Lennie Hayton was a good friend of Dad's from the Paul Whiteman days, but I couldn't understand what they were talking about. Jesus, what *did* happen to him? Did he die? Did he do something wrong and get thrown in jail? What? Much later I figured out what they meant. Lennie Hayton's great sin was that he had married Lena Horne, a black woman he loved, and the old Irish bigots who were running the business put the hammer on him. He had been slated for great things, but after that they didn't want to know him.

My relationship with Sophie came to its own natural end without any help from the general or my father. One morning I woke up in the hotel room bed with my usual hangover, and when I turned to face her I saw that her eye was swollen closed, her lips puffed up and the side of her cheek all bruised. I couldn't begin to remember how that might have happened. When I shook her awake she told me. I had done it. We'd had an argument the night before, and in the rage of the moment I had lashed out with my fists and worked her over. I couldn't believe I'd let myself do something that awful, but I knew it was true. I wanted to cut my throat. Instead, I uncorked a jug and poured myself a stiff drink.

We kept to the room until she was straightened away enough to go back to work. I watched over her while she slept and fed her soup and put ice packs on her bruises and kept on talking and apologizing for what I had done. At first she was so angry and hurt she wouldn't listen, but after a while her anger cooled down. She knew it didn't have anything to do with her. She knew I was striking out at the Army and Dad and God and the whole damn universe, and she forgave me. I didn't forgive me. I don't forgive myself to this day. She never did tell me what started it, and I didn't press her. That wasn't important. There was no excuse for it, no earthly way to justify it. Sophie was more than my lover. She was my friend. She had saved my ass too many times to be anything but the best friend I ever had.

The fact that I could mangle someone that close to me and not even know it scared me to death and made me close off even further. I was terrified it might happen again, but the fear only made me drink harder and black out more often.

We stayed together until the bitter end—sort of—but there was no more talk about getting married. I was so crazy about her that I had wanted the marriage more than anything in the world, but now I had to take off the rose-colored glasses and face reality.

"Wait a minute, man," I told myself, "you aren't ready to get married to anybody. The way you are and the way it's gonna be for you, you're just a sinking ship. If you care for this woman at all, you better just leave her be."

The day I headed back to Tinseltown, my discharge in my pocket, we said good-bye at the train station. We promised each other we would write and stay in contact and get together soon, but we never did. That was the last I saw of her.

I still wouldn't acknowledge it, but by the end of my two years in the Army I had turned into a full-fledged alcoholic so dependent on my daily quota of booze I would go into withdrawal seizures if I didn't have it. Not having it wasn't usually a problem. God knows I kept myself well supplied. But three or four times it was. Word would come down that the inspector general was arriving in the morning to inspect the post, and since I wouldn't be able to hide my stash of jugs I'd finish them off that night. The next day rumdums like me were told to disappear somewhere so we wouldn't embarrass the commanding officer with our incompetence. I'd head straight for the PX or enlisted men's club to restock, but they'd be boarded up tight for the inspection. I'd be feeling all hinky and nervous, counting off the hours until I could get a drink under my belt, when an A-bomb would explode inside my brain and I'd suddenly black out. Someone would find me thrashing around on the ground, twitching and shaking so hard he'd have to stick a handkerchief in my mouth to keep me from biting off my tongue.

The next thing I knew I'd be staring up at the ceiling in the locked ward of the hospital's neurological section. The first time it happened I thought maybe I had snapped out and they'd put me away. I looked over at the steel door with no handle, noticed how it was all blackened with soot from where someone had tried to set fire to it, and told myself, "Woo-oo, you're in the snake pit now, Jack." The possibility was confirmed when the male nurses refused to let me have a match for my cigarette or the belt to my bathrobe or even a sharpened pencil. I tried not to let it get to me. "So I'm in the snake pit. So what? I'm still doing my time, still chalking up them days. Might as well do 'em in here. They bring me my meals. I get to watch 'Time for Beany' on television. It's almost like a vacation. Hell, I know I ain't crazy." Beneath the bravado, though, I wasn't so sure. I knew I was coming unglued from all the booze and pills. I knew my temper was completely out of control. Part of me did want to toe the line and was scared to death I'd be thrown in the brig for being such a wild man and fuckup, but another part couldn't care less, and the tension between them was tearing me into pieces. I was so down and depressed, it didn't seem like I'd ever be able to get any good thoughts going and straighten myself out.

Maybe the doctors did think I was nuts, but after endless rounds of spinals and brain scans and EEGs they decided I had epilepsy. They didn't associate the seizures with the fact that I had been forced to cold turkey for a day and, without the alcohol my body now needed, all the circuits in my nervous system had shorted out. Neither did I. I didn't discover that until three or four years later. I can't say their diagnosis caused me much concern. It was just one more piece of bad news. After I'd rested up a few days and was starting to get thirsty again, they explained how I'd have to live with epilepsy for the rest of my life, handed me a prescription for Dilantin, then cut me loose. I headed straight for the nearest bar and stayed loaded until the next time the inspector general came around and I landed back in the hospital again.

When the old man heard about my illness, he sent off a cable asking if I wanted him to come over. I told him not to bother, of course, so he said whatever he had to tell me by mail. His letter tried to stay upbeat and supportive, but he couldn't resist the opportunity to moralize. My bad habits had caught up with me. If I didn't want to ruin my health completely, I'd better cut back on the heavy eating and drinking and stop running around.

Given his natural bent toward secrecy about anything personal —which was pretty near everything outside of the official public image—I wasn't surprised by his concern that I might go shooting off my mouth about my "problem," as he called it. The appeal had about as much impact as his advice to improve my eating and drinking habits. I didn't give a damn who knew about it. On the contrary, I used it as material for bar jokes.

"Whee, I got epilepsy."

"Really? No kidding?"

"Sure, watch me fall on my head."

Chapter Thirteen
Back on the Loose

Alcoholics are scared to death of change. Give us a rut and we'll furnish it. Just as the Army and I were parting company, Rosey hit me with the news that he'd signed me to a movie contract with Fox and had lined up a whole string of nightclub dates. For all my pessimism about the future, I was back in show business. But the new lease on life didn't seem to make a bit of difference. I was still the same guy, operating with the same headset. Instead of bouncing off the walls with relief and gratitude, all I felt was guilt.

"C'mon, man, you've been shut off from the business for two years," I told myself. "If that happened to anybody else, they sure as hell wouldn't be coming home to a movie contract. They'd be back to busing dishes and hustling the agents in the afternoon."

I stayed on in Europe as long as I could, then groped my way back to the United States. My first night in New York I got myself so loaded that when I woke up the next morning in some seedy hotel room off Times Square I had to check the cover of the Bible on the night table to find out where I was. Still snoring away next to me was an ancient hooker who looked like Tony Galento. I couldn't remember how she had gotten there either.

Fox started me off as Pat Boone's fast-talking, wisecracking sidekick in a low-budget "youth" movie called *Mardi Gras*. I had been acting that personality in real life for so many years now, I could play it half bagged—and I did. Pat, of course, came from the other end of the universe. He was as clean-cut and straight as I was bent, and although he was a pleasure to be around, we weren't exactly sidekicks when the cameras stopped rolling. But I had enormous respect for him. I watched the way he ran his action, and I could see he was genuine. He was a good, natural, straight dude who never acted holier-than-thou or tried to make you come over to his way of thinking. In the double hip world of show business, where everyone is so slick and cool, he had to take an awful lot of kidding for being Mr. Virtuous, but he took it well and didn't let it change his style. He'd laugh right along with you, then continue to live it. He had a solid core of inner strength, and that made him happy.

I'd look at him on the set and say to myself, "Boy, it must be something to be that good and be that happy about it." It seemed to me that most of the so-called "good" people I'd known were really boring, pinch-faced and miserable. They were so busy trying to be good that they missed out on life. But not Pat. He wasn't missing out on anything. Sometimes I'd catch myself thinking, "Jesus, if only I could be like that, it would be so great. God, it would be wonderful. It would make the old man so pleased." But that was just a passing thought. I knew that never in a million years could I even begin to hack it.

Back in L.A., I rented a one-bedroom house up on Sunset Plaza Drive, bought myself a mean-ass little watchdog I named Shifty and continued on my wicked ways. Sammy Davis, Jr., and Herb Jeffries lived right down the hill, and we partied it up at Sammy's house till all hours of the day and night. One of my favorite drinking buddies was Don Rickles. Whenever he came to town to work at Slate Brothers, I'd go over to the club and juice with him till the place closed; then we'd come back to my joint and juice some more. At some point in the middle of the night Don would always want to phone his mother in Florida.

"She'll never know we're drinking," he'd say.

"Don, it's four-thirty in the morning here," I'd try to tell him. "Where she is it's seven-thirty. If you call your mother at seven-thirty in the morning she's gonna know you're not sitting around eating ice cream and cake, Don."

"Nah, she'll never know."

He'd put in the call, and naturally she nailed him the moment she heard his voice. After finishing up his conversation, he would pass out on the couch under the living room skylight. When I stumbled back into the room about noon, the sun would be beating down on him, the sweat would be pouring off his forehead and his entire suit would be soaking wet. We'd pull it together, get him back to his hotel, then start over again the next night with the same routine.

Don tore it up pretty good in those days, but even he couldn't keep up with me. After a couple of nights of carrying on he'd have to tell me, "Hey, kid, I gotta work. I gotta perform. I can't keep doing this all the time." So I'd have to find someone else to play with for a while. That wasn't hard. The bars were filled with swingers like myself looking to hang out until the sun came up. One night I ran into Sydney Chaplin, Charlie's son. By the time we ended up back at his place I was so drunk that when he staggered over to my chair to tell me something I shushed him up with the line, "Y'know, Syd, the trouble with you is you don't know what it's like to be the son of a famous father." He laughed so hard he collapsed right on top of me.

It wasn't all fun and games, of course. Once I had a few drinks under my belt, it didn't take much to trigger my temper, and whatever happened happened. I didn't care. I reacted the same way whether I was in a workingman's bar or some Beverly Hills mansion. The night I got into a scuffle at the party for Carl Sandburg at Milton Berle's house, I damn near punched myself out of the business. Some corporate big shot who was even drunker than I was started in on me about the name, and instead of walking away as expected, so the high rollers could enjoy their cultural evening unruffled, I lashed out at him with my mouth until he took the first swing, then I went for him, slapping him hard in the face. The fight was broken up in a second, but the room was jammed with press people and the news was sure to be in all the gossip columns the next morning. I could see the headlines:

"Gary Crosby At It Again—Disrupts Uncle Miltie's Party for Poet." It would have happened, too, if Milton's wife, Ruth, hadn't gone out of her way to keep the roof from crashing down on my head. The next day Rosey called to tell me how she went to bat for me.

"Well, kid, you sure lucked out on this one."

"What do you mean?"

"Well, Ruth Berle stayed up half the night calling every newspaper guy in town to make sure they understood the other fella started it. So it looks like you're gonna be all right—this time."

There were other times, though, when the other fella didn't start it and nobody was around to keep me from messing myself up with the powers that be. After *Mardi Gras* I went on to make three or four more quickie movies for Fox. The titles were different, but my part stayed exactly the same. I was still playing the hero's wisecracking sidekick. When you do only one thing all the time, people begin to get the idea you can't do anything else, so I went over to Fox to talk to the executives.

"I've done the garbage now for you guys. I've done everything you want. Now can't you put me in something halfway decent? Can't you give me a good small part where I get to stretch a little?"

I guess I was knocking their pictures to them. I didn't mean to. I thought they knew they were garbage. But if they did they didn't want to hear it from the likes of me. In a couple of years there wouldn't be any more parts, but for the time being I continued on with more of the same.

I did not make a lot of friends for myself on the set, not where it counted. Oh, the extras loved me. I sat around kibitzing with them between takes and ate lunch with them, which was considered very bad form, and when someone was stiffed out of the full money due him I'd tell the director, "Okay, that's it. I ain't working today until you fix this guy's problem." Playing Don Quixote like that didn't exactly endear me to the hearts of the producers. Nor did the way I showed up for work totally wasted and bedraggled from the night before. I'd be popping bennies and juicing all morning just to stay up there enough to hit the mark and say the lines. When we finally broke for lunch, I'd either crash in the trailer for an hour or run to the nearest bar and

247

throw down three or four fast doubles and get properly wasted.

Some days I didn't show up at all. When I came home at five in the morning I'd shave and shower, then lie down for a few minutes, and the next thing I knew it would be two o'clock in the afternoon and I'd blown the whole day. The phone had been ringing for hours and Rosey had been pounding on my front door, but I hadn't heard them. I'd walk onto the set the next morning like nothing had happened. "Hi, guys. Let's go to work." I'd do fine that day and maybe the next week, but then I'd blow it again. I never started out meaning to blow it. I'd go out the night before, just intending to have a little fun. But a little was never enough. I was still running the old tape: "When I was a kid they wouldn't let me out of that goddam jail long enough to have any fun, and now that I'm over twenty-one I'm gonna make up for it and I don't care what happens."

Part of me did care and tried to talk some sense into myself, but of course I wouldn't listen. And the more I lectured myself, the angrier and more bullnecked I became.

Rosey must have tried a hundred times to get my head straight. And I heard him. I knew what he meant. If I'd been in the frame of mind to listen to anyone, it would have been him. But I just wasn't in that frame of mind. I didn't want to hear about being a good boy. I didn't want to hear about being responsible. I didn't want to hear about making people like me. I had been listening to that horseshit all my life, and I was tired of it.

"Jesus Christ, man, you can't keep doing this shit," he would tell me, more like a buddy than some kind of high and mighty authority. "They're gonna catch up with you. That shit's cute once, maybe twice, if you're a big star, but that's about it. You know, those people put money into that stuff. You're fucking with their pocketbooks now. You ain't just thumbing your nose at them. God damn, Gary, you got a lot of ability and most of the time you're a pleasure, but, Jesus Christ, kid, you keep going off like that and they're not gonna hire you anymore. You're gonna be out of the business."

To anybody else I'd have answered, "Aw, fuck you, get lost," but with Rosey I sat there and listened. And every now and then what he was saying did get through to me. Then I'd tell him,

"Yeah, Rosey, you're right. I'm really sorry, and I swear to God it won't happen anymore. I'm gonna clean up my action, I promise you." And while I was saying it I believed it, just like any drunk believes it when he promises someone he loves. And because I believed it Rosey believed it. Yet a day later, or a week later, I'd be back in the same shithouse again, not knowing how and not knowing why and not knowing what the hell it was all about. The only thing I knew was that I needed to drink. I needed to drink to hide. I needed to drink to stay away from feelings. I needed to drink because I was angry. I needed to drink because I was scared. I needed to drink because I hurt, because my heart and soul just ached with pain all the fucking time.

If I was mayhem on the movie set, I was mass murder in nightclubs. Putting me in those gin mills was like sticking a diabetic with a sweet tooth in a candy store. Go to work in a joint where they served you drinks? Holy God, it was a license to steal. Well, I was supposed to be a big boy now. No one was supposed to be watching out for me. I was supposed to be watching out for myself. But I hadn't even admitted I was an alcoholic yet, much less done something about it. "Handle it? Why, sure, I can handle it," I told myself as I put on my tuxedo and opened my bar tab. "No problem."

I was loaded almost every gig I played. I'd have seven doubles before the first show just to loosen up, then half a jug more while waiting out the hour and a half to go on again. If it wasn't for the uppers I would have passed out for sure by the second show. As it was, most of the time I played it completely by rote in the grand tradition of the other show business lushes.

I loved juicing in those saloons, but I sure hated playing them. I hated the moldy backstage dressing rooms. I hated having to go out there by myself and work "in one." With Louis Armstrong and Les Brown I was just a small part of the show, and that suited me fine. Now I had to carry the whole thing by myself, and my ego wasn't up to it. More than anything, I hated that damn Bing Crosby medley that was my big closing number. It was like looking forward to death twice a night.

When I was first putting my act together, I picked out the kind of music that meant the most to me, largely soul tunes and blues like "Please Send Me Someone to Love," "Nobody Knows You When You're Down and Out," and the Lambert, Hendricks & Ross song "Gimme That Wine." Everyone kept asking me which of Dad's things I was going to use, and when I told them I hadn't planned to use any of them, they always reacted the same way. "What do you mean, you're not gonna do any of Bing's songs? Are you kidding? Of course you have to do them." Finally Sammy Cahn and Harry Crane came up with a medley of eight bars of every record he ever made and laid it on me, insisting I use it. Well, they were top songwriters and knew a whole lot more about the business than I did, so if they said I had to have a Crosby medley I guess I had to have a Crosby medley. But there I was again, riding the old man's coattails.

I suppose it was a great piece of material. The customers loved it. The rest of the act they weren't all that crazy about, probably because I wasn't giving them what they expected. But having to do that tribute to Dear Old Dad twice a night was driving me batty. When I tried to drop it, Harry Crane, Rosey and all the others kept telling me, "Man, you can't. Let's face it, that's what they come to hear." That would really ruffle my feathers because I knew it was true. So I kept it in, deliberately messing it up and doing it sarcastically and wise-assed to salvage some small shred of self-respect. It was just one more reason to get myself stoned.

The fact that the medley never failed to bring down the house didn't exactly enhance my sense of self-worth. If I hit one bad note while I was out there and all the rest were perfect, that would be the one I'd remember. When I came offstage I'd be so crazed I wanted to beat my head against the wall till my brains spilled out of my ears. When I didn't do it to myself, there was always some drunk in the audience ready to do it for me.

"Aw, you stink! You can't sing fer shit!"

He may have been a paying customer, but I dealt with him the same way as the GIs back in the service clubs in Germany. At first I'd resurrect a few of the old jokes all performers use to defend themselves against hecklers.

"Pardon me, sir, but when you go to the movies do you talk to the screen? . . . Oh, you want to do lines with me? Wonderful, I'll check my brains and we'll start even."

But I ran out of patience fast. If he was too drunk or hostile to quiet down, and if the bouncers didn't hustle him out the front door, I'd segue into a more direct approach.

"Hey, dummy, shut your fuckin' mouth or I'm gonna knock your head off!"

If that didn't stop him, if he tried some kind of comeback line —"Oh, a tough guy, huh?"—then I snapped completely.

"That's right. You want it here or what?"

By now I'd be moving through the audience with the mike stand in my hand, ready to bash his brains out. Once a heckler started in on me, all my concentration went to him and I forgot about the two hundred other people in the room. I didn't realize I was scaring the bejesus out of them. Inside my befuddled mind I was back in San Jose, where everyone talked and acted tough. But I guess I had them cringing in their seats.

The management would try to talk to me about it afterwards. But I was too hot to listen, and I'd be just as hostile with them.

"Hey, look, I did some lines at the guy. If you assholes can't get down there and haul his ass away before there's trouble, then there's gonna be trouble. You hire bouncers. Use 'em. Get those motherfuckers off my back!"

"Well, that's not the way to handle it."

"Yeah? Well, that's the way *I* handle it! I ain't gonna stand there and take shit from some drunk forever. If I run out of lines, I'm gonna go for him."

I was not what you would call America's gift to the fine art of nightclub singing.

I hardly saw the old man during these years. He was going his way, I was going mine. I was out of his house, living the way I wanted. In October 1957, six months before I came back from the Army, he had remarried, and now he was busy making a new life for himself.

Despite all the gossip to the contrary, I didn't really care that he had married again. I figured it was none of my business. Oh, I would have cared if he had dumped my mother and left her to rot while he took off with another woman. I would have cared plenty. But the way it was, Mom was gone and there was no reason for him to stay single the rest of his days if he didn't want to. If anything, I was glad he had married again. Between his loneliness after Mom's death and the recurrent kidney stone attacks, he had become so miserable and short-tempered that I had thought if he found a lady to love it would probably mellow him a little. It would certainly give him something else to think about besides me and my brothers, and God knows we could use the breathing space. Before the wedding to Kathryn, I even used to fantasize about who he might end up with. "Yeah, Rosie Clooney would be great, but of course she already has Joe. Well, maybe it'll be Mona Freeman. That would be good. She's nice people."

As for Kathryn Grant, I had only seen her once before the marriage, and she seemed okay too. Dad had invited my brothers and me over to the house to meet her, and she struck me as a bright, energetic, positive human being. I think the four of us might have frightened her some, which showed she also had good sense. We weren't the little Katzenjammer Kids anymore. If Linny and the twins hadn't yet become quite the terror I was, they weren't all that far behind. There had been one awkward moment at the dinner table when the old man and I were talking about ball and she jumped in with the line, "Gee, I think it's wonderful young boys like you are interested in sports." "What is this young boy stuff?" I grumbled to myself, knowing she was six months younger than I, and I threw her a dirty look. But then I realized, "Oh, hell, she's just trying to be ingratiating," and dropped it. She seemed to be making the old man happy, and that was the important thing. Anyone who made him happy and kept him off our backs was all right with me.

The press, though, didn't seem to want to see it that way. It was no longer a secret that Dad and I were on the outs, and the reporters kept bombarding me with questions about the marriage, trying to get me to say something that would make a good headline.

"So how do you feel about your father remarrying? What do you think about Kathy Grant?" they would ask, cocking their eyebrows as if they expected me to blurt out, "Man, I'm really mad about it. I'd like to kill that bitch."

I was easy enough to bait, but this time around I wouldn't go for it. If I was angry at anyone it was the reporters for trying to build something that wasn't there.

"Hey, what the hell business is it of mine? He's an adult male. My mother's dead. Who cares what I think?"

"Well, what about his new wife? Any truth to the story you don't get along?"

"Jesus Christ, I don't even know her. How can you not get along with somebody you don't even know?"

If I wasn't drunk and hostile enough by now to tell them to go fuck themselves, they'd press on with the next question calculated to get a rise out of me.

"Well, do you think she'll be able to replace your mother?"

That one was too absurd to even merit an answer. They were talking to me like I was still a little kid, but I was a grown man twenty-four years old.

"Hey, I told you guys what I have to say. That's it."

"Uh-huh. Well, if you don't give us any more, we'll have to write the story the way we see it."

"Fine. You write anything you want."

And often they did.

If anyone was upset about the marriage, it was Dad's friends. The vitriol that spewed out of their mouths at the beginning just amazed me. A lot of them seemed to assume I felt like they did, and when I ran into them at a studio or bar they'd start bad-rapping Kathryn the second they laid eyes on me.

"Oh, it's such a shame," they'd complain, "such a damn shame how she's taking him away from everybody, how she's cutting him off from you and your brothers."

I wouldn't rise up to defend her. That wasn't my business either. But inside I'd be thinking the atomic bomb couldn't drive us any further apart than we already are.

I'd stand there nodding silently while they went on to take her inventory from top to bottom, saying all the classic dumb things people say when they're unhappy that a friend has remarried.

"Oh, she's so much younger than him . . . She's just a fortune hunter out to grab all his bread and take it away from you guys . . . Listen, did you catch what just went down, how she charged this and bought herself that?"

When they paused and looked up for some kind of response,

I'd answer, "Well, I really don't know what's happening there, man. I don't talk to him that much, y'know. We're not exactly buddy-buddy. But if what you say is true, well, she sure grabbed the wrong cat to pull that shit on. He'll turn her hair gray trying to cop his money. She'll die in the attempt if that's what she's up to." Nothing struck me as being funnier than the riff that Kathryn was looking to do my brothers and me out of the old man's fortune. I figured we were the last persons in the world he'd give it to anyway, and that didn't bother me in the least. Hell, it was his money. He earned it. He could do whatever he wanted with it.

Sometimes I'd watch his cronies cheer themselves up by trading off old man–young wife jokes.

"Hey, did you hear the one about the night Bing came home late from the studio? He comes into the house and calls out, 'Kathryn, honey, I'm home.' But there's no answer. 'Kathryn!' he calls out again. Still no answer. 'Kathryn? . . . Gary?'"

I'd laugh right along with them, but I didn't think the humor was particularly funny. I'd notice a bunch of squares at the other end of the bar, their eyes bugging out of their heads, and realize that although the guys were just kidding around, these people were taking the *tummel* halfway seriously.

Until they learned better, I guess they were afraid they were going to lose the old man. Not that they had him in the first place. Most of them only had the persona, not the genuine article. There weren't that many people he was really close to. But he was such a charmer that he was able to make someone he didn't see from one year to the next believe he could barely exist without him. Dad was sensational with that stuff. He had tons of what I had none of, and I had to admire him for it. It was a whole lot better than being an asshole like me, who told everybody to go fuck themselves. At the same time, though, you never really knew where you stood with him, and I suppose those who loved him were scared to death he'd drop them. That didn't happen, of course. Marriage didn't change his life that much. He still went fishing with his fishing buddies, still played golf, still did all the things he used to. Eventually even his most jealous cronies came to realize that and were able to stop bad-mouthing Kathryn and relax.

A little over a year after Dad and Kathryn married they had their first child. A few months later the old man gave an interview to Joe Hyams that rocked me back on my heels. Under the headline "How Bing Crosby 'Failed' His Four Sons" he went public for the very first time with the news that he wasn't exactly the all-wise and all-loving father he had always been painted in the press.

"I guess I didn't do very well bringing my boys up," he confessed. "I think I failed them by giving them too much work and discipline, too much money and too little time and attention. But I did my best and so did their mother. I'm getting another chance with Tex (Harry Lillis Crosby, Jr., aged five months), and with Kathy as help I'll do better. . . . I used to get them together for talks all the time and get nowhere. They'd yes me along beautifully and say, 'You're so right, Dad' and go out and do it all over again. I used to have mass whippings—not very often, but I kept a big leather belt hung on a hook upstairs as a sort of symbol. It got so I just had to start for the belt and everything would quiet down. . . . It made me feel like a heel to be bawling them out all the time, and the endless pleading, the coaxing and arguing grew tiresome. I've had so many heart-to-heart talks with Gary I'm embarrassed when I say, 'Sit down, Gary, I want to have a few words with you.' . . . I think maybe I did too much talking while they did too little. It seems that maybe we got out of the habit of communicating. You've got to get kids started talking to you and keep them at it. I never had much success talking with mine."

Except for the line about giving us too much money and too little attention—from where I stood, it seemed like exactly the opposite on both counts—everything he said was true, and that shocked the hell out of me. Dad never talked that openly to the press—or to anyone else, for that matter. When the reporters came around to interview him he always played his standard balmy, hail-fellow-well-met routine on them, and if they had the audacity to ask a serious question he'd throw out a gag line and get them laughing and off the subject so fast they wouldn't even realize they were being turned around. I was used to that stuff, but this was completely unexpected and I didn't know what to make of it. "Whoa, what's happening here, Jack?" I found myself wondering. But I knew he had said it. Without a doubt the words were his.

Coming from my father, it was a huge admission. Up to now he had never let me think for a single instant that he wasn't 100 percent right and I wasn't 100 percent wrong. If he had any uncertainties about it, he kept them to himself. After the interview hit the streets he still acted that way. The next time I saw him it was like it never happened. We went right back to the usual superficial talk about sports and show business. And he never did acknowledge the interview to the day he died. That's the way he was. He was one of those men who just don't have it in them to express their emotions face-to-face. He could only do it through the back door. He had been the same with my mother. When he went on the road, he wrote her tender, beautiful letters saying how much he loved her, but once he came home he reverted to the jocular, offhanded way of dealing with her that kept all real feeling at arm's length. Still, the interview was as close to an apology as he had ever come, and that was something.

I suppose I might have gone to him and said, "Hey, Dad, that was wonderful. Reading what you told that guy really made me feel good. Let's talk some more." I didn't. I was too busy killing off every bit of human instinct in me for love, warmth or sincerity to even consider opening up to that kind of sentiment. To my way of thinking, all that crap could do was get you hurt, and I knew damn well I didn't want to hurt anymore. Looking at it now, I can see that the interview was Dad's way of signaling that he was ready to end the war between us. But I didn't see it then, didn't want to see it. I wasn't ready for him yet. "Oh, great," I grumbled to myself, "it's a little late in the day for him to start talking that shit. How the hell did they get it out of him anyway? What did they do, catch him drunk or something?" Another part of me that begrudgingly had to admire him for his honesty answered, "Well, hell, man, at least he did it, y'know," but I shut that voice up real fast.

Predictably, the interview generated a lot of follow-up stories with headlines like "Bing Calls Self a Flop as Father" and "Crisis for the Crosbys: What's Bothering Bing's Boys—A Report on an American Family That Might Have Done Better by America."

And, just as predictably, the reporters tracked down the kids to record their reactions to the old man's confession. My brothers played it straight the way they'd been taught from childhood and acted like they didn't even know what he was talking about. "I don't know why he made that statement," Linny told Louella. "No one meant to do any wrong, and we're all working hard." Phil's line was, "None of us feels the way Dad does about it. Sure, we had a few problems. Any family runs into that." And Denny added, "So far as being strict is concerned, I remember we used to get a few cuffs now and then, but everybody gets those. I don't recall any lickings." If anyone was keeping score of the old man's defenders, I imagine I must have been conspicuous by my absence.

The same month the Army shipped me over to Frankfurt Denny and Phil finished up their tour of duty in Germany. When their route back to the States brought them through Frankfurt, we were able to get together for a few days. It was the first time we'd seen each other in ages, but the second we touched base we immediately fell back into our old familiar rap.

"Hey, Gary, how you doin', asshole?"

"I'm doin' fine."

"How you like the Army?"

"Oh, fuck you guys. I'm just serving my time."

"Well, we're short. We're headed home."

"I know that, you shits. So get the hell out of here, will ya. Don't be hanging around grinning at me. Go on back and be civilians."

Over the next three nights we hit every soldier bar in town and tore it up pretty good. They were drinking as hard as I was by now, but I didn't worry about their juicing any more than I worried about my own. Hell, we were just three swingers and rounders. Nothing wrong with us. Everybody carries on the way we do—everybody we know. Anyone who doesn't is a square asshole.

The boys hadn't really figured out what to do with themselves now that the Army was cutting them loose, but to keep Dad off their backs they had promised to return to school and finish up their degrees. "Well, good luck with it," I told them as we said good-bye, knowing full well their hearts weren't in it. "Hope you guys make it."

In between lectures Dad kept me posted about their progress. I automatically took their side whenever he came down on them, but the truth of the matter was they didn't seem to be making out all that well. They sure as hell weren't keeping him too happy. From the sound of Dad's letters, neither was Linny.

I couldn't really understand why the old man kept writing me about his disappointment with my brothers for quitting school and failing to give their lives a more positive direction. But looking at it now, I suppose he was already reaching out and trying to strike some kind of truce. I suppose now that Mom was gone and the younger kids were turning into everything he feared they might, he needed emotional support from somewhere and hoped to get me on his side by sharing his concern. But I was the very last one to turn to. I was in worse shape than they were and didn't expect to be getting any better. Besides, I was still convinced he was the one who stuck me in the Army in the first place, and as much as I shucked and jived him the few times I actually wrote him back, I was still furious. Sure, now that the prick has me where he wants me he can afford to make nice when he isn't bawling me out.

Occasionally he tried a different tactic to bring me around, exposing his own insecurities, I suppose to give me a glimpse of the flesh-and-blood human being behind the invulnerable facade. First he was apprehensive about the recording sessions coming up with Buddy Bregman because he was afraid he'd lost his beat. Later on he confided that he sounded so bad to himself on his last bunch of sides that he was going to quit recording altogether. I didn't go for that one either. It was inconceivable to me he could ever doubt himself for a minute. He might well have meant exactly what he said, but rather than making me sympathetic or concerned, all that kind of self-questioning did was get me angry.

By the time the Army cut me loose, Denny had gotten married to a showgirl who was working the Tropicana Hotel in Las

Vegas. Four months later Phil married her buddy from the same chorus line. They had a third one all picked out for me, but I fooled them. I was back to running with hookers and wasn't about to tie myself down with anyone. Dad hoped that marriage would make the boys shape up and give them some sense of direction, but it didn't seem to change them much, not even after their wives became pregnant. Phil cut a couple of records and invested in a chain of taco stands. Denny had an afternoon disc jockey show in L.A. But they were both mostly just marking time while they partied. When Linny finished up his service the following year and moved in with me, I could see he didn't know what to do with himself either. I watched the three of them drifting around, doing a whole lot of nothing, and began to wonder, "Why are my brothers sitting on their asses like that when they're all talented? They all can sing. They all can talk into a microphone. They all can be funny. Maybe it just didn't occur to them, but wouldn't it be great if the four of us joined up and went to work together?" When I sprung the idea on them, they liked it and so did Rosey, so we chipped in the money to hire a bunch of top professionals to create an act for us and started rehearsing.

To get the act up on its feet, we put in three months of hard work at a rehearsal hall in L.A. We mostly sang together as a quartet, but each of us also had a solo spot and in between songs we did some comedy patter and even a little dancing. Denny was the only one who could dance worth a damn. The rest of us clumped around the stage like three bull elephants, but our choreographer was so good he was able to teach us enough soft shoe to sneak by. Just watching us try not to knock each other down got everyone laughing, so I started throwing in one-liners and that made it even funnier. Our big finish was the Crosby medley. It didn't bother my brothers, but I still hated it and everything it stood for.

We opened in Tucson, then moved on to Chicago, Cleveland and Washington. The act seemed to work. The people liked it, which made the bosses breathe easier about all the money they were paying us, and the press was more than kind. "The boys have a chance of becoming one of the top acts in show business," the critic for the Arizona *Star* wrote about our Tucson debut. *Va-*

riety was just as enthusiastic when we played the Chez Paree in Chicago. "Bing Crosby's four sons have a superlative act that is likely to abash those skeptics who surmised the boys would trade mainly on the lustrous family name. . . . A rouser of an entry for the big rooms and vaudeo."

The success of the act should have been tremendously gratifying, but I was still the same cynical, negative lush who couldn't seem to get pleasure out of anything. I was always looking to find fault, even though working with my brothers was a joy compared to doing a single. It wasn't so cold and lonely out there when the jokes died or a song didn't go over. We could throw lines at each other—"Oh, you messed up that one good"—or play around for a minute to ease the tension, and the audience was able to have fun with the mistakes. But not me. They still drove me crazy.

We put the act together without any help from the old man. Respecting our wishes to make or break it on our own, he kept his distance. Every now and then word would filter back through Rosey or Bill Morrow that although he worried about our drinking he was pleased we had at least gotten up off our duffs and were doing something. "Gee, your dad's really proud of you guys," they would tell us, but of course I didn't believe them. I wasn't proud of myself, so how could he be? "Well, what else are they gonna say?" I'd rationalize. "They're in his corner anyhow, so it's just more bullshit." But it wasn't. That was his way of letting us know he was more or less happy with us for the moment.

When we opened at the Sahara in Las Vegas the end of July 1959, Dad was off fishing in Alaska with Morrow and Phil Harris. I suppose because that interview with Joe Hyams was only four months old, the story about how we weren't getting along still had some life in it, and the reviews all made a big point of the fact he wasn't sitting there at ringside cheering us on. The next day the regular press picked up on it.

"Where's your father?" the reporters kept asking. "How come he didn't show up? Anything wrong?"

It was obvious that they were trying to get us to say something they could use against him to sell a few papers, but there really wasn't anything to say. The rift between us wasn't any wider than it had ever been. Linny and the twins made the appropriate denials. Phil even read them the telegram Dad had wired us from Alaska: "Take 'em by storm. Catching lottsa fish in this part of the country. See you soon." If I had kept my mouth shut too, the whole thing would have blown over in twenty-four hours. But the reporters continued hammering away with the same questions and, as had to happen, one night I was juiced and hostile enough to give them what they were waiting for.

"We just don't get along," I told them. "The other boys can invite him if they want. Ain't gonna bother me in the least. Dad did some things last Christmas that I felt were far from right. But he's done a lot of things in the past that I didn't like. I'm sure no one knows him as well as I do, although a lot of people think they do."

That's all they had to hear. "Gary Reveals a Quarrel with Father, Bing Crosby," screamed one headline. "Gary Crosby Peeved at Dad: Admits Rift with Bing Wide," read a second. "Behind the Bing-Gary Break," promised a third. The "things" Dad had done that I had felt "were far from right" were to get angry at Linny and return his Christmas present because he had turned down the old man's invitation to Thanksgiving dinner to spend the holiday with me. But the papers all had their own ideas about what was bugging me. One claimed I was bitter that Dad had remarried. Another insisted I was miffed because he had moved Mom's things out of the house when Kathryn moved in. A third said I didn't like what he had told Joe Hyams about how he had raised us. When the four of us signed to appear on Bob Hope's television special, some of the papers even read that as a direct insult to the old man. Why else would we go to work for his rival?

The foolishness didn't end until Dad turned up to catch our act at the Moulin Rouge in Hollywood three months later. After the show the reporters trailed him back to our dressing room to witness the big reconciliation. The boys and I had to be as juiced as we always were, but I'm sure we straightened up on the spot the moment he strolled through the door. "Nice job, fellas," he told us. "You were in tune most of the time, you didn't bump into the furniture and you all finished together. That was terrific." Aside from the obligatory photographs of Bing and the kids, that's about all that happened. The whole visit couldn't have lasted more than twenty minutes, but it was enough to send the press guys running to their typewriters. "Peace reigns once more in the Bing Crosby family" read the morning papers. "The crooner and his eldest son Gary settled their differences last night and posed for pictures with their arms around each other, joined by Bing's other grown sons, Dennis, Philip and Lindsay."

When Dad wrote me in November he seemed pleased that the act had gone so smoothly in Pittsburgh and expressed the hope it would hold up just as well when we moved on to Montreal. The way it worked out, it didn't hold up at all. A week into the gig the whole thing came crashing down around our heads. Less than six months after the four of us got together our partnership was over.

To this day I'm not entirely clear about what happened. I know the constant boozing had to have a lot to do with it. We were juiced all the time, and when we weren't juiced we were hung over.

Not that my brothers didn't have reason to drink. Their personal lives had gotten all tangled together, and they were making each other miserable. The friction was creating worse and worse turmoil the longer we stayed together. I didn't have a personal life to speak of—no wife or steady girl friend—and maybe that gave me a little more objectivity. "Hey, if you guys don't cut this shit out, you're gonna end up killing yourselves," I tried to tell them. "Stay away from each other when you come offstage. Go in different directions until showtime tomorrow." But I was no beacon of clarity. By the time we reached Montreal I was so disgusted that I had thrown enough nasty lines at them to place myself in the middle of the cross fire despite all my own good advice about keeping out of each other's business.

The boys had their own share of gripes against me. None of them liked the way I fooled around with the tribute to Dad at the close of the show. I'd throw out sarcastic Jack E. Leonard wisecracks, roll my eyes in exasperation, punch the piano player on the arm while the other guys were singing, do anything I could think of to make it clear how I felt. The band and the comics in the room would crack up, but the rest of the people thought I was being disrespectful to my father. So did my brothers. They kept telling me to stop messing with the medley, but I hated it so much I wouldn't listen. Maybe that's what we fought about.

Or maybe it was because I cut the show short that night and walked off the stage after twenty minutes. I had a bad habit of doing that. There were nights I was so hostile that if the audience didn't laugh in the right places or didn't seem to appreciate what they were seeing, I'd just fold it up on the spot and split.

"Okay, that's it for tonight, folks. You don't like what we're doing here? Terrific. Doesn't bother me. Only means I don't have to sweat up another suit. See you later. Good-bye."

You can't indulge yourself in that kind of insanity if you expect to stay in the business. But I was crazed and drunk and angry enough to try it.

Whatever the reasons, when I came back to the dressing room that night the boys were laying for me. The second I walked through the door all three jumped me. Two of them were crying as they pinned my arms to my sides. The third doubled his fists and started punching away. I was too drunk to know what it was all about, but that didn't matter. The important thing was that they had agreed to gang up on me. Three against one just wasn't our style, and I was so disgusted I don't even know if I even made much of an effort to fight back.

The scuffle was over in five minutes, but my feelings still hurt the next day. Well, if the boys didn't want me around, the hell with them. I wasn't going to stay. I didn't want anything more to do with them either. I called everyone together into my hotel room and told them I was leaving.

"You can't do that. We got a contract. We'll sue," the owner of the club threatened.

"Fuck you," I told him. "Sue anybody you want to sue, but that's it. I'm done with this thing. As far as I'm concerned, it's over . . . Okay, guys, here's the arrangements. Whoever wants to stay with you can stay. I'm going home."

My brothers took one plane back to L.A. and I took another. When the reporters waiting for them at the airport asked what had happened, they denied the split-up and said the engagement was cut short because I had come down with a sore throat. "We had a little disagreement, but there was no fight," Linny told them. "We wanted to get Gary to see a doctor. He is like the old man. He doesn't want to give up." We paid off the club to settle our contract, then canceled the rest of our bookings. The following May Linny and the twins regrouped and tried doing the act as a trio, but after a while they ran out of steam and closed it down for good. With no place to turn, I went back to working the joints as a single.

Chapter Fourteen
Second Chance

The first time I saw her I knew I liked her. Barbara was working the line at the Sahara Hotel in Las Vegas when I opened on the same bill with Joe E. Lewis seven months after the fight with my brothers in Montreal. I wasn't looking to get into anything serious. I was a confirmed bachelor by now, with so little self-esteem when it came to women that I'd automatically write off any lady dumb enough to want to have something to do with me. Still, that tall blond dancer in the chorus line definitely caught my attention. Between shows I watched the way she ran her action, and I liked her independence, I liked her sense of humor, I liked how she didn't take crap from anybody or bend over for the bosses.

At first she wouldn't let me come near her, which showed she also had good taste. I was still hiding behind my fast-talking, finger-popping bullshit personality, and she didn't care for that guy at all. "Hey, doll, what's happenin'?" I'd rap out of the side of my mouth when I passed her backstage, desperately trying to start some conversation so I could get to know her. But she kept right on moving like I wasn't even there.

"Hey, how does a person go about getting to meet Barbara?" I asked her friend Patti, who danced in the same chorus line.

"Just talk to her. Barbara's easy to talk to."

"Well, she doesn't talk to me. I can't even get a hello out of her backstage. Can you give me some help here?"

"Sure. You come with me."

Every night after work Barbara met a pack of her girl friends at the Flamingo Hotel. Then they'd all go out to eat and visit the clubs. Patti conspired to take me along. Everywhere they went I went. If there was an empty seat next to Barbara I'd grab it, and little by little I managed to worm my way in.

Late one night about fourteen of us were having breakfast at the Desert Inn with Frankie Laine and his wife when a drunk staggered up behind me, whacked me hard on the shoulder and growled, "Hey, Crosby!" I found out afterwards he was some big-shot hotel man from Houston who had mistaken me for one of my brothers, but I didn't know him from Adam and assumed he was just another hostile lush looking for trouble. Before he could straighten me out I had him down on the floor with my thumbs hooked in his throat. His eyeballs were bugging out of his head, and I was so full of rage I was ready to kill him. The security guards were still trying to pry me loose when, from the middle of the tumult, I heard Barbara say very quietly, "All right, Gary, cut it out and sit down." To my great amazement, that's exactly what I did.

"Jesus Christ, you must really love this girl," I thought to myself. "When the hell did you ever hear someone talking to you when you were that mad, much less do what they told you?"

It may sound like a strange way to fall in love, but that's how it went down. Later that evening her date put his arm around her shoulder and announced, "Hey, this is my girl, and I'm gonna marry her." "Oh no you're not," I found myself answering. "You better not go to the men's room, Jack, because she won't be here when you get back. *I'm* gonna marry her!"

I'd only known her a few weeks, but my mind was already made up. We began seeing each other privately every day. With no crowd of people around, I was able to relax my Mr. Cool defenses just enough to begin to talk to her like a reasonable human being. Whenever she caught me jiving, she busted me on the spot. "No, Gary, don't talk *at* me, talk *to* me," she'd say, and once I got the hang of it it wasn't all that hard. When I left Vegas to work in Reno I called her two or three times a day to tell her how much I loved her. The night I proposed I kept her on the phone seven hours and wouldn't let up until she finally said yes.

When I notified the old man about my wedding plans he was about to leave for Rome. He fired off a quick note advising me to take my time and be sure I'd made the right choice.

Well, I hadn't taken my time, and I wasn't sure about much. Oh, I was sure I loved Barbara and wanted to marry her, but I didn't think it would last. I figured it might take her a month or two to get tired of me and then she'd dump me real quick, so I played the whole thing for laughs. I rented the Bugsy Siegel Suite at the Flamingo Hotel for the ceremony. Don Rickles was my best man. When we went to buy the wedding bands he was so nervous he dropped a trayful of rings on the floor and was doing one-liners while we were down on our hands and knees trying to put them back. Then he had me bouncing off the walls with his *tummel* to the jewelry store owner.

"Want a ring at a discount. The kid doesn't have much. His old man's got all the money. You're gonna have to wait for the big score. Come on, *landsman,* haven't you got something nice at a better price?"

When the elevator carrying Barbara and her maid of honor up to the ceremony broke down, I was certain she had run out on me. Rickles and I were pacing the carpet in our suits, watching the minutes tick by, when he turned to me and wisecracked, "Well, I think she got smart. I think somebody told her something at the last minute, and she's on her way to Mexico." "Probably," I answered, trying to conjure up a smile. Finally she arrived, and the judge married us. He was so drunk he wrote the wrong name on the papers, and we had to have them redone the next day. Neither of us knew most of the people at the reception. At one point Harry James popped his head in the doorway and asked, "What's going on here?" "It's supposed to be a wedding," someone answered. "Oh, really? Who got married?" "I did," I told him. "Oh, good. Congratulations. Is that the cake?" He cut himself a slice and continued on his way. When the phone rang the next morning and a male voice said he wanted to meet with Barbara, I went crazy—even after she explained it was only a young guy she used to take care of years ago when his parents weren't around. "What the fuck is this?" I ranted. "Meet with my wife, my ass! I'll hammer his head in the sidewalk!" That's how secure I was.

After the wedding Barbara quit her job and we moved back to L.A. A few months later we were joined by her five-year-old son from her previous marriage. Steve had been living in New York with Barbara's mother, but now that she was done with the long late-night Vegas hours, she wanted him with her. Quite suddenly, without any real thought or planning, I seemed to have a full family of my own.

When Dad and Kathryn returned from Europe, I took Barbara to their house in Holmby Hills to meet them for the first time. It had to be done, but I was more than a little apprehensive. "Honey, y'know, he's kind of a cold fish," I told her on the drive over. "He's not warm like you are. So don't be grabbing and hugging at him like you usually do with people. That's not his style." She laughed and answered, "Well, I'll try. If I can remember, I'll keep my hands to myself." Before I could even finish the introductions, she threw her arms around him and gave him a big bear hug. He was as embarrassed by the display of affection as I knew he would be and tried to back off. But she wouldn't go for it. She went right up against his coldness like it wasn't there and destroyed it on the spot. On the way home she told me he even hugged her back a little when they said good night, but I don't know.

That was Barbara. She came from a large, warm Italian family in New York's Little Italy, where everyone hugged and kissed each other all the time. If you went downstairs for a pint of ice cream, they'd all have to throw their arms around you before you left, then embrace you again five minutes later when you came back. I had my own problems with that one in the beginning. On our way down to Mulberry Street to meet them, Barbara warned me, "Look, Gary, don't be surprised, because my Aunt Margaret and Uncle Paul will hug and kiss you and my cousins—Tommy and Lena and Richie and Johnny and Moe—will hug and kiss you. Everybody will hug and kiss you. That's how we are." "Well, I don't hug men," I grumbled. "In my family, you do," she snapped back, and that was that. At first I didn't know what to make of it and just let my hands dangle down at my sides. But little by little it got easier, and soon it was no problem at all.

The Cosentinos were a New York version of all the happy families I'd known as a kid—the Rosses I used to stay with when Mom was alive, the Wilscams and Benedettis and Donovans I visited over the weekend in high school. Tommy worked in the post office. Richie was a hairdresser. Lena had a job in the garment district. They were all good, down-to-earth, unpretentious people who loved and took care of each other and laughed together when things were going well and cried together when they weren't.

Every week the whole Cosentino clan, complete with husbands and wives and children, would crowd into Aunt Margaret's tiny apartment for Sunday dinner. There'd be huge trays of antipasto waiting for you on the dining table, pots of spaghetti bubbling on top of the stove, chicken and meatballs and sausage and God knows what else cooking away in the oven. You'd eat and eat until the eyeballs were bulging out of your head, then here would come Aunt Margaret with a big platter of something else. If you had the audacity to say, "No thank you," tears would come to her eyes and her chin would start to tremble, so you always had to have some more. When there wasn't strength left in your arms to raise your fat body from the chair, Tommy would run down to the corner and pick up a few dozen cannoli. We'd eat for about six hours, but Aunt Margaret still wouldn't be sure everyone had had enough. "Are you full yet?" she'd ask. "How was it? Was it good?" On your way out the door she'd slip you a brown paper bag of leftovers to take home.

I became part of all that and was grateful for it. Whenever I played New York, the cousins and uncles and aunts would be there every show to take care of me. I remember one night at the International when maybe thirty of them turned up at one gigantic table—and that wasn't even half the family. They happened to be seated next to four businessmen who kept on discussing business while I was singing. The guys weren't loud enough to bother me—I didn't even notice them—but the Cosentinos thought they were being disrespectful. Aunt Margaret turned around and shushed them a few times—"You be quiet while my Gary's singing"—but she was just a little old lady and they ignored her. Finally she became so exasperated that she picked up her purse and whacked one of them over the head. When they looked up they saw a wall of faces, which might have come straight out of *The Godfather,* glaring back at them and didn't say another word the rest of the performance.

Barbara didn't know about the drinking until after we were married. I had temporarily stopped doing it right before we met. It wasn't a matter of choice. While I was preparing the act in L.A. I suddenly lost all feeling in my body one night and found myself temporarily paralyzed from the neck down. An ambulance rushed me to the hospital, where the doctor said I had suffered a partial heart block from the digitalis in the new kind of diet pills I'd been taking to reduce the liquor bloat. He told me I had damn near croaked and wasn't to do any work or even take a step for the next six months. "Bullshit," I answered. "You sign a contract in Vegas and you better show up. They don't want to hear excuses." He thought about it awhile, then agreed to let me go under the condition I take B_{12} and Dexedrine shots before every show, get lots of rest and cut out the booze and carousing. I was into that routine when Barbara and I first met and stayed on it until we moved to L.A. after the wedding. But once the doctor told me I seemed to have recovered, out came the vodka bottle again and away I went.

I was starting a new life. I had a new wife and a son. But I hadn't changed. I was still the same asshole. About the only difference was that now I was hurting the people I loved as well as myself.

The first time I came home drunk Barbara thought I had only gone off on a little toot the way new husbands will do when they feel the walls closing in. She put me to bed and went back to studying the plans for the new house we had just bought in the Valley. But one binge led to the next. I'd disappear for two or three days at a time, then turn up all wasted and bedraggled, without the slightest idea of where I had been. When I didn't have work to keep me halfway straight, I'd start juicing at ten or eleven in the morning and be so whacked by late afternoon that she'd have to send Steve to his room when he came home from school to keep him from seeing me that way. That hurt her. So did the decision to stop having friends over to the house. Barbara was a gregarious, fun-loving woman. She loved people and she loved life. But once I got loaded she couldn't tell what kind of havoc I might wreak on whoever happened to be sitting around the living room, so the friends had to go. I wasn't much of a replacement. A lot of nights I'd take off alone to one of my bars and end up so blind the bartender would have to call her to come get me. The nights I did stay home I disappeared into the den with a jug and watched late movies on television till my eyes glazed over, while she cried and prayed in the bedroom.

She did what she could to make me stop. She tried hiding the bottles, but I found them. She tried talking to me about the drinking, but I wouldn't listen. I was always full of remorse the next morning for whatever outrages I had committed the night before. "My God, I really didn't mean to say that to you. Jesus Christ, hon, you know I would never hit you. That wasn't me. I swear it'll never happen again." But I still couldn't admit I was an alcoholic. I could confide in her about Mom and Dad and my childhood. I could talk openly about my brothers and even admit how much I regretted the act breaking up. But when it came to the booze, all I could say was, "Hey, everybody drinks. Everybody gets drunk once in a while. It's no big thing."

As much as I wanted to deny it, the truth of the matter was that a decade of constant juicing had caught up with me and I was coming unglued. The night the D.T.'s took over I was watching television in the den when the Indians crawled out of the picture tube in their war paint. I was still safe in the dark, but I knew they could see Barbara silhouetted against the doorway when she stopped by the room.

"Get down!" I screamed. "Get down, honey!"

She did like I told her but didn't seem to understand what was happening.

"What's the matter? What's wrong?"

"It's the Indians. The Indians are gonna attack us. But don't worry. I'm here, and I'll protect you. You get Steve, and I'll find us some shelter."

My reassurances didn't seem to do much good. She looked scared to death. But she went off to fetch Steve, and I crept into the living room to search for a safe place to hide. I was climbing up the hill looking for the cave when I slipped on a rock and went crashing down to the bottom. Barbara heard the clatter and came running. When she saw the blood she called the doc, who gave me a shot of Demerol. It didn't put me to sleep, but the Indians were frightened off and disappeared back into the TV set.

I woke up the next morning with a throbbing pain in my back. I looked in the mirror, and there was a large red welt running from my shoulder to my hip.

"Wow, what happened here?" I asked her. "How'd I do that?"

"Don't you remember? You were ranting and raving in the den last night, then when you went into the living room you fell over the coffee table and broke it in half."

That sounded crazy to me but, sure enough, when I checked it out the large stone table was split in two.

Another morning, shortly after Steve went off to school, the vampires came to get us. But I was too smart for them. I pretended I was still sleeping until Barbara entered the bedroom, and then explained what was happening.

"Get into bed. Lie very still. Be very quiet. Now look over at the closet doors."

"What's the matter with them?"

"Well, the vampires are inside in their coffins. But don't be afraid. I know what we have to do. We have to make wooden crosses and put them on our chests. That'll ward them off."

"All right, Gary, I understand. I'll take care of it."

When she returned with the crosses I had her get back into bed.

"Just lie down, angel, lie down. They can't hurt us now. The crosses will keep us safe."

But something was wrong. Two burly vampires in white coats slipped into the bedroom along with my doctor and ordered me to come with them. The crosses didn't seem to work, so I had to fight them off with my fists. That did the job and they returned to their coffins. When the coast was clear, I left the house with Barbara and the doctor and headed for fresh sanctuary.

I came to—the next day? two days later?—in a bed in St. John's hospital. That's where all the big-time Hollywood Irish Catholic drunks went to dry out. The rooms were beautifully decorated, and you could even order in from Chasen's if you wanted. A huge, hairy bear of a man in a white coat was sitting in the room with me. Tree trunks grew out of his sleeves and he must have had a twenty-inch neck, but he was friendly and polite and spoke in a pleasant, well-modulated voice.

"How do you feel, Mr. Crosby?"

"Oh, I feel fine."

"Well, that's good. All right now, Mr. Crosby, we're gonna be nice and not make any trouble for anyone, right? We're just gonna stay in our room and take our medication and relax."

"That's right. Whatever you say, pal."

I wasn't about to tangle with him. He looked like he could handle a hundred of me.

I knew the routine. It wasn't the first time I'd been there, and it wouldn't be the last. I went along with the program like he told me, sleeping and resting and letting them shoot me up with dope to keep the heebie-jeebies from coming back. I laid around for three or four days until I was detoxed. Then, after promising never to do it again or whatever it was I had to tell them, they cut me loose and sent me home. I couldn't wait to get back to the house and crack open a jug. Those people had been driving me nuts. It was always "those people." There was nothing the matter with me. I was fine.

Once I was off on a bender there was no telling where I might end up. Some nights I even drove over to the old man's house and sat around the kitchen like I did when I was a kid, laughing and joking with the help. I don't know what I had in mind. I probably forgot I was a married man with a home of my own and thought I still lived there. Maybe I also wanted to shove in Dad's face the fact that his son was loaded to the gills to see what he would do about it. If I was trying to get him angry, it didn't work. All he did was beat it back upstairs and call Barbara to come get me.

The old man wasn't much for facing unpleasant facts—even when they were shoved in his face. He could deny I was an alcoholic just as easily as I could. One night I called him on the phone in a drunken muddle and asked him to come over. I had just checked out of St. John's again and was back in the bottle, and the whole routine was getting to be too much for Barbara. She hadn't slept or eaten in two or three days and couldn't seem to stop crying. I guess I had to reach out to somebody, and he was the only one there. By the time he drove up I had invited a bunch of other people over to party. I was juicing with them in the den when he walked into Barbara's room. He asked her what was wrong, and when she told him he wouldn't buy it.

"I don't understand this. My son does not have a drinking problem. I think you're making it up, Barbara. Gary told me he hasn't had a drink in five years, and I believe him."

She was so stretched out she just blew.

"All right, Bing. If you don't believe me, go into the den and look behind the bar. You will see your son on the floor with a quart of vodka in his hand, chugalugging it down."

Slipping into the den, he asked the other boozers, "Gary really hasn't been drinking that heavily, has he?" Of course they all answered, "Oh, no. Certainly not." You don't tell God what he doesn't want to hear. But when he peeked behind the bar, there I was, just like Barbara had said. He turned on his heels and made a beeline for his car. The incident was never acknowledged by either of us.

Predictably, the more insane I got with the booze, the more I messed up at work. I disappeared on my way to a gig in Milwaukee, and the club sued me for not showing up. When the audience at the Trade Winds in Chicago didn't laugh at one of my jokes, I told them to go fuck themselves and stormed offstage. The owners called Barbara in L.A. and told her, "Listen, you better come get him right this minute. We don't want him around anymore." She was so terrified by the prospect of what might happen if she left me alone that she headed straight for the airport and arrived in Chicago in the middle of the night. When she walked into the hotel room she found me in bed with a woman. I was too drunk to remember I was married until I saw her. Then I got so crazy with guilt I shoved her out into the hallway without so much as a hello. And, of course, my guilt gave me good reason to drink even more.

For the next four days I stayed loaded in my room while Barbara gathered up my music and tuxedos and negotiated with the powers that be to let me out of my contract without having to pay them a fortune. One night while she was sleeping I sneaked downstairs to the bar, then came back to the room an hour later with some total stranger, another lush I must have picked up on the street. I have no idea what was going through my drunken mind, but I shook her awake and forced her to write the guy a check for a hundred dollars.

Barbara did her best to watch me every second, but I was uncontrollable. On the flight back to L.A. I conned the stewardesses into plying me with booze in the lavatory. Then an hour out of Chicago I tried to jimmy open the emergency exit and walk off the plane. Barbara grabbed me just in time. I don't think I wanted to kill myself. My Catholic upbringing said that if I did I'd go to hell. I only wanted to drink myself to death or provoke someone else into killing me. The cops were waiting at the airport, ready to haul me off to jail. Barbara somehow talked them out of it and promised she wouldn't let me drive home. That's all I had to hear. The moment they disappeared I pushed her out of the driver's seat and tore back to the house at eighty miles an hour.

The craziness wasn't over yet. The next week the bartender at one of my places called Barbara and told her to take me home. For some reason I didn't understand, he'd thrown me out and told me never to set foot in there again. On the ride back Barbara was angrier than I'd ever seen her. Usually she suffered in silence, but this time she was really steaming.

"God, Gary, you are such a jerk!" she shouted at the top of her voice. "You really are. I don't want anything more to do with you. Just go away."

"What did I do? Tell me what I did."

"I thought I knew you. I thought you were a kind person with a kind heart. That's why I married you. But how could you try to beat up a cripple, a man with only one arm? I have no respect for you anymore."

I refused to believe my lying ears. Sure, I'd fight when I had to, but I wasn't a bully. I didn't pick on anyone. I would never go after some guy who couldn't defend himself.

"What? Jesus Christ, Barbara, tell me I didn't do that."

"No, you did it all right. That's why I'm so damn furious. You're not only hurting me and Steve and yourself. Now you're

275

going out there and hurting innocent people who already have their own problems."

I started to cry, as much for myself as for my victim. Even with the booze and the pills, I still thought of myself as a righteous human being, but there was no denying it, I had buried that guy six feet under and had turned into everything I hated. I cheated on my wife. I fucked up at work. Now I had tried to beat on a cripple.

"Sure, go ahead and cry," she answered. "It's not going to help that man. And forget about apologizing to him. None of the bartenders knows his name. They've never seen him before. It's too late to make amends."

A week or two after that Barbara left me. I'd taken off for Vegas on another binge, and when I dragged myself home three days later she and Steve were gone. So were Anna and Ralph, the couple who worked for us. I sat in the house the rest of the day waiting to hear from someone, though in my heart of hearts I knew perfectly well what had happened. I'd treated her miserably the entire eleven months we'd been married. The more she tried to love me, the worse I behaved. I was so full of self-loathing I didn't want her love. I wasn't worthy of it and did everything in my power to turn it into hate. The capper had been the night I left for Vegas. My old high school buddy Tom Wilscam was down from San Jose, and the three of us were supposed to go out to dinner. But I was so drunk I started ranting and raving at her in front of Tom, then stormed out of the house in a rage. Tom had stuck with me the whole three days, trying to keep me from doing myself in. He kept saying, "Come on, Gary, that's enough drinking and carrying on. Let's go home. Why don't you call Barbara and tell her you're on your way?" But of course I wouldn't listen. Now I was going to have to pay the dues for acting like such an asshole.

Towards evening Anna appeared at the house to pick up some changes of clothes and Steve's school books. There were tears in her eyes, and she begged me not to ask her where Barbara was staying. Well, if that's how Barbara wanted it, that's how it had to be, so I didn't press her. Every few days Anna returned for more of Barbara and Steve's things, while I continued to sit there thinking about what a mess I'd made of everything. Finally the phone rang. It was Barbara's attorney. He told me to get hold of my lawyer and bring him to his office Thursday morning at ten o'clock.

Barbara was already there when I showed up, but she stayed silent and let her lawyer do all the talking. "Your wife loves you too much to see you kill yourself," he said. "So you'll either go to this place in Connecticut to dry out and never take another drink the rest of your life, or she's going to leave you. What'll it be?" Barbara was taking a chance. She knew I was not a guy to accept that kind of ultimatum kindly. Throw a challenge in my face and I'd automatically throw it right back at you just out of principle. But something clicked in my head—the same way it had that night at the Flamingo when she told me to stop beating on that stranger and get back in my seat. I may not have shown it much, but when all was said and done I loved her and I loved Steve and didn't want to lose either of them. I still didn't think I had a drinking problem, but since she did I had to go along with her. "Okay," I answered, "I'll do it. Make the reservations."

It had all been taken care of beforehand. Barbara drove me to the plane the next morning. I'd hidden a jug of vodka in my flight bag, and by the time I arrived at Silver Hill I was too drunk to see straight. But at least I was there.

Silver Hill was a rich man's dry-out clinic. I had a beautiful room. My window overlooked flowers and rolling lawns. Each week I stayed there cost a bundle. Barbara told me later that the old man footed the bill, but he never did own up to it.

I had gone there to placate Barbara, so I'd still have a wife and son when I came back home. But a lot of things about the place made sense. The first thing they did was put me on a regular schedule. I got up and went to bed the same time every day. I ate my meals at a certain time, went to the workshops and played sports and saw the shrink at a certain time. Gradually I got back on the same timetable as the rest of the world, and that felt good. I began to remember what sunshine looked like and how food tasted. I even painted a picture and made a pretty good tray in woodworking shop. When my head hit the pillow at 10 P.M. I fell right off to sleep.

I met with the shrink daily. He was an expert at treating lushes like me and had no trouble making me face up to the unpleasant fact that, however much I wanted to deny it, that's what I was. All he had to do was hand me a little yellow card from Alcoholics Anonymous listing twenty questions, then leave me alone while I read them down to myself.

1. Do you lose time from work due to drinking?
"Yes."

2. Is drinking making your home life unhappy?
"Yes."

3. Do you drink because you're shy with other people?
"Sure."

4. Is drinking affecting your reputation?
"You bet."

5. Have you ever felt remorse after drinking?
"All the time."

6. Have you gotten into financial difficulties as a result of drinking?
"Yes."

7. Do you turn to lower companions and an inferior environment when drinking?
"Nah, my companions are all better than me."

8. Does drinking make you careless of your family's welfare?
"Family? . . . What family?"

9. Has your ambition decreased since drinking?
"Mmm, I don't think so, but it sure hasn't increased."

10. Do you crave a drink at a definite time daily?
"Yes. Every waking minute."

11. Do you want a drink the next morning?
"Sure, if I'm not still up juicing."

12. Does drinking cause you to have difficulty in sleeping?
"No, I pass out real good."

13. Has your efficiency decreased since drinking?
"Yes."

14. Is drinking jeopardizing your job or business?
"Yes."

15. Do you drink to escape from worries or trouble?
"Sure."

278

16. Do you drink alone?

"You bet."

17. Have you ever had a complete loss of memory as a result of drinking?

"Frequently."

18. Has your physician ever treated you for drinking?

"No, since I never went to him for it."

19. Do you drink to build up your self-confidence?

"Sure."

20. Have you ever been to a hospital or institution on account of drinking?

"Well, here I am."

Down at the bottom of the card I read the bad news:

If you have answered YES to any one of these questions, it is a definite warning that *you may be an alcoholic.*

If you answered YES to any two, the chances are you *are an alcoholic.*

If you have answered YES to *three or more, you are definitely an alcoholic.*"

Well, there was hardly one I hadn't answered "yes" to, so that was that. When I read them over again to make sure they weren't rigged against me, I had to admit they were all pretty fair. They were just questions of fact, without any moralizing. I knew damn well any normal person would answer "no" down the line to every one of them. From that moment on there was not a doubt in my mind that I had a problem. But then I picked the wrong solution.

I knew I was an alcoholic. I knew alcoholism was a disease like TB or cancer. I knew I wanted to get well and could never drink or use pills again. That was real progress and helped me a lot in the years to come. What I didn't know was that I had only taken the first step.

I desperately needed a program to get my life back on the right track. But, out of egotism or fear or just plain ignorance, I wanted to do it on my own. The psychiatrist tried to talk me into joining Alcoholics Anonymous. Later on so did Barbara. But I was too muleheaded to listen. "I'm a loner," I told them. "I'm not a joiner. I can do it by myself." When the shrink handed me the AA book, I went straight to the personal stories—the drunkalogs—in the back, skipping over the first 160 pages that detailed all the information about alcoholism I needed to know. If I had read them then, the next nineteen years of my life would have been different. I would have saved myself a lot of mistakes. I would have made my problem a lot better. I would have gone to AA meetings and found myself with people who were just like me, who experienced the same down feelings and negative thoughts and helped each other learn to cope with them. But I guess I wasn't ready for that. I have to look at it that way. I either say I wasn't ready or that I wasted the next nineteen years of my life, which is about what I did.

After six weeks at Silver Hill I'd had enough. The only way I could get out of there was to be caught drunk, so I set it up for that to happen. I went to town Saturday morning, conspicuously bought myself a pint of vodka at the busiest bar on the main drag, then hid out the rest of the weekend. When I came back Monday they said, "Mmm, Mr. Crosby, looks like you've been off on a bender." I admitted that was so. "Well, that means you will have to leave here," they answered. "We're going to call your wife to come get you." The moment Barbara appeared I took her off to one side and told her, "Don't panic, hon. I know what I'm doing. I'm not drinking anymore. I'll never have another drink as long as I live."

She didn't really believe me. Once we were home, every time I headed for the front door I'd see that same look of fear and disbelief on her face that all alcoholics inspire in their loved ones. But this time I kept my word. I white-knuckled myself off the booze, and then I cut out the speed, which in some ways was even tougher. I crashed so hard that for a couple of months I thought I would never wake up again. As long as my mouth kept moving I could function, but the second I shut up I began nodding out. I'd fall asleep sitting in a chair, standing up, walking—anywhere. Eventually I got past it, and then almost automatically I came off the downers because I no longer needed them to counteract the speed.

One day, after a few years of staying sober, I noticed how that look wasn't there on Barbara's face anymore when I left the house by myself, and that was a wonderful moment. But I still wasn't sane. My mind was still alcoholic. I hadn't lost the self-centeredness of the drunk. I hadn't lost the self-will run riot. I hadn't lost the overwhelming sense of impending doom and the feeling of powerlessness to do anything about it. All I had done was quit using the anesthetic, and without that the pain had become even more intense.

Now that I was sober I wanted to go back to work and make good for all the fucking up I'd done when I was drunk. I wanted to work every day to show them that this time around I could do it right. Work became the whole focus of my existence, the one and only measure of my self-worth. "If I can just get that going again," I'd tell myself, "I'll be able to feel good about my life and my family and everything else in the world, and I'll be okay." Every day I didn't work I was a failure. And every day I was a failure just reiterated one more time what a bum and a loser and a no-good bastard I still was. Without work I was nothing. I was what everybody thought I was—a rich dilettante, with no talent, just living off his old man's money. And each day I didn't work that's how I saw myself. And I hated that image.

My dream was to work in good things, to do movies, records and shows I could be proud of twenty years later. Not like the old man. Not every time out of the box. I never had the audacity to put myself on a competitive level with him, to try to top or equal him. I knew that was impossible. I just wanted some work I wouldn't have to be ashamed of when I said, "I'm an actor and a singer." But for the time being the dream could wait. The quality of the show or part didn't matter. As long as I was working, it was another chance to show up on time, know the lines and be no problem to anyone.

But it wasn't that easy. I figured I'd have to take some heat for a while and then I'd work again, but it didn't happen. All through the years of carrying on I'd gotten away with murder, and now that I'd finally straightened out the dues had caught up with me. The jobs weren't there. Nobody wanted to hire me. And when a gig did come through, more than once some anonymous heavyweight in the front office would put the kibosh on it and it would suddenly disappear. Maybe I had straightened out too late. That was the only explanation I could think of. It was as if the producers and the club owners hadn't put it all together while I was behaving like a maniac, then the day I went off to dry out they had a meeting and brought each other up to date. I could hear the dialogue in my head. "Y'know, that Crosby asshole didn't even show up for the job," one guy says, opening the discussion. "Really?" chimes in the next. "Well, he pulled the same bullshit with me." "Yeah, and he told me and my customers to go fuck ourselves," adds a third. "Okay, gentlemen, that's it for the sonofabitch. From now on no more work." Meanwhile I'm on the plane to Connecticut, flying off to get well.

I carried the same bad rep with me for years. Not that I did a hell of a lot to destroy it other than to stop drinking and using. I didn't tell the powers in the business that I had cleaned up my act. I didn't write any letters of apology offering to make amends. I didn't go around to the hangouts and show off the new, improved me. When I wasn't working I just disappeared into a hole. Barbara tried to fight me on that one. "If they don't see you, how can they know you've changed?" she would ask me. But I really hadn't changed.

Every morning at nine o'clock I called my agent. If he didn't have a job for me I was a failure for the rest of that day, and I remained furious with frustration until the next phone call the following morning. "Damn it to hell, why won't they give me the work so I can prove myself?" I would rage. "How can I make it up to them if they don't give me the chance?" I couldn't understand why it wasn't happening. To my way of thinking, I was doing everything right. I was toeing the line. I had my nose to the grindstone. I was as straight as an arrow. I was living so clean I squeaked. I was a good husband. I was a good father. I was even a good Catholic again. After I cleaned up I had gone back to the Church and gotten right with God, but even that didn't seem to help.

I would get down on my knees and beg and plead with Him for just one decent shot. "Please, God, please give me a job. I'll do whatever You want. I'll go to church every day—anything. What do I have to do to prove to You I'm all right?" But He didn't seem to be listening. He started to become like the old man to me. There wasn't any way to please either one of them. It never dawned on me that things happen according to His will and His time, not my will and my time, and if He didn't send me what I thought I needed He'd send me something else. I pored over each day with a microscope, searching for reasons for His silence. "Well, I swore three times this morning, and this afternoon I got mad at the line in the grocery store. Maybe that's it. Maybe that's why I didn't get the gig." I was down to nothing. I had no more stories left. But even then I didn't understand what was wrong.

The main thing that kept me from going back to the booze and pills was that Barbara and Steve, two human beings who loved me, were counting on me to stay straight. I could do it for them, even if I hadn't yet come to realize that, like all alcoholics, I had to be able to do it for myself.

Barbara did everything in her power to shake me out of my negativity. She was a positive thinker and gave me a whole shelf of books to read: Maxwell Maltz's *The Magic Power of Self Image Psychology*, Norman Vincent Peale's *The Power of Positive Thinking* and Walter M. Germain's *The Magic Power of Your Mind*. I read them all and tried to make them work, and they did work until I came up against the next big rejection. Then I'd throw them against the wall and fume, "This is shit too!" I was driving her into the ground with my cynicism, and, of course, the way things were going it made it look like I was right.

I felt my life was sliding straight down the tubes and I was dragging her and Steve down with me. I started thinking, "I shouldn't have ruined this poor woman's life like this. I love her too much to see that happen. Maybe if I weren't here to pull her down, a good dude who earns a decent living might come along and make the two of them happy." A year or so after I returned from Connecticut I asked for a separation. I moved over to the other side of the hill into some guy's apartment and began running with hookers and bums again like the same wild man I was before, only this time I didn't drink. I was so miserable that after a year of it I was ready to come home. "Maybe I'm wrong," I told myself. "Maybe I can do the job." I knew Barbara felt I'd run off only because I wanted to cut loose, but thank God she took me back anyway.

Shortly after that I left Rosey. He'd always handled a certain amount of Dad's business and also represented my brothers, and it seemed to me that maybe that was too many Crosbys for one man to sell. I thought I might do better if I went with some other agent. It was not a brilliant career move. Over the next few years I tried them all—the big factories, where you were lost in the shuffle, and the little guys who couldn't get their feet in the door—and one was the same as the other. At the beginning everyone seemed to assume the Crosby name would work its magic in bringing in the commissions and welcomed me with open arms. But when that didn't happen they soon lost interest, and I moved on to the next one.

The one bright thing I did was to start taking acting lessons from Bennes Mardenn. Up to then I had no technique as an actor, and I knew it. I could play the same fast-talking bullshit clown I impersonated in real life, but if I had to do any serious acting I was in deep trouble. I'd be frightened to death. Bennes changed all that. He got me past my introversion and opened me up. He made me play effeminate roles. He made me play girls' parts and hoods and spectacled accountants. They were a painful stretch for me at first, but he was such a passionate, skillful teacher that he made you want to work for him, to do what he told you and do it right. I went to him every day from early morning to late afternoon, and after a while my confidence began to build. When I scored a role in a "Twilight Zone" episode I had to play a bad-news sonofabitch of a thief who flips out, a total departure from the usual lightweight wiseguy I'd acted in the past, and thanks to Bennes I was able to do it. When it came time for that character to be afraid and go crazy, I was afraid and I went crazy. I didn't care whether the people on the set might think I was an asshole. I forgot who I was and became someone else. For maybe the first time in my life I wasn't embarrassed to cry or whimper or scream or be frightened in public. I was able to get past my self-consciousness and show my emotions, using them like a real actor to portray the character I played. And that felt great.

I won't say the world suddenly turned around after that. The dry spell did not end overnight. I was not miraculously born again into a brand new human being. But I did build up some new confidence as an actor and maybe that helped me get back to work. A few people did take a chance on me. Danny Thomas cast me as the second lead in "The Bill Dana Show." Jack Webb put me in "Adam-12" and some of his other series. Suzanne Pleshette recommended me for a part in her TV movie. I got to do a production of *The Odd Couple* with wonderful actors like Tony Randall, Mickey Rooney and Arnold Stang. My old reputation as a bum and a lush still followed me. Hollingsworth Morse, Jack Webb's director for "Adam-12," had to put his own job on the line when someone at the network didn't want me hired because he'd heard I had a drinking problem. And even when I did have a gig, all I could think about was that it was going to end tomorrow, or next week, or next month, and I'd be out of work again. But at least I was staying alive.

I was so busy living in the wreckage of my past and the anticipated wreckage of my future that I didn't leave room to enjoy the pleasures of the present. When I was working I could take Barbara out to dinner or even to visit some friends. But when I wasn't working—and that was almost always—I couldn't go anywhere. That's how badly I had tied my self-worth to my job. All I wanted to do was hole up in my room with the TV set and vegetate. I became a recluse.

I didn't know how to act in public. I'd never had any kind of real social life except when I was drunk. As a kid I was scared to death to go to dances or parties because I didn't feel socially equal to anyone. Then I discovered booze and, oh boy, I was all over the place. When I drank you couldn't keep me home—I forgot I had a home. I was a wild animal. I couldn't stay locked up for two minutes. And now that I had quit drinking, once again I pulled in. I gradually stopped going everywhere that was uncomfortable for me, and pretty soon I didn't go anywhere at all because everywhere was uncomfortable.

I hated the social tap dance. Parties were an agony for me, just one built-in trap after another that had to be avoided. Everyone would be smoking dope or snorting lines of coke or downing eight glasses of booze, and I wouldn't know what to do with myself other than stand in the corner like a guy from the temperance union. And my career was so nowhere I'd be scared to death someone might ask me a question and make me justify my existence. I didn't have any lines ready like the other out-of-work actors, who could give you forty-five minutes on how they had this play coming up and that picture and this other television series. I always thought they were telling the truth, and I knew I didn't have that going for me. When a stranger asked, "So what are you doing now?" I'd answer, "Nothing, man. Nothing at all." "Well, what do you have lined up?" "Nothing." That would end the conversation. He'd move off to someone else while I stood there digging my toe in the carpet for the rest of the night. I was afraid of myself too. The normal social flirtations got me crazy. "If anyone comes on to my wife tonight," I'd grumble, "I'll kill the motherfucker where he stands. I'll drown him in the pool." I would have, too, and now that I'd sobered up I didn't want to start in with that nonsense again. I didn't want to fight people anymore. I was tired of it. Well, if that's the way you envisioned going out for an evening of fun, it makes a lot more sense to stay home.

It was rough on Barbara. She was an outgoing, gregarious person, and I loved that about her and didn't want her to change. I wanted her to take off with her friends at night and go to parties and openings and shows and have herself a terrific time. I could enjoy them vicariously when she came back and told me about them. That seemed like a reasonable relationship to me. But alcoholics don't have relationships. They take hostages, and Barbara became the hostage of my own self-imposed isolation. Like a good wife, she gave up her pleasures to stay home with her husband, and as the years went by the walls closed in around her.

The one thing that kept me from going insane from all the empty time on my hands was Steve. When he came out to L.A. to join us, he was frightened to death of everybody and everything. Barbara's mother had to leave him alone a lot and had put all sorts of fears into his head to keep him out of trouble while she was gone. "If you open the front door the monster will get you. If you go out to the street you'll be killed by a car. You can't have a bike because you'll fall down and hurt yourself." I could see right off he needed a father to help him grow up strong, to give him a little confidence in himself and some sense of family roots. That became my job. I helped him with his schoolwork, saw to it he was showered and cleaned up, and put him to bed on time. Much to my surprise, I enjoyed it. And it was good for me. The more I did for him, the more I did for myself. I even started thinking, "Well, man, maybe that's why you're not working. Maybe you're supposed to be here in the house to take care of your kid." Suddenly that little guy was there counting on me to bring him up right, and that meant I had some purpose in the world.

Given the kind of son I'd turned out to be, I probably should have been filled with apprehensions about becoming a father. Strangely enough, I wasn't. The marriage to Barbara had happened so fast that before I could even think about it I had adopted Steve and had a son of my own to raise. Once I stopped drinking, my responsibility was clear. Not that I had much of an idea what to do about it. About the only thing I knew for certain at the beginning was that I didn't want to be like the old man to him. I didn't want to set myself up in his eyes as God. I wanted him to know I was just a poor, fumbling human being trying to do the best he could. I didn't want him to be afraid of me. I wanted him to be able to talk to me whenever he felt like it. I wanted him to be able to invite friends over to the house and have fun without feeling that I was getting in his way. I wanted to be able to roughhouse with him, put my arms around him and hug him.

I empathized with Steve so strongly that at first I couldn't bring myself to impose on him any of the things I had hated when I was a kid. Well, no child likes discipline, but now that I was on the other end of the stick it didn't take long to realize that some of it was necessary. I saw that I couldn't just let him run wild in the streets doing whatever he liked. That wasn't good for him either. I saw that there had to be limits, rules, and some form of punishment when they were broken. I felt I owed him an explanation so he wouldn't think they were just judgments handed down from on high, without any love or reason behind them. He got enough of divine authority from the priests and nuns at school. I felt that I had to listen to his excuses when he had them, and let him off the hook when they made sense. I praised him just as heavily when he did something good as I yelled and screamed when he was bad. I wasn't a martinet. But compared to the fathers of his friends, I was tough.

Barbara helped me work out the problems of parenthood. We sat down together and made up what we thought was a pretty good set of rules and regulations. Then we made sure we stuck to them and presented a united front at all times. Sometimes, though, I was too much of a stickler. I could be just as rigid as the old man. If I told Steve to come home for dinner at six o'clock, he had to be home by six on the dot, not one minute after. I'd stand in the driveway with the watch in my hand counting off the seconds. He was such a good kid that it seldom reached the point where I had to give him a licking, but if that was the promised punishment I made myself do it. I hated it. I hoped each time would be the last. Then one day it was. I caught myself taking out on him all the pent-up hatred and frustration I felt for everything else in my life and was so appalled I never laid another hand on him.

I began to see it wasn't so easy being a parent. I'm not sure if that helped soften my attitude towards the old man, but it had to have some effect. As the years went by I bumbled along like most other fathers, trying to strike the middle ground between too permissive and too strict, and through none of my doing Steve grew up into a bright, happy kid who was comfortable with himself and the world. When his schoolmates gave him shit for being Bing Crosby's grandson, he had the capacity to laugh at them for the assholes they were and just walk away. He was so much smarter than I was, and that gratified me. I knew by now that my way wasn't right. I wound up distrusting people and hating them. I didn't want Steve to turn out like that, and I would always tell him about where I went wrong, hoping he could profit from my mistakes. I don't think he really had to. I think he was just born with the natural smarts I never had. I'd watch how he ran his action and think to myself, "God, I wish I'd been like him. It would have saved me so much grief."

The old man loved him. He was the one thing we could both point to with pride.

"Boy, that Steve is really something," he'd say, shaking his head in wonder.

"Yeah, he really is," I would answer. "But not due to me. Believe me, it was nothing I did."

"What do you mean?"

"Well, I don't know, Dad. It's just that he was always the kind of kid who'd volunteer to help around the house and things like that."

"*What?*"

"Yeah, when he finished his chores he'd go up to his mother and ask, 'Is there anything else you'd like me to do?'"

"Holy Christ, I may adopt him myself."

The war ended so gradually that I was still fighting it after it was already over. There was no sudden cessation of hostilities. No formal declaration of peace. No dramatic making of amends. He did not tell me, "Well, son, I apologize for being so rough on you, and I'm certainly glad you straightened up." I did not say, "Gosh, Dad, I'm sure sorry I gave you all that trouble, and now my life is on its way." One day it just didn't seem to be there anymore.

Once I stopped drinking and got halfway straight, Barbara simply would not allow the battle to continue. Neither, I think, would Kathryn. She kept asking us over to their house in Hillsborough even though I kept turning her invitations down. I wasn't going anywhere those days and certainly wasn't about to travel all the way up to San Francisco to visit my father. There didn't seem any point to it. I could see myself sitting there like a lump, just like when I was seven years old, watching my p's and q's, afraid to eat dessert or do anything else that might incur his displeasure. There would be the same tension-filled silences and long, drawn-out dead spots there had always been, broken only by an occasional bit of banter or small talk about sports. We certainly wouldn't get down with each other and converse about something real. I'd just be counting off the minutes until it got to be ten o'clock and he went to bed. So what would it accomplish?

"Oh, come on," Barbara would coax, trying to talk me into it. "Your brothers are going to be there."

"Well, screw my brothers. They're grown men. They can do whatever they want. If they can handle it, fine. But I don't want to go. I told you what it's gonna be like. We're gonna have to talk him into taking the lock off the icebox door so you can get something to eat after he goes upstairs. We're gonna have to tip-toe around the house because he sleeps light. We're gonna have to smoke in the bathroom so Kathryn won't be bothered by the smell. It'll be like going back to jail again. What do I need it for?"

Since I wouldn't go to the old man, Barbara arranged for him to come to me. At a quarter to six she'd announce, "Mmm, listen, Gary. Better get ready, hon. Your Dad's in town and he's coming over for dinner in fifteen minutes."

I'd go crazy.

"What do you mean my father's gonna be here in fifteen minutes? You're kidding, right? He's not really coming to dinner, is he? He can't be coming. Uh, I have a television show I want to watch at six-thirty. How can I watch it if he's here?"

"I guess you can't, Gar. Don't you think you ought to wash up?"

I'd still be ranting and raving—"Goddamit, you should check with me before doing something like that!"—when the doorbell would ring and there he'd stand. I'd automatically straighten up on the spot, reverting back to the mealymouthed phony I hated for the next two hours, then start in bitching and moaning again the moment he left.

It took me a long time to get it through my noggin that the hours we spent together weren't so awful. Eventually, though, I began to notice that he didn't seem to be coming down on me anymore. He wasn't acting so cold and disapproving. He wasn't lecturing me about all the things I was doing wrong. He seemed to be accepting me pretty much for what I was. I suppose to his way of thinking he no longer had that much to bitch about. I had stopped drinking and using. I had married a good Catholic woman he liked. I was raising a son and not doing too bad a job of it. I wasn't carrying on like a maniac when I worked. I looked halfway responsible to him, and now that I was a lot closer to what he wanted he was able to let up. Most likely he was sick and tired of the fight anyhow.

I began to realize he probably hadn't been fighting me for years, but because no truce had been called I'd been keeping the war going all by myself. He started running his tape on me when I was a little kid and kept running it until I was grown, and now that he had stepped away from it I'd taken over running it for him. And I ran it harder and longer than he ever could because I was with myself twenty-four hours a day. I didn't need to hear his voice pointing out my faults and telling me how to act. It was always there anyhow, and the battle continued to rage inside my head without his presence.

When I stopped to think about it, I could see that in his own peculiar, indirect way he had been sending me peace signals from the time I quit drinking. Once I got off the booze, word began filtering back about how pleased he was that I had finally straightened up. I'd run into Phil Harris, Rosey or one of his lawyers, and he'd tell me, "Well, your dad sure is happy you went on the wagon, got married and are starting to settle down." As soon as he left the house after one of his visits, Barbara would recount how he had laid on all kinds of compliments while I was out of the room, how he was delighted I had trimmed down and shaped up and done some decent work. Kathryn would say the same in her letters.

At first that kind of report would make me grumble, "Well, why the hell can't he come to me and say it himself?" It took me a while to accept the fact that just wasn't ever going to happen, so I might as well relax and be happy I got it secondhand from other people. Sometimes I'd fantasize about trapping him into saying something nice directly to my face, but I never could figure out how to do it. He was so good with words that he could spot a trap a mile and a half away. To the end, the best I could get out of him was, "Hey, saw you on that show the other night and, well, you did a pretty good job." Then he'd immediately rush into some of the leftover lines from his old routines with Bob Hope. "Did they pay you? Bite the nickels to make sure they're real. If they gave you a check, head straight for the bank and cash it at once."

About as close as we came to a direct acknowledgment that the war had ended was the afternoon I was visiting him up in Hillsborough and he came looking for me in the den. "Why don't we take a walk?" he asked. That was a bit unusual right there. He had never sought me out to walk with him before. I said okay. He selected a stick from the cane stand by the front door, called one of his dogs to come with us and we headed down the driveway and onto the path around the garden. The stroll didn't last more than half an hour, and on the face of it nothing extraordinary happened. Yet, compared to the other times we'd been alone together, there was a whole different feeling and a whole different subtext. He talked to me more like one adult to another. He asked me the same questions he always did, but now he asked them as if he expected an answer back for a change and was interested in whatever I had to say.

He wanted to know what was happening with my career, and I told him how hard it was getting it going again. Then we talked about my brothers. He said he wished they had some direction in life and would stop being the fuckups he thought they were. I tried to defend them. The boys and I had long since made up, and although I didn't see much of them since I stopped drinking, we still loved each other.

"Well, you know where they come from, Dad. We've all got problems, including me. It's not that easy being a famous man's son. They just haven't figured out yet what to do about it."

It wasn't much of a defense, of course, because he couldn't understand what I was talking about. It was inconceivable to him that the outside world wouldn't treat us the same as it treated him. He had never experienced being on the receiving end of hatred and anger. He liked everyone, and everyone liked him back. He was a very civilized man. We were not civilized. We were wild Indians, and he didn't have it in him to comprehend why we drank and carried on and did all the dumb things we did. But he took in what I was telling him—"Yeah, well, maybe . . . maybe you're right"—doing his best to make sense of it.

By the time we headed back to the house, nothing had changed and yet everything was different. He hadn't apologized for a single, solitary thing, yet he had apologized. He never said he was wrong in any way, yet he had said he was wrong. On the walk up the driveway I think I put my arm around his shoulder.

Whatever it was that happened that afternoon seemed to change the way I felt about him. I wasn't afraid of him anymore, and I was no longer angry. Once he got off my case I was able to relax and take another look at him. I found myself thinking, "All right now, this man has done some good things in his life. Try to name some of them." That wasn't hard. He made millions of people happy through his talent. He contributed God knows how many dollars to dozens of good causes. He played hundreds of benefits, giving away for free what he could have been selling for a bundle. "Okay, suppose some other man did these things. What would you think of him?" Well, hell, I'd think he was a damn good guy, really a good man, a straight dude. "Well, if he did them, then he must be a good guy too, right? That doesn't make for a bad person." I had to agree with that. So the anger was only about the way he had been with me and my brothers, and about how the people who bought his persona judged us by what they thought him to be.

But he wasn't to blame because his fans found it inconceivable that such a wonderful man could father such horrible, rotten, ungrateful children. And if he did make a mistake in raising us, he couldn't really be blamed for that either. The mistake wasn't intended. The old man believed what he believed, and he thought he was doing right. He wasn't any tougher than a lot of fathers of his generation. And a lot of kids can handle that kind of upbringing without any difficulty. It was too bad that my brothers and I didn't buy it and turn out the way he wanted. That would have made it very comfortable for everyone. But, whatever the reasons, we didn't. Linny and the twins clammed up like a shell. I bulled my neck and fought him tooth and nail all the way down the line. To my own destruction. The discipline just didn't work with us. But regardless of whether what he did was right, wrong or somewhere in between, at least he had some kind of plan. At least he was trying to bring us up the best way he knew how. At least he tried. And that's more than can be said for a lot of fathers.

He was so much better with his second group of kids—Harry and Mary and Nathaniel. Not that he suddenly turned around and became the sweetest, kindest, most sensitive old gentleman in the world. He was still a disciplinarian and could still be rough on them.

One afternoon I was eating lunch with him up in Hillsborough when Harry, then a young teenager, came bounding into the dining room all bubbly with excitement. "Played eighteen holes this morning," he blurted out, "and guess what, Dad? Didn't go into the woods once. Hit every fairway straight down the middle." The old man didn't even glance up from his plate. He just said, "Yeah, and I bet you three-putted every green, didn't you?" I looked over at Harry, and he was crestfallen. "Oh, Christ," I started thinking, "here he goes with that there's-no-way-you-can-please-him shit again." But then I caught myself. I knew by now that this was just his way. I guess he figured Harry was secure enough to understand he was only kidding. But you aren't at that age. Your heart is lying there, wide open, and it's easy to punch. And if it gets punched enough it gets awfully hard. I didn't want to see that happen to Harry, so after dessert I took him aside and talked to him.

"Listen, your old man really loves you, and I'm sure he's proud of what you were trying to tell him. So don't get the idea in your head that he doesn't like you or isn't pleased with you, because that's bullshit. I used to think like that, and I was wrong. He just doesn't want you to get cocky. Y'know that's a big thing with him."

While I was talking I realized all of a sudden, "Hey, man, that's what it was with us guys too." Up to that moment it hadn't really occurred to me. But I didn't dwell on it. Our part was already over and done with. There was no sense going back to look at all the roads not taken. I'd gone through what I had gone through, and there was no changing anything. Still, it was good to make that discovery.

Well, if the old man hadn't changed completely, he had still changed a lot. After putting one wife in the ground, then turning around to see that his four sons were fuckups, he couldn't have been looking forward to too much happiness in the remaining years of his life. But then he was given a second chance, and his whole life brightened up. And he made the most of it. He softened.

I only peered in through the window every now and then, but there seemed to be a much better feeling around the house. The kids weren't afraid of him. They could play and joke with him. They could even disagree with him and voice their opinions.

They still had to do what he said. I'm sure they thought he was strict—and he was. Their mother was pretty strict with them too. But at least they felt free to wheedle and cajole and argue. As they got older and wanted to spread their wings and grow the way children must, there were the usual arguments that happen, and ought to happen, in any family. But that was completely normal. It reminded me of all those healthy, happy families I'd been watching my whole life. About the only difference was that this one was living in a big, rich house, and the big, rich house didn't really matter because the dialogue was the same.

"Get the grades up. Do your chores. Be home early."

"Aw, geez, Dad, do I have to?"

"Oh, come on now. Yes, you have to, so stop the beefing."

There was love there and even some leniency. Sometimes, when the kids pressed him too hard, I'd catch an expression on his face that seemed to say, "Hmm, in the old days you wouldn't have gotten away with this." But then he'd look over at them and smile and let it slide. And I think he was a happier man for it.

The difference between the second family and the first was the difference between Dad's British majordomo Alan Fisher and Georgie, our old housekeeper. Georgie was the lord high execu-tioner. She carried out the letter of the law with an iron fist. God help you if she caught you doing something wrong. Fisher was the exact opposite. He ran the house magnificently, displaying such fun and good humor that he kept everybody smiling. He loved to get together with Barbara and gossip. "Oh, so-and-so was heah lahst week. Veddy, veddy rich, you know. It's called stinking rich, dahling." Then Barbara would regale him with the latest Hollywood dirt. "Ohhh, my deah," he would cackle. "Is it reahlly so? Ohhh, my God." He was as different from Georgie as day from night.

Strangely enough, I didn't feel any jealousy toward Dad's new children. I examined myself very carefully to make sure. "They've got it so much better than you," I'd tell myself, "why don't you feel bad about it?" I could only answer, "I don't know why, but I don't. I just feel good for everyone concerned. The kids are doing so well. The old man's happy. Kathryn's happy. I'm glad for the whole bunch of them." Sometimes it crossed my mind that maybe their happiness gave my own existence some meaning. Maybe all that fear and anger and hatred and strife weren't just a waste. Maybe they had something to do with how the old man handled his second chance and helped make a healthier life for the whole family.

It never occurred to me that the old man was mortal. Are the mountains mortal? The sky? God? Then, on the last day of 1973, he had to go into the hospital to be treated for an inflammation in his lungs. At first the doctors thought it was pleurisy, then pneumonia, but they didn't really know what it was. The unspoken fear was that it might be cancer, even though he had long since stopped smoking his pipes. Two weeks later they diagnosed it as a rare fungus infection he'd picked up in Africa. It didn't respond to the usual antibiotics, so they had to operate. When they opened him up they took out an abscess the size of a tangerine and removed almost half his left lung.

The whole family was plenty worried while sweating out the operation. Dad was almost seventy years old. Nathaniel worked hard to keep a smile on his face when I took him over to the hospital after the surgery, but his father looked so ashen and weak he had to hold himself back from dissolving in tears. Dad tried to cheer him up—"Oh, I'll be out of here soon. Don't you worry about a thing"—but seeing the old man like that was hard on him. It was hard on all of us.

"How you doing?" I asked him after Nathaniel left the room.

"Well, it's pretty rough," he answered.

"Do you need anything for the pain?"

"No, I'm okay. I don't want to get wrecked out of my gourd."

"Well, don't be a hero."

"I hope he makes it," I thought to myself on the way back to the car. But I didn't get overly sentimental about it. I was sure he would. Barbara wasn't quite so optimistic. "I think this might be the beginning of the end," she told me. "I think your father's dying, honey. I don't want to make you paranoid and put you through a lot of changes. Just try to accept it and spend some time with him at the hospital." I knew that Barbara had a little clairvoyance, just enough to make you nervous, but I sloughed her off with a joke. "Die? Shit, he'll never die. What, are you kidding? He'll outlive all of us. He'll put us all in the goddam grave. He'll be standing over me saying, 'I told you you didn't do it right.'" But inside I was thinking, "Well, Jack, it's true. He's gonna check out just like everyone else. Not today. Not right this minute. But it's gonna happen soon."

After he recuperated he went back to work with a vengeance. Before the operation he had been gradually phasing himself into semi-retirement, but now he suddenly seemed renewed and began making all kinds of personal appearances, TV specials and records. It was as if he realized he was getting close to the end and wanted to kick up his heels and go out swinging. He even went on the road with Kathryn, the kids and his old pals Rosie Clooney and Joe Bushkin. When I caught their show in L.A., it tripped me back to the days he took me along to play army bases and bond drives during World War II. The kids seemed a whole lot happier to be out there with him than I was, but I could hear the same little quiver of fear in Harry's voice from trying to be good enough to please him. I wasn't so dramatic as to think, "Well, this is the last time I'll ever see the old man perform in person," but I knew it wasn't far from it.

Then, in March 1977, he took another bad shot. He was taping a TV special in Pasadena celebrating his fiftieth anniversary in show business, and just after finishing his bows to a standing ovation he fell off the stage and plunged twenty feet down into the orchestra pit. That one worried me. He was seventy-two years old now, and at that age a spill on the sidewalk can be enough to do you in. Luckily, he grabbed a piece of the curtain as he fell, and that probably saved his life. When I saw him at the hospital he made light of the accident and took all the blame. "It's my fault," he admitted. "I forgot they changed the routine and told me to exit through the audience. I automatically headed for the wings like you normally do when you're finished, only they'd folded up that part of the stage." As much as he downplayed it, he had still ruptured a disk in his lower back and was laid up in the hospital for over a month. But he was a strong man with a strong will. By October he was feeling well enough to go off on a concert tour of Great Britain.

The operation and the accident had prepared us for the end. It happened on his way home from England, when he stopped off in Madrid to play a round of golf. He won the game by one stroke, and just as he was leaving the eighteenth hole he died of a heart attack. It was over in an instant. "I can't think of any better way for a golfer who sings for a living to finish the round," Kathryn told the press a few hours later. When the details of the story got back to me, I felt the same way. He had hit a good shot onto the eighteenth green and sunk the putt. Some people on the veranda gave him a hand. Then he turned around and, without any pain, went straight to God. I thought to myself, "Well, isn't that just like him? Everything's perfect. He went out doing what he loved most, doing it successfully, taking a bow, knowing he was in good shape with his Church and his God and his fellow man. How many guys get to die like that? What an ending."

The funeral was exactly the way he wanted. My mother's had turned into such a three-ringed nightmare that he never forgot it. I remember him telling Kathryn, "When it gets to be my time, don't be going into that joint and buying the biggest, most expensive, ornate casket in the world. Just get me a plain wooden box and put me in the ground without any pomp and ceremony. I don't want a lot of people around or any big shows."

That's how she did it. The service was held at six o'clock in the morning at the small chapel in St. Paul's Church in Westwood. Only about thirty-five people were invited: the immediate family; some longtime business associates; and a few close friends like Phil Harris, Rosie Clooney and Bob Hope. Kathryn told me the night before that she wanted my brothers and me to be pallbearers. A lifetime of fucking up flashed before my eyes, and I tried to talk her out of it.

"Are you crazy, Kathryn, or what? Good God, we'll probably trip and drop him on the way to the grave."

"Well, Harry and Nathaniel will help you."

"Oh, wonderful. They both weigh about 120 pounds with an anvil under each arm. Pallbearers? God have mercy."

"It'll be all right, Gary," she answered, and somehow it was.

There were tears at the chapel when the casket was opened, but Kathryn and the kids tried hard to keep themselves from getting too down. He had lived seventy-three full, mostly happy years, and now he had gone to his Maker. When I took my last view of him, the first thing that popped into my head was,

"Jesus Christ, how small he looks in there. How could such a small man strike so much terror in my soul?"

He was buried in the family plot at Holy Cross Cemetery, next to Grandma and Grandpa Crosby and my mother.

Since then it hardly seems like he's gone. You keep hearing his records and seeing his movies on TV. You keep reading about him and hearing the stories. Christmas rolls around every year, and here he comes again. They get out the records of "Silent Night" and "White Christmas." They rerun the specials. I don't get to be with him for Christmas dinner, but that's about the only difference.

I'm happy we made some kind of peace before he went. Neither one of us backed up and neither one of us apologized, yet we made it. We were able to give some love to each other before it was too late. And I'm happy that the last years of his life he was satisfied with me. That's nice. I like that feeling. I'm glad I gave him a little something to be proud of towards the end. I'm especially glad I didn't do it for that reason. I'm glad it just happened that way, that I more or less straightened out on my own and that's what it took to please him.

I was pleased with him, too, at the end, though I still couldn't quite believe it mattered. It still seemed a little like saying, "I am pleased with you, sky. Mountain, I am pleased with you." Old habits die hard. To this day it's still kind of strange not having him around to fight anymore, not having him sitting there in his chair passing judgment and meting out punishment, goading me into all kinds of crazy carryings-on just to spite him. He was a hell of an opponent. But when all is said and done, I figure I managed to get a tie out of him, and that's not too bad. I'll settle for that.

Chapter Fifteen
Getting Straight

After eighteen years of marriage Barbara gave me my walking papers. I was hurt and so confused I didn't know what to make of it, but after a while I began to understand why. All that negativity, anger and reclusiveness just got to be too much for her. I was destroying her, and she had to get away from me. We divorced.

But I was lucky. I was handed a second chance of my own. It started after the breakup, when I turned around and found Andrea, a warm, good-hearted woman with a wonderfully wild, offbeat sense of humor. At first we were only buddies, and then one day we looked each other in the eyes and knew we were ready for more than that. I fell in love all over again.

But I was still the same old me. I stayed away from people to keep my monsters under control. The instant the traffic light turned green, I was screaming at the car in front of me to move. Every waking hour of the day I was pressuring myself to succeed, succeed, succeed, and because the jobs weren't coming the way I wanted and thought they were supposed to, I was constantly furious at everybody and everything. The frustration was driving me straight up the wall, and the adrenalin was surging through my veins thirty or forty times a day.

Inevitably it caught up with me. The doctor looked up from

the angiogram and announced he was shipping me off to the hospital immediately for a triple bypass. "You're what we call a Type A personality," he said, "and you have to change, or you will die. If you stop smoking and can learn to control your anger after this operation, I'll guarantee you thirty more years of life. You buy that?" "Let's see, live to seventy-seven? Yeah, sure, I'll buy that," I answered.

The night before they opened me up—after I'd made out my will, spoken to the priest, and was lying there alone, counting off the hours until I went on the table—I realized that I really did want to live. Before then I wasn't so sure. It seemed to me that life wasn't that big a deal and it didn't matter much whether I lived or died. But there, in the quiet of the hospital room, the closer I came to the knife the more I realized that was bullshit, that I wasn't ready to die. I hadn't done anything yet. I hadn't made a mark on the world worth a damn. I had a new wife, and my life was only beginning. "Please bring me through this thing," I prayed. "Just let me get to the other side of it, God, and I won't ask for a whole lot more."

He heard my plea and gave me even more than I asked for. After I recuperated I went back to my shrink, Dr. Vivian Gary, and I guess she heard the same old familiar anger coming out of me that was there before the operation.

"You know, I think you better go to AA," she told me.

"Aw, come on," I answered. "What the hell is AA gonna teach me? I don't drink or take pills anymore. I'm nineteen years dry."

"Yes, well, there's a lot more to AA than just helping you stop drinking and using."

"Yeah? So what are they gonna do for me?"

"I can't tell you. You're gonna have to go there and find out for yourself."

"Oh, for Chrisake, Doc, don't do this to me. I'm not a joiner. I'm not about to do that."

"Well, I'll tell you what. If you don't go down there, you can't come back here. That's it."

I was furious at first, but then I began to cool down. I reminded myself that Dr. Gary had probably done more than anyone on earth to help save my life and sanity. I love her and trust her and, as much as I may rant and rave, I know it makes sense to listen to her.

The next morning I called up a good friend of mine. When he began having trouble with the booze, I had sent him to AA myself. Over the past nineteen years, ever since I had gone public with the admission I was an alcoholic, I had sent a lot of people to AA. As a result of articles about my problem and talks I gave to youth groups, people would come up to me and ask my advice about how to stay sober. I'd tell them, "Don't do it my way" and suggest they check out Alcoholics Anonymous. Not that I really knew anything about it. I only knew there had to be a better way to handle the problem than the one I'd chosen, and maybe that was it.

"Hey, man, what the hell's goin' on down there?" I asked him.

"Can't really tell you, pal," he answered. "You have to see it with your own eyes."

"Oh, no. Not you too."

Then one night he managed to pry me loose from the TV set to attend a meeting, and the rest of my life started.

The moment I stepped inside I realized I was in the right place. It was the first time in my life I ever walked into a roomful of strangers and didn't feel hostile, defensive or afraid. Up to that moment I had thought I was crazy because I got so angry all the time and couldn't seem to control it. I was certain nobody else in the world was like that, but as I sat there listening to them talk about themselves I saw they felt almost exactly the same and I knew I wasn't alone anymore. I knew I belonged there. The only difference between us—and it was a big one—was that they had a program to let them handle it so they could lead happy, productive lives.

"What do I have to do to get to be like you guys?" I asked them.

"Read the AA book," they answered. "Keep coming to meetings. Don't drink in between. And just keep on listening. Sit down, shut up and listen, and you'll get the message."

I did what they told me, and they were right. Everything I needed to learn was waiting there for me. It had been waiting all along, but I guess I wasn't ready for it.

I learned that staying dry for nineteen years doesn't make you sober. Because sobriety is a way of thinking and living. By itself, cutting out the booze and drugs isn't enough. You still lose your wife and family. You still lose your career. You still lose your future. It just takes longer.

I learned that we alcoholics are creatures of self-will run riot. We want the world to work our way, and when it doesn't we get depressed and angry and hateful. We are egomaniacs unable to think about anything but ourselves, but to live only in yourself is to die. I learned that when you're in a tight spot or have a lousy day, instead of beating yourself up for being a failure you have to put yourself aside and do something for someone else—go help another drunk.

After thirty years, drunk and dry, of messing up my life, I learned there's a power greater than I am that can manage it just fine if I'll only get out of the way. Once I've done the legwork—gone to the auditions, given the readings—what's supposed to happen will happen and it's all for the best, all part of the plan—His plan, not mine.

I have so much more to learn. I'm almost fifty years old now, but I'm just a beginner. Yet it seems to be working. The old feelings of helplessness and impending doom aren't there anymore. I don't get so angry, and when I do start to fly into a rage I know I have it in me to put on the brakes before I explode out of control. I'm no longer so consumed by the idea of having to prove myself through my career. I'd like it to happen, but if it doesn't, well, then it's not supposed to and I'll have to accept it. It's not going to make my whole life come crashing down around my head, making me and everyone close to me miserable. If I do get the shot, I know I'll do fine. I never felt that kind of confidence before. Maybe I used to be so driven because I wasn't really sure I could cut it. I had to keep finding out for myself every show, every record session, every day.

I think I may even be getting past the egomania of the alcoholic. If I did have an ego problem I'd be in big trouble, because I'm starting to get lines from people I meet on the street like, "Who are you? What do you do for a living? Are you still in show business? Didn't you used to be Gary Crosby? Which Crosby kid are you?" Sure, sometimes that bothers me a little, but it doesn't hurt bad because it's just reality. If you don't get the gigs, after a while people forget who you are.

It's even a kind of blessing. In the old days everybody expected me to be a carbon copy of their idea of the old man, and because I wasn't that and couldn't give them what they wanted they were disappointed with me. Now that wall between me and the world is starting to crumble. As I grow older, more and more younger people I run into don't even know who Bing Crosby was. They damn sure don't know who I am, so they don't expect anything from me. What they see is what they get, and they either like it or they don't. Well, that's what I always wanted, and I'm happy to take my chances with that.